CH00666043

ADVICE TO YOUR YOUNGER SELF

A unique collaboration of reflections, lessons and advice, inspiring you to fulfil your unlimited potential

ADVICE TO YOUR YOUNGER SELF

A unique collaboration of reflections, lessons and advice, inspiring you to fulfil your unlimited potential

Research by Mark Stokes

Cover Design by Avnie Shah

Email: mark.stokes@equaSSAS.co.uk

www.SSASalliance.org

www.markstokesuk.com

All rights reserved. No part of this publication may be reproduced, stored in a retrieval system or transmitted in any form or by any means electronic, mechanical, photocopying, recording or otherwise, without written permission of the author in advance.

© Copyright 2019 EquaSSAS Limited

ISBN:	9781527242630
Edition:	1st Edition
Title:	ADVICE TO YOUR YOUNGER SELF – Volume 1
Subtitle:	A unique collaboration of reflections, lessons and advice, inspiring you to fulfil your unlimited potential

Printed and Bound by Amazon KDP Print on Demand.

The views and opinions expressed in this book are those of the individual chapter authors and do not necessarily reflect those of the book author, or any related companies.

The author shall not be held responsible for any misuse, re-use, or application resulting from the content of this book and accepts no responsibility for loss, damage or injury to persons or their belongings as a direct result of reading this book. Always do your due diligence and take advice from qualified professions where appropriate to do so.

All people mentioned in this book have been used with permission and may have had names, genders, industries and personal details altered to protect confidentiality and privacy. Any resemblance to persons living or dead may be purely coincidental.

DEDICATION

This book is dedicated to three particular groups of special people:

1. My children: Ben, Jack, Katy, Emily and all of our relatives and close friends, both now and in the future.

2. All the children, nephews, nieces, grandchildren and future relations of every one of our magnificent chapter authors.

3. All children and young people making their way in the world.

I wish you all every success, happiness and love in your lives as you gain inspiration and fulfil your glorious potential and go on, in turn, to inspire future generations.

TABLE OF CONTENTS

FOREWORD

Greater than the sum of the parts

Setting out to write a book of this magnitude was certainly an eye-opening prospect yet, in truth, it had been something that had been gnawing away at me for several years. To think that one person can collate all the vital lessons learnt to support and guide the next generation would probably be impractical, and most certainly arrogant!

Given that I believe humility is one of the greatest qualities one can have as a business leader, I was not about to falter into the latter category and once the concept of a collaborative work was seeded, taking the synergistic 'greater than the sum of the parts' approach, the book soon gathered unstoppable momentum and infectious interest.

In many ways this book represents a tremendous opportunity:

- To the contributors in passing their valuable lessons to the next generation.
- To all those that savour the incalculable value within this book, absorbing and apply its contents.

From a personal perspective, this book forms part of a lifelong reflection and determination to be the best version of myself and of giving back to future generations both in knowledge, application and in monetary terms.

The undoubted hardship that can occur in business and life can certainly be eased very significantly with the astute embracing of the lessons of others that went before – enablement, evolution and progression – forming the spine of the advance! By seeking to understand the lessons learnt from those that have gone before us, we equip ourselves to minimise failure, prepare ourselves for the certainty of change and condition ourselves for the continuous improvement cycle of life.

'Walk a mile in another person's shoes'

The self-belief and confidence of knowing that you have a toolbox of life lessons to serve your future direction and prepare you for many of the uncertainties that await, is incredibly valuable. It will enable you to uncover the many exciting business and life opportunities that await you – often hidden in full view but missed by the many and harnessed by only the few.

The alternative? Well, for some, it is awaiting one's fate, 'it was meant to be', a 'hands off the steering wheel' approach to life, often leading to dejection and a troubling entitlement culture.

But not for those that read and embrace this book!

The gifts contained within the following pages are based on experience, trial and error, failure and success in equal measure. They are priceless beyond measure, finely honed through a multitude of lives, backgrounds and circumstances.

Over the years I have had the privilege to meet many gifted and talented people who possess sómething special. To invite their collaboration in this book was the logical next step, given I had worked closely with many and enjoyed and respected their company, wisdom and reflections.

I have reached out to a very select few people who come from all manner of backgrounds and experiences, each with sincere wisdom to be shared. This powerful diversity has enabled the book to shine brightly as a lighthouse of knowledge and guidance for future generations. It was such a pleasure to see all the authors rise to the challenge and embedding and embracing the deep values contained within the book.

'It is amazing what you can accomplish if you do not care who gets the credit'

Harry S. Truman

The chapter authors all gave their time freely and generously and for many it was to prove a cathartic and reflective experience – to some opening up new thoughts and opportunities, for others creating closure and transition.

This book is uniquely designed for everyone – children, teenagers, adults, parents and grandparents all with a passion for supporting the positive growth of confident custodians of their future society, planet and self. It is for the young and the old, for personal development or passing the baton to future generations. There are many timeless lessons and golden nuggets throughout, just waiting for you to uncover and apply them.

So, whether this book is a gift for others, or for your own personal growth, there is something for everyone. My wish, hope and desire is that once you have read this book, you then take the next defining steps to achieving your fullest potential in life, and to take the necessary steps to take control of your personal economy.

And remember that 100% of the profits from every book will also go towards helping those less fortunate than ourselves, to equip them with choices and to enable lives fully lived.

Thank you for supporting this exciting book that will be a defining 'Force for Good' in so many ways across society. I know this special book will resonate with so many people, directly and indirectly, and will be strengthened by the personal contribution of each and every one of our chapter's authors and their wonderfully eclectic backgrounds in business and life.

The energy that awaits you within these pages has the power to unleash massive momentum in your life and it is there for you to reach out for, to harness and to embrace.

My very best wishes to all who read and embrace the contents within these pages and to all those that benefit from its wisdom.

Mark Stokes

BOOK CONTRIBUTORS

This book is all about the chapter authors – my unreserved thanks and appreciation goes to each and every one of the chapter authors who gave their time graciously and freely for the benefit of others. You are all amazing.

Rehman Akhtar

Natalie Bailey

Greg Bateman

Sabrina Ben Salmi

Paul Bingham

Michelle Bryant

Ryan Carruthers

David Clouter

Eddie Collman

John Corey

Ross Crawford

Justin Davis

Matt Everson

Steven Fawke

Nigel Greene

Andrew Greenhalgh

Darren Grigas

Mo Haykir

Chris Henry

Andrew Hubbard

Alex Impey

Richard Kennedy

Ron Li

Richard Liddle

Kunal Makwana

Luke Mann

Ian McBain

Ray McLennan

Nellie McQuinn

Halstead Ottley

Diksesh Patel

Chris Paton

Tatiana Preobrazhenskaya

Juswant Rai

Angelos Sanders

Avnie Shah

Rob Spencer

Kim Stones

Akash Vaghela

Bronwen Vearncombe

Shaz Watkins

Rob Wilkinson

Doug James   Zoe Williams
Kal Kandola   Neville Wright
Ian Kavanagh   Aaron Yahaya

A huge thank you to the talented Avnie Shah who has not only contributed a wonderful chapter of the book, but also designed our wonderful book cover. You continue to be amazing Avnie!

A big thank you to Steve Baker at Ebooks By Design for his experience and advice in preparing this book for print.

My sincere thanks and gratitude to my Mum, Rachel and my wife, Sharon for their proofreading skills – many thanks to you both xx

And finally, and by no means least, a huge thank you to my wonderful wife Sharon for supporting the book during its many stages and helping in the significant organising and logistics required to finalise this book.

My sincere thanks to you all.

MAKING A DIFFERENCE – OUR GOOD CAUSES

The genesis of this book is firmly placed in helping other and creating massive shared value over multi-generational timescales.

The compounding of the knowledge contained in this book will certainly achieve this shared value for those ready and willing to embrace it.

The profits of the book are being distributed to a number of extremely worthy causes:

- **British Heart Foundation** – Heart disease remains the largest cause of death in the UK and we are proud to support the great work of the British Heart Foundation. This extremely worthy charity was the chosen beneficiary at the funeral of our great friend Peter Abbott, who left us far too early. This book, and its proceeds, serve as a memory to the wonderful person Pete was, touching so many people's lives.

- **B1G1** – we are proud to be a member of B1G1, a social enterprise and non-profit organisation with a mission to create a world full of giving. Unlike conventional giving models, B1G1 helps small-and medium-sized businesses achieve more social impact by embedding giving activities into everyday business operations and creating unique giving stories.

- **Discretionary Fund** – we are allocating the third proportion of the profits for other very worthy local causes.

REHMAN AKHTAR

Make happy memories

"Until one is committed, there is hesitancy, the chance to draw back — concerning all acts of initiative (and creation), there is one elementary truth, the ignorance of which kills countless ideas and splendid plans:

that the moment one definitely commits oneself, then Providence moves too. All sorts of things occur to help one that would never otherwise have occurred. A whole stream of events issues from the decision, raising in one's favour all manner of unforeseen incidents and meetings and material assistance, which no man could have dreamed would have come his way.

Whatever you can do, or dream you can do, begin it. Boldness has genius, power and magic in it. Begin it now"

Johann Wolfgang von Goethe

ABOUT THE CHAPTER AUTHOR

Rehman was born in Pakistan and came to live in the UK at the age of four. The first of four children, his formative years were spent in London living either as a lodger in other people's houses or on a council housing estate.

From this humble beginning, he started a remarkable journey that saw him gain higher than average grades at school, a degree in Mechanical Engineering and post-graduate studies at The Cranfield School of Management.

He now works in The Middle East as a senior HR professional in one of the world's largest companies, specialising in professional development. Before this he had a varied career in the UK spanning financial services, pharmaceuticals and Information Technology.

Rehman has had a lifelong interest in public speaking and stand-up comedy, taking to the stage at the age of eleven for his very first act. Subsequently he has performed all over the world and is now in high demand as a public speaker and master of ceremonies – especially at corporate events in The Middle East.

Rehman recently launched his own podcast "Make Happy Memories" in which he aims to help young people through life's experiences.

Rehman is recognised as one of the pioneers of the stand-up comedy industry in Saudi Arabia – which has recently mushroomed into a huge industry.

Despite all this, Rehman describes himself as an 'ordinary guy, living an extraordinary life'. He has battled against many difficult periods to get to where he is. He attributes much of his success to a strong upbringing by traditional Pakistani/Muslim parents and a very strong wife.

MY CHAPTER

Let me set the scene and give you some background.

As I start typing, I am sitting on a plane with my younger son, thirteen-year-old Haroon, who is resting his head on my shoulder watching a movie. We're heading to Heathrow from Saudi Arabia, a country our family have called home for the last eighteen years, having emigrated from the UK.

As soon as we land, I'm going directly to my daughter Nadia's house to meet my first grandchild, Yusuf, for the very first time. Nadia and her husband Azhar had this lovely addition to their family just five days ago and I honestly can't wait to hold him in my arms!

Following closely behind us, on another flight, are my elder son Wasim and his wife Arwa who also live with me in Saudi Arabia. They arrive in London shortly after us. It's going to be a really emotional family holiday. We'll be enjoying the last few days of the Holy month of Ramadan with my mother, my siblings, their kids and grandkids followed by a great Eid celebration together.

You may have noticed two key relatives missing in the above introduction: my father and my wife. Both were instrumental in my life journey and both are unfortunately no longer with us.

My father passed away over 5 years ago, two weeks short of his eightieth birthday, having moved to the UK in the mid-1960s, bringing up four children through sheer hard work and perseverance in the face of sometimes overwhelming odds.

My wife Shaafia left this world exactly seventy-two weeks ago today. A mere forty-six-years-old. Yes, I'm still counting the weeks. I can't bring myself to define it in years. I find comfort in feeling like she was with us in the recent past, just weeks ago, rather than years. I fell in love with Shaafia at first sight (sounds corny I know, but it really was a strong, instant attraction!). We had twenty-eight amazing years together and despite prolonged periods of financial hardship, our love and respect for each other never wavered. It only grew. All I can remember of the almost three decades together are the happy memories we created together, regardless of our circumstances. Hence, the title of this chapter, "Make Happy Memories" – more on that later!

So, as I sit here talking to my younger self, the first thing I want to say to him is "Well done Rehman for choosing the right partner in life". It took me just a few minutes to make this choice but it positively affected the course of my life and ultimately led to the success that I am now enjoying, albeit without my wife by my side.

Key take-away? Behind every happy, strong, successful person, there is usually a stronger partner who had faith in their ability to deliver a brighter future who stood shoulder-to-shoulder with them, providing unconditional support in good times and bad. Our family are living proof of this because our lives are based, first and foremost, on love and respect. Everything, absolutely EVERYTHING else is secondary.

Apart from the above life-changing decision, what could (or should) I have done differently? Part of me instinctively says, "Don't change a thing!" because it is the total human experience (good, bad and ugly) that mould us into who we are today, but since that would defeat the purpose of this book, let me think it through and give it my best shot!

Here are the pieces of advice I would give to 'younger Rehman' (in no particular order of priority):

1. Read a book called "The Slight Edge" by Jeff Olson

Apply the beautifully simple, yet powerful techniques, to live a more empowered and fulfilled life. I apologise if that sounds like the blurb you may read on the back cover of the book, but it really did fundamentally shift my attitude to life and allowed me to excel in areas that had been pipe dreams until then. I just wish I had read the book earlier in life!

2. FOCUS longer on key strategies

I spent too much time in my 20s and early 30s reinventing myself. Switching between jobs and continually having self-doubts and second thoughts. This resulted in having to do menial jobs to put food on the table while sorting out my main career. While I am happy that I did whatever it took to put food on the table, I could certainly have benefited from:

Focusing on
One
Course of action
Until
Successful

3. Make health and fitness your central pillar

Make it a foundation for everything else. Success in all other aspects of life is severely diluted if you are not in a position to fully embrace and enjoy the results. Good physical health also enhances your ability to cope with the mental stresses that life will inevitably throw at you. Mental and physical health have a positive correlation. I was never a couch potato, but I didn't always eat healthily.

It's the combination of physical activity and a healthy diet that lead to good health. This was a tough one for me to grasp, because my favourite way of spending a night out was always stuffing myself with good food in the company of great friends. It's only later on in life that I understood the power of moderation when I managed to lose around 20kg (and still going strong). I wish I had started earlier!

4. Know that true happiness lay in FEELINGS, not THINGS

In today's world of consumerism and instant gratification, too many of us subscribe to a strange notion of happiness that is based on the possession of 'things'. Things that we sometimes can't afford and ironically things that we have often been brainwashed into desiring by social media influences. Is your life really not worth living if you don't get that latest phone, that flashy high-specification car, that designer dress or handbag?

While in reality, in my humble opinion, there is just as much personal satisfaction in taking a walk on a beautiful summer day along a river bank with the love of your life or a good friend, talking about nothing and everything. You're making happy memories that will last long after those flashy items have gone out of fashion!

5. Network a lot, get mentored, but be careful who you trust

There is definitely an advantage to networking to get a diverse set of opinions and guidance. I have enjoyed being mentored by amazing people throughout my life. In fact, I have never been without mentors (formal and informal) since my teenage years. They have shaped my way of thinking and driven me towards positive outcomes in various aspects of my life.

However, here is where I'd like to strike a note of caution to my younger self: think twice before trusting people. Being a positive person, I gave too much 'benefit of the doubt' to people I worked with – especially in my business ventures. I took people at face value and did business with people because they were nice people and I couldn't possibly imagine them harming my interests. I learnt my lesson the expensive way. Nowadays, the personality of my business partners accounts for around 10% of the decision-making process, the other 90% via thorough research – backed up by legal agreements!

6. Pay it forward

No man is an island. As you gain experience in life, achieve success and make money, remember to pay some of it forward. Reach down and give people a helping hand up the ladder, just as others helped you. Mentor people, especially youngsters who may not have all the tools yet to make the best decisions in life. When you are financially comfortable, remember to help others less fortunate than you. This brings great balance to your life and helps you to avoid becoming arrogant about your own success. You can't help everyone, but you can make a significant difference to a small number of people. Just do it. You will not believe how much personal pleasure there is in giving.

7. Work hard, play hard

Go easy on yourself. Ambition is a great thing, but don't forget that every day on this earth may be your last.

When your time comes, you don't want your family to just have memories of an absent hard worker. They want to remember the vacations, the laughs, the movies and shows you watched together, the funny moments you shared, the catch phrases you used, your smiling face, rather than a stressed frown. When you are gone, it is these memories that will sustain your loved ones and help them cherish your absence, rather than just feel the void. I know this because my late wife has left me memories that will keep me and my family smiling as long as we live.

Conclusion

We have started our final descent into Heathrow. I look forward to the 30-day adventure that awaits my family and I in the UK before we return to Saudi Arabia. There will inevitably be tears when I meet my grandson for the first time because I would have loved to share this moment with my dear Shaafia. However, there will also be many tears of joy as we continue her legacy and I continue making happy memories with our children until she and I meet again 'upstairs' and stay together for eternity – God willing.

NATALIE BAILEY

Control gives you freedom

"The significant problems we face cannot be solved with the same level of thinking which created them"
Albert Einstein

ABOUT THE CHAPTER AUTHOR

I was born and raised in London but am now based in Mallorca. I moved to Mallorca in 2011 chasing the 'dream life' and so lived in the sun and worked in bars before I changed my path and became a personal trainer. I realised I wanted to make people feel good, not give them a hangover. Health and fitness is high on my list of values and I continue to work on this with my businesses today.

I now run two property businesses with my Mum, Paula Bailey. We do commercial to residential conversions and serviced accommodation. I also have an online store for fitness equipment and I am a confidence coach, helping to give people the keys to unlock their lives in order to be more confident and successful.

We at Bailey Enterprises are also on a mission to combat loneliness through property by creating community. We do this both online and offline, with the message 'Better Together' which can be found on Facebook. It's this which makes the difference for us and the lives of many.

I'm an avid traveller which is what took me to Mallorca in the first place. My 'dream life' is now being able to travel but I help others to be more confident, creating a legacy where they too can build a property portfolio and have the income they require to do what they want in life. This is where the difference lies in what I do – helping people to be fully present in their own lives and by having 100% belief in themselves helps them to succeed.

Confidence is the foundation to your success.

www.baileyenterprises.org

MY CHAPTER

I know what you're thinking: control gives you freedom? Come on, really?

Bear with me while I explain and let you into a little secret which changed my life. And that is that implementing control over myself, gave me freedom which is something that you can attain too. That's why you're reading this isn't it? To learn how to be free?

Being young and carefree is supposed to be where it's at – the highlight of life. This is why so many people look back on their younger days wishing they had done more, or maybe less, when times were easier and when there wasn't a level of responsibility to be upheld. How many times have you been told "do it whilst you're young enough" because when you get older it's not 'right' or 'acceptable' 'at that age'.

This chapter isn't going to tell you to stop having fun, that you need to be controlled and dim your light on who you are. Or that you need to suppress your personality to fit in. In fact, it's going to be the complete opposite. It's going to let you know that you can be who you want to be, and have fun, without judgement, without being anyone but you.

When I say 'control' I don't mean the overbearing rigid routine or having someone stand over you. What I mean is that you have control over you and your life.

It's hard growing up, figuring out who you are, what you want to do, who you want to be. It's a time of exploring, saying: "Yes", being "crazy" and having fun.

You want to do all of the fun things without the consequences, with no repercussions. Well, what if that was possible? Just by having a little control.

Without some semblance of control, of a routine, your life will be in disarray. Without a goal in life you have no purpose, no direction, nothing to drive you forward. What you have is a feeling of being lost.

It's important to set yourself on a path to success. Not thinking, "I can figure that out later" because 'later' never comes. The only way you can be successful in anything is through being consistent in your actions. When you have the control over your mind to do the daily tasks required to achieve a goal, you have success, and that is what will set you free.

Being young and carefree doesn't mean you can't have more in life, and younger in life, it is something that should help to drive you forward.

Learning to enjoy what you do in life in order to create a successful life is key. If you are seeing your daily tasks as chores, it will hold you back, allow you to procrastinate and stop you from doing what needs to be done. Find your passion by trying things out, keep a journal and look for your purpose in life, all whilst having fun. Life is for living.

I lived my 20s like you 'should' do – travelled, partied, had fun and laughed a lot. I also experienced a vast amount of grief, stress, overwhelm and struggles which were hard to let go of. It's these things in life which shape you into the person you are today. You are the sum of all the parts of your life.

Spend time with people who matter, create memories – laugh until your cheeks are sore. Take photos and videos and look back on these times often. Be present with the people in your life. Get off your phone and talk to each other because you cannot beat looking into the whites of someone's eyes. To feel that real connection with them you have to be present. This means listening. It's a key skill for great communication and it will take you the furthest in life.

Don't worry about spending time with 'cool' people – make yourself that person who people want to be around. By adding value, fun, passion and being there. Surround yourself with the right people and they will lift and inspire you to do more, to be better and you will create an amazing life for yourself. Life can be lonely, especially when you are starting a new venture, but it doesn't have to be that way. Use social media for all it's good for, but never forget to get out in the real world in order to truly connect.

Get to know yourself. You are going to live with you until you die, so you had better be your best friend. Learn to forgive yourself when you make mistakes – and you will make many. Accept that, embrace your flaws as they are what make you. Strive to be the best person you can be, not by comparing yourself to others, but by comparing yourself to you. How you react to situations out of your control will tell you a lot about yourself. Do you get angry and have a tantrum, shouting at the people you care about the most, or do you see the positive in the negative and create something special instead?

Sometimes the best decisions in life are the 'fuck it' ones, the spontaneous ones, the unplanned things which turn out to be amazing things. But don't forget to spend some time planning, working out what you want in life, what you're really passionate about and create that life through a mixture of discipline in your day, and spontaneous trips.

When you learn to control your emotions and gain emotional intelligence you will become much more confident in yourself and your abilities. This will also mean you have better relationships with people. Remember, it's not about the number of people in your life, but the quality. When I was 16 we organised a party for a friend's birthday, there must have been 200 people turn up but was I close to all of those people? No. The real friends at the time I could count on one hand, and they are the ones who really mattered. Stay close with people who lift you, and away from people who lead you to do things which go against your values.

Feed your mind, body AND soul. I wish when I was 18 that I had learnt about meditation and tapped into my soul, learnt then how to control my emotions, to respond proactively rather than reactively. To be a leader. A leader of self.

Exercise is what will help you to stay young, live, be strong and be connected with your own mind. What you put into your body shows on the outside. In order to be the most confident person you can be, you need to learn the art of being comfortable in your own skin, to get out of your comfort zone, to understand your mind and to push your mind and your body to places you didn't think possible. This will help you move forward.

The world is a huge place, with many cultures from which you can learn. That's why I love travelling so much – to see the way people live and take the best of it home with me. You can do that too.

The key thing here is to respect yourself. Make decisions which help you to grow and don't degrade yourself by thinking you aren't good enough, that you don't deserve to be happy or to have friends or be a part of the club. You DO!

Have fun, be young, enjoy yourself, but not to the detriment to your self-respect. Exercising a modicum of control will help you more than you'll ever realise right now.

If you follow the advice in this book, you'll be set for a great life. Remember that confidence is the foundation to your success. So, go and be crazy, but do it with control and you will have the freedom you desire.

Confidence is the foundation to your success.

GREG BATEMAN

Growth mindset

"…once the storm is over you won't remember how you made it through, how you managed to survive. You won't even be sure, in fact, whether the storm is really over. But one thing is certain. When you come out of the storm you won't be the same person who walked in. That's what this storm's all about"

Haruki Murakami, Kafka on the Shore

ABOUT THE CHAPTER AUTHOR

Roles: Professional Rugby Player for Leicester Tigers, Entrepreneur, Media Personality and MBA Student.

While playing professional rugby Greg is the only player in Premiership Rugby history to start in all three front row positions. He has built successful (and unsuccessful) business ventures, created craft ales and launched the first podcast from within a sporting organisation. In June 2019 he posted about his own battles with mental health to support others from his particularly masculine and stoic environment, especially for males, where mental health is rarely talked about. Post-professional rugby-player Greg is quickly making a name for himself in personal performance coaching, offering advice, consultancy and an impressive network built up during his playing career.

Instagram: @gregbateman
LinkedIn: Greg Bateman

MY CHAPTER

As I sit here thinking about what advice I'd give to my younger self I recognise it's not the first time I've had this conversation with myself. I notice I've had this dialogue for years when I've wondered if I'd played this differently or done that differently would my life look like this? Ultimately one of the key things I've learned is you can't undo the past, but you can let it not define your future by not viewing everything as a match or a game to win or lose.

Growth Mindset

I've always been competitive. I vividly remember thinking I knew the answers to things teachers were trying to teach us in school. I remember getting fucked off with my dad for trying to show me how to use a power drill at the age of 10. I've always thought I can do things. It can be a gift and a curse. To believe in yourself is one of the most powerful superpowers around. However, fundamentally not having an appreciation that the more meaningful things in life aren't won or lost, right or wrong requires a more 'craft' than 'success' mindset.

Carol Dweck's book 'Growth Mindset' changed my life. We had an ex All Black coach who was so inspiring and encouraged us to read on our personal development. Admittedly this was to teach us about the craft of training and honing our skills. Taking it further and applying a growth mindset to my personal life has massively helped me reduce my anxiety on whether I'm winning at something immediately.

How to be in love for example is not a success or winning game. It's a never-ending relationship, learning together, growing together and holding the other person's needs and dreams as high as your own. There is no scoreboard in a true meaningful loving relationship.

Identity

In 2017 I split up with my wife, the mother of my children. I quickly found myself lost. Not because I was particularly bothered about the relationship break up as we'd been holding off splitting up for years, but because my identity – which I'd told myself was a husband, father, rugby player and entrepreneur – was gone. Sure enough the business went and my kids were moved to Devon and I see them every 4-6 weeks. I felt like my identities were lost and I didn't know who I was.

I battled with depression and anxiety for a lot longer than I realised but eventually reached out to get help through medication and talk therapy. One of the most important things I have ever done was to get to the root causes of my issues, rather than just deal with the symptoms.

So now I'm in a much better place, I've spent a lot of time working out what happened and how I found myself so far away from who I thought I was. I think what I had was a belief in what those identities were – but they were something I 'did' rather than who I was. I've grown a lot in this time of reflection and can honestly say

I now look for things that are me, my character 'who I am' rather than 'what I do'. I rang a leading expert in social identity theories while in this transition and asked him what I should do now I know them. He explained that was my first problem – your identity isn't a doing thing, it's a self-awareness thing. That blew my mind!

Furthermore, in an extreme sense, the way to build resilience is to lean on the identities that build you up in times of hardship. So if rugby is shit, focus on your kids, if they're annoying then spend more time in the business. That way you build your self-esteem by leaning on the identities that build you up.

Preparation + Perfect Practise = Performance

<u>Preparation</u>

Preparation is like dragging a Swiss ball full of water up a mountain for me BUT I have found some really helpful, fulfilling ways of being more prepared hugely helps my performance on the pitch, in my personal life, in my business life and overall wellbeing.

Week Planning – every Sunday night or Monday morning after my weights session, I sit in the changing room with my weekly planner sheet – write down all my sessions, my date night, my time for studies, business or meeting times and, arguably most importantly, golf practice!

By planning my week, firstly it helps me see what sessions I'm targeting but I then plan what I want to achieve from those sessions – do I need some extra running? Do I need some more scrums? That way I don't aimlessly make my way through a training week hoping my needs are picked up by someone else.

Also, and the thing I love about it most, is it allows me to be fully present. When I'm playing golf, I'm not thinking about whether I've done enough training that day, because I've planned it. When I'm out with my Mrs, I'm not thinking about the golf course. I can be fully present with her and give her all of me. This is one of my values to live by.

Perfect Practice

Malcom Gladwell suggested 10,000 hours is the time to master a skill. I have driven a car for far more than 10,000 hours, however I am not yet (despite my various speeding fines) Lewis Hamilton! That is not because he's put in more hours than me. It's because his hours are focused, specific and targeted towards a style, a way of driving, inching towards performance. So, you see, it's not about the hours you put in, it's what is inside those hours you put in. This is a way of describing process goals whereby you focus on how you perform your tasks and focus on them and the result 'takes care of itself'. That way you're not overwhelmed with what you want to achieve, rather you're focused on the rugby thing at that given moment.

Performance

Performance is not an end in itself. Approach your craft to improve, to learn to get better, to focus on the process and the result will follow.

Have more fun, challenge yourself, create things, be brave and tackle life head on. As far as we know, we don't get another go at this so give it your best shot and I'll be right there cheering you on ☺.

SABRINA BEN SALMI

Just know that you are enough

"The journey of one thousand miles, starts with a single step in the right direction with the loving and caring support of your village"

Sabrina Ben Salmi

ABOUT THE CHAPTER AUTHOR

Mother of The Year Award Winner Sabrina Ben Salmi BSc is an award-winning author (Dreaming Big Together, Mamas Secret Recipe, and Lone Parenthood), multiple award winner and public speaker. She is now a proud mother of 5 entrepreneurial children who are also multi-award winners and award-winning authors who have their own brands and signature programs. They are aged 5yrs to 18yrs old who she refers to as her Fantastic 5: 18yr old Lashai aka Dreampreneur – Stepping Stones Formula™, YouSmart™, and Kidz That Dream Big™, 14yr old Tray-Sean aka I'm That KID, Kidz That Dream Big™, I'm That KID™ and Child Genius™, 11yr old Yasmine aka Lovepreneur, The Choice Is Yours™, 10yr old Paolo aka Pint Size Adventurer™ and 5yr old Amire aka Mr Intelligent – Because

I Am Intelligent™. Sabrina's background is in Computer Science and Sabrina is co-founder and Director of Harris Invictus Academy (Ofsted Outstanding Secondary School). Sabrina is founder of The Mobile Single Parents Project™, Dreaming Big Together, Mamas Secret Recipe™, MindSet-ReSet Now™, The Conscious Entrepreneur Blueprint™ and Shift Happens™ transformational Programs. It is said that Sabrina is the mentor of many successful and famous individuals, responsible for local and global personal and professional connections that have gone on to influence business and individuals across the globe. Sabrina is a Make Your Mark Ambassador, PRECIOUS AWARD finalist, British Library case study and has attracted the attention of both National and International media across TV, newspapers and radio, ie BBC London News, BBC Radio, Colourful Radio, Channel 4 documentaries (The Secret Millionaire etc). She is also a fellow of the School of Social Entrepreneurs (SSE), A Glimmer of Hope award winner, Urban Futures award winner, an Unltd Award winner and nominated to carry the Olympic Torch in 2012.

Facebook: https://www.facebook.com/sbensalmi

MY CHAPTER

In life I have come to learn that the most important journey that you could ever embark on is the journey of self-discovery. I would definitely tell my younger self to enjoy the journey more. Allowing myself to get away hasn't always been an easy thing for me to do because my driven nature can keep me going, which makes it hard to slow down and give myself permission to step away. I would encourage my younger self to ponder on these questions as often as possible.

What do you want most?

Is it money, love, health, wealth, happiness, fame, power, contentment, peace of mind etc?

I encourage you to take your time to establish your individual skills, talents and sacred gifts so you can go on to identify your philosophy of life, if you're searching for a definite goal in your life's journey. I highly recommend that you take responsibility to deal with your past, take control of your present and go on to create a compelling future.

Believe in yourself, even when others do not – it is absolutely paramount that you honour your internal guidance system (your emotions and gut instincts) as it will navigate you in your life's journey.

Before beginning adulthood, you could benefit hugely if you recognise the fact that:

Good company in a journey makes the way seem shorter — Izaak Walton

I am absolutely exhilarated about sharing this TRUTH with you that: "You Are Enough".

enough

I can still remember sitting down during my childhood worrying about whether I was good enough, if my thoughts and suggestions were good enough, trying to impress others, trying to be the same as my peers as I feared being rejected.

If I knew then what I now know with regards to self-love and self-acceptance, I could have saved myself all the time that I wasted seeking external validation.

As I grew up, I questioned why I expected people who couldn't see my vision to give me permission to pursue it. I am here to encourage you to be yourself no matter what others say or do because you are enough, just the way you are.

I am so in love with the continuous and organic unfoldment of life, the contrast, the unexplainable encounters, the sweat, the tears, the attachments, the fears, the discomfort, the moments of sadness and despair, the unexpected pleasantries in abundance and so much more.

It is such a deep profound feeling to know that life has taken me on a journey of self-discovery from feeling unworthy to a sense of self-love and self-acceptance.

That which initially presented as a so-called pain, has gone on to become the premise for my thriving. I have come to realise that my so-called darkest days were merely contrast and have now become my blessings beyond words. I have certainly learned that one can choose to grow through life or go through life. One thing that I truly believe is that life is a journey of market research and what you choose to do with the data is up to you. Life is always giving us feedback and when we learn the lesson that each experience has come to teach us, it will equip us for the next phase of our life. At times it will not make sense in the present, however we connect the dots when we look backwards.

<u>The question is, what will you choose?</u>

Life will give you feedback. However, what have you been choosing to delete, distort and generalise?

You are enough, therefore:

- Take the gift of life seriously and convey gratitude
- You have nothing to prove to others
- You are unique, so there is no competition
- Take care of yourself
- Pursue your deepest dreams and desires
- Know that you are worthy
- Maintain faith and focus on thriving
- Take a deep breath and fully reconnect with your inner core
- Stop rushing, get into alignment and then life will come to you
- Trust yourself
- Trust your intuition
- Give up the belief that you have to work hard to create your desired outcomes
- When contrast presents, choose to learn the lesson that it has come to teach you

- You can choose to be in the choice

- Express yourself

- Being vulnerable is the first step towards success

- Meditate daily to allow you to reconnect

- You are a unique gift to the world

- There is no such thing as failure, only feedback

- All contrast helps you to fine tune that which you do not desire in order to fine tune you

- Just know that you are exactly where you need to be, simply surrender to the process

- Stop settling for too little

- Your opinion matters

- You make a difference

- Forgive yourself, others and let go

- Slow down and simply be fully present to this very moment – that's the difference that will make the difference

- Allow yourself to become an excellent giver and an excellent receiver

- Learn to fall in love with yourself. So much so that you enjoy being alone in silence listening to your inner being and align

- You are a speaker and the world is your stage

- You are an artist and life is your canvas

- You are a musician and life will respond to your unique rhythm

- Know that people are in your life for a reason, a season or a lifetime

- You are an author and the pen is in your hands

- Take the gift of life seriously and convey gratitude for all aspects of your life as often as possible

- Acknowledge, appreciate and support those who support you within your life journey

- Redefine success according to you

- Say "How does it get any better than this?" as often as possible

- Convey gratitude for yourself and others

- Know that your emotions are your internal guidance system

- Honour your needs and desires

- All problems are problems of the mind, therefore all solutions are also solutions of the mind

- Just know that contrast assists you to fine tune that which you do not desire and empowers you to powerfully pivot towards that which you desire to experience

- Walk in nature barefooted and allow yourself to reconnect with nature

- When you have a negative thought simply say "Who does this belong to? I return to sender with consciousness attached"

- Use things and value people
- Acknowledge your strengths and weaknesses
- Stop trying so hard
- Being vulnerable is a strength
- Stop blaming others and tap into your inner power
- Ask for help when needed
- Trust the process
- Step outside of your comfort zone
- Dance like no one is watching
- Create systems and processes to make life run smoothly
- Honour your thoughts by saying "thank you for sharing"
- Stop trying to impress friends, family and/or colleagues
- When surrounded by crabs in the bucket trying to dilute your vision, always respond saying "I'm just getting warmed up"
- In life you can either watch the movie, be in the movie and/or direct the movie
- Reconnect to your inner core
- Take aligned action
- Choose to be like water and adapt to life with flexibility

Embody the positive learnings for yourself and the future. Go ahead and take three deep breaths, with each breath that you take notice how relaxed you are becoming. Now let's try this powerful breathing technique that our family mentor (Juanpa Barahona) taught us:

Take a slow and controlled deep breath to the count of 4 seconds.

Now hold your breath for 4 seconds and then slowly exhale to the count of 4 seconds.

Excellent – well done, now let's go for 6 seconds.

Take a slow and controlled deep breath to the count of 6 seconds. Now hold your breath for 6 seconds and then slowly exhale to the count of 6 seconds.

Excellent – well done, now let's go for 8 seconds.

Take a slow and controlled deep breath to the count of 8 seconds. Now hold your breath for 8 seconds and then slowly exhale to the count of 8 seconds.

Excellent – well done

Please allow me to share this poem with you, it's called 'On Children' and it inspired me to parent my children the way I do today:

"Your children are not your children.
They are the sons and daughters of Life's longing for itself. They come through you but not from you, and though they are with you yet they belong not to you. You may give them your love but not your thoughts, for they have their own thoughts.
You may house their bodies but not their souls,
For their souls dwell in the house of tomorrow,
which you cannot visit, not even in your dreams.
You may strive to be like them, but seek not to make them like

you. For life goes not backward nor tarries with yesterday. You are the bows from which your children as living arrows are sent forth. The archer sees the mark upon the path of the infinite, and He bends you with His might that His arrows may go swift and far. Let your bending in the archer's hand be for gladness; For even as He loves the arrow that flies, so He loves also the bow that is stable."

By Khalil Gibran

I trust that you have noticed the shift after reading the above.

PAUL BINGHAM
People begin to become successful the minute they decide to be

"Life is a journey, not a destination"

Ralph Waldo Emerson

ABOUT THE CHAPTER AUTHOR

Hi, I'm Paul Bingham (43yrs old), married to Julie and father to three wonderful boys: Barney, Toby and George.

Five years ago, my life changed dramatically and started to take a new direction following a pivotal moment in my life. During this time, I've had many low moments and confronted many personal demons, however I've also had time to reflect on my true personal identity, wants and desires. When Mark asked if I would like to contribute to the book, I had no hesitation in saying yes so I could get my insights and learnings out of my head and onto paper – in the process hopefully sharing my experiences with others.

What I thought would be a simple process has turned out to be a major challenge and I've had to dig deep to complete the exercise. All I can ever hope for is that the younger generation find value in my story and life learnings so they can ask the big questions early in life to maximise the precious time we have in this world.

As an early innovator in the emerging 'Intelligent Buildings' and 'Smart Cities', I enjoyed a successful career as a business leader specialising in sales, marketing and strategy, operating in the technology, IT and telecoms sectors. I have worked alongside many of the industry's pioneers and helped them to scale and deliver next-generation digital infrastructure projects including Wembley Stadium, The Shard and The Olympic Park in Stratford.

During this time, I got to see how technology was changing and disrupting the Financial Services industry. Fortunately I followed my instinct (Lesson 1 – follow your gut) and deep down I knew IT & Telecommunications was going to disrupt every industry globally and I wanted to be part of something new, innovative and fast paced (Lesson 2 – choose to align yourself or business to a high-growth industry).

I've taken an active interest in property development having grown a small portfolio of rental properties in Rickmansworth, Herts before moving into development, learning everything about modern property development and investment strategies. I aligned myself with individuals and companies who are making an impact in the industry.

Two years ago, I decided to build upon my experiences, extensive connections and industry insights to form Smart Connected Buildings Ltd. The company's mission is to:

1. Simplify, innovate and disrupt the status quo in how technology is procured, delivered and funded in large property development and refurbishment projects.
2. Advise building owners on how to attract and retain increasingly tech-savvy occupiers through the use of smarter, more flexible and productive digital connectivity infrastructure.
3. Deploy next generation digital infrastructure to help drive premium rental and sale values whilst also providing scalable infrastructure for the future (5G, IoT, AI, VR, Smart Buildings etc).

www.smartconnectedbuildings.co.uk

MY CHAPTER

My journey – the pivotal moment

Five years ago, my life changed forever!

On the 26th May 2014, my mother died after losing her battle to Cancer. This was the most difficult period in my life to date. It was also the trigger point that set my life on a new path of self-discovery. They have been, and still are, the most difficult years of my life – but also the most rewarding.

After mum's passing, I went on a mission to seek the answers to the many questions I had and within three years my life had undergone a major transformation. I turned 40, my wife gave birth to our 3rd son, I quit corporate life, set-up 2 new companies (Bing Property Group Ltd and Smart Connected Buildings Ltd) and wandered into the wilderness to see where life would take me.

It's been difficult but I've learnt more about myself in this short space of time than the previous 20 years combined.

Why?   What changed?   What's different?

Simply put, after mum died, I was no longer scared – the shackles were off and I was going to live life on my terms! I wanted my life back, I wanted control and I wanted to spend time with those I loved most.

The biggest change as I see it, was in the questions I was asking myself.

The questions you ask determine the decisions you make.

"People begin to become successful the minute they decide to be."

I can't remember when and where I first heard this phrase, but it's always stayed with me and I've pondered its meaning for a long time.

Did I feel successful? NO! But from the outside looking in, I was a success. I had a wonderful family, perfect wife, great job, successful career, business leader, good earnings and a large house etc.

Was this my definition of success or was I conditioned to believe this?

Is this what society defines as success? Perhaps parents? Schooling? Media?

Once I started to ask myself these questions I realised what I really wanted was fulfilment and contentment. Once I came to this realisation I was then, and only then, ready to start the process of making life and career changing decisions.

Anyhow, after mum died, I was no longer scared to make the tough choices and cut the shackles of modern corporate life. I was going to become successful (fulfilled) but not how everyone else wanted me to be! I was going to do it on my own terms.

It should be made clear that I am still only starting out on the road to true fulfilment, and as I've explained since changing the direction of my life, I've learnt more than I could have ever imagined.

My experiences and learnings over the past five years are where I feel the most value lies when advising my younger self.

1. Follow your gut

Intuition is one of my strongest traits. However, decision making is something I've realised I need to sharpen up. Big decisions I find easy; small decisive actions are where I struggle and tend to overthink and explore every angle trying to find the optimum answer.

My wife helped me unlock this pattern recently by noticing I was struggling to make a decision; she could see me asking others for their opinion and without realising it seeking their validation. She took me to one side and said I needed to be more confident in my conviction and followed up with these extremely insightful and wise words:

"You are the only person that can make the right decision because you are the only one with 100% of the information".

Think about that for one second. It is so true. Every previous life experience, past thought and learning, presents your present self with the correct answer that is personal to you. I firmly believe that gut feeling and intuition are extremely powerful and we should all learn to listen and tune in to what our heart and soul tell us day-to-day. There is a much larger force operating here (but that's for another time).

Your gut (which is also known to be our second brain) provides deep insight and understanding into complex decisions. It draws upon every conscious and subconscious moment ever experienced to present a solution.

My advice is to go with your gut and don't sweat the small stuff!

2. Align yourself and business to a high growth industry

I'm fortunate that intuition early in my career presented me with the foresight to recognise that technology and telecoms would be one of the fastest growing sectors globally and if I could find a role within the industry that suited my own unique abilities (Ninja skills – life lesson 3) I could ride the growth wave, have fun, and most importantly, be a part of something new and exciting.

If I was starting out again today, I would tell my younger self to spend time examining and understanding the global macro environment, research global trends and find a market sector that is set to explode with high growth potential. If you can find a growth industry and become a specialist/thought-leader within it, you will be moving with the flow rather than against it. The inertia and momentum will propel you along and reduce friction (really important when starting out on a journey).

A smart move for anyone starting out would be to look at your own unique 'Ninja' skills and find (or create) a role that amplifies you in an industry that is about to explode. Current sectors to explore would be Augmented Reality (AR), Virtual Reality (VR),

Artificial Intelligence (AI), 5G, Blockchain, Space Travel, Energy & Sustainability and Bio Sciences to name a few.

3. Explore, study and learn everything to know about YOU

Ninja skill: a unique personal strength, skill or character trait that sets you apart from everyone else.

What's your 'Ninja skill' in life?

I've always loved to learn and I enjoyed my educational journey through to university. However, much of the curriculum and delivery of content was painfully dull and didn't work for my style of learning. Exams didn't come easy to me and I had to work extra hard to achieve good results.

From an early age it's important to fully understand your unique passions, skills and learning style and then to focus on developing them through organised and structured extra-curricular activities. On the flip side you should also be clear on where you have weaknesses or blind spots and develop strategies to overcome these.

4. Don't reinvent the wheel, just make it better

Many successful people I've met throughout my life I have observed and recognised that they intimately understand the market in which they operate. They seek to truly understand the companies and other leaders within their industry and place their own unique spin on the product or service they are delivering. They take the best of what works and apply their own special sauce to the recipe to make it better:

- Apply best practices from other non-related industries and apply to your own

- Use technology, systems and new ways of working to package your product or service differently

5. Life-long learning and expanded horizons

Living a life of continual learning is critical in my opinion and something I wish I had focused on from the moment I left university. Upon completing my degree, I didn't want to take another exam ever again, and had subconsciously become lazy when learning about new ideas and concepts and seeking to learn from others around me (point 6 below).

However, once again my intuition and passion for personal development pushed me to read many books on business and personal development during my 20s and 30s – however, in hindsight, I didn't read anywhere near as much as I wish I had.

In the past 5 years I've read and listened to more audio books than ever before and these have provided frameworks/methodologies around which I have built my businesses.

6. Embrace the knowledge and resources available whilst in full-time employment

During employment your areas of responsibility are clearly defined and typically you are paid to do something that you are competent at and are supported by a team of people around you. However, the moment you go it alone and become a business owner your role expands to every position within the business and from painful experience this leaves you totally exposed and you have to face many harsh realities; primarily you are NOT good at most things and therefore need a strong support network around you.

My advice to people currently in full-time employment is to leverage the resources, knowledge, experience and expertise you have around you. During corporate life I've worked with some amazingly talented people and many experts within their respective fields. I've worked closely with them on many ground-breaking projects, each playing a critical part in the successful delivery of the project.

In hindsight, I wish I had taken a far more proactive approach by seeking to truly understand their function and speciality. At the time I was unaware of how invaluable this knowledge would be later in life and that I would be running two companies and dealing with all aspects of commercial, legal, financial, technical and operational affairs.

William Blake once said, "Hindsight is a wonderful thing, but foresight is better". For me it's definitely a journey of lifelong learning.

MICHELLE BRYANT

Dare to be different

"Twenty years from now you will be more disappointed by the things you didn't do than by the ones you did do. So throw off the bowlines, sail away from safe harbour, catch the trade winds in your sail. Explore, Dream, Discover"

Mark Twain

ABOUT THE CHAPTER AUTHOR

I am Michelle Bryant, a Kiwi living in the heart of London. One of three, to the best Mum and Dad you could ever wish for and Aunty to four nephews.

I was raised on a dairy farm in Northland, New Zealand; I had an idyllic childhood. I have vivid memories of school lamb and calf days, fishing, water skiing, picking mussels and oysters from rocks and catching a lot of sun.

I moved to the big smoke, Auckland, to become a Chartered Accountant. This, and my desire to travel, led to the Banking world of the City of London and into the field of Project Management (Financial Services).

I have now lived out of my native country for (circa) half my life (to date).

The distance has brought family closer and more appreciated. I return annually for nice lengthy stays to spend precious time with them and life-long friends.

I remain passionate about animals, often seen at my local city farm reminiscing about pet lambs.

I now enjoy the world of property and invest in NZ, London and the regions. I am a Landlord, Consultant, SSAS Trustee and an Ambassador of an incredibly successful Fintech.

A health and fitness lifestyle is important to me – I go to the gym a lot.

You get one precious body, so why wouldn't you look after it?

I love adventure and try to live life to the full.

Always open to new opportunities and challenges, as you never know what and to whom they may lead. I am a loyal friend, I have a positive mindset and I'm no quitter.

I laugh every day and love to hear the sound of others doing the same – it's such a tonic.

If I can help anyone I will. I like to add value, from an introduction, a beneficial connection to a potential new business idea. Nothing beats the buzz from helping others and I enjoy celebrating their successes.

I thrive on the unknown.

www.Michelle-bryant.com

MY CHAPTER

Just prior to receiving the privileged invitation to contribute to this fascinating, collaborative book, my gorgeous sister had her first baby.

"Daniel Richard Anstis, welcome to the world – my precious new nephew.

One day you may enjoy reading some of this."

Looking back, I am sometimes surprised at how life has turned out, but who really has their life mapped out? The things that have stayed the same are:

- – Who I am
- – My values
- – The colour of my eyes
- – My inquisitiveness and
- – My sense of humour (hopefully!)

Fast forward to today: I live on the other side of the world from where it all started. Little did I know how many adventures awaited me when I arrived in London back in my early twenties, whom I would meet and the opportunities that would come my way. Potentially it was quite a brave thing to do, back in the day where one had to post a letter to stay in touch and communication, with the time difference, was not as easy as it is today.

I have gone down a few unplanned (but exciting) roads and am fairly independent. With a bit of life experience comes the appreciation of time. Hence, one of my prime goals is to be able to work remotely from anywhere in the world enabling myself to be the master of my own time, maximise moments with family and friends around the globe and follow the sun.

I have summed up a few things that I have learnt along the way, and if I could go back in time and hang out with my younger self for a day, here is what I would share.

Whatever happens, do not be that person looking back at their 'older self' in the mirror, wishing they had lived a fuller life. Live a life with no regrets. Jump at the opportunity to try something new. It is a proven fact that people regret the things they have not done.

What you say "no" to is more important than what you say "yes" to. You are never too old to change or start something new. Age is just a number. Never let anyone tell you otherwise.

There have been long hours, in challenging environments. Hard work and perseverance pays off. There is still much to achieve adventure wise, personally and in business.

Life can change for the good or bad in a heartbeat; it is so important to have incredible memories and stories to reflect back on, to laugh at again and again with friends. 'Create' and 'bank' memories.

Go out there and chase adventures – from a weekend summiting Ben Nevis to bungee jumping, paragliding off the French Alps, to cleaning out a well-known rock star's mini bar.

Grab each opportunity while you can. Life is so precious. There is no 'someday'. Don't put anything off. No one is promised a tomorrow.

There is a lovely little saying, "It is not the number of breaths you take, it's the moments that take your breath away that count".

Travelling was your first big dream, to go to New York, onto London, to work and travel the world. To have a lifetime of exotic holidays with loved ones. This stuff is happening!

Becoming a Chartered Accountant was a great foundation for opening new doors, project and programme management, travelling with work and investing in property. The ongoing opportunities that arise when you start to pursue things you are passionate about, can be endless. Not to mention the people you meet on the way.

Continuously make goals, focus on one thing at a time and nail it.

Achieving goals can lead to real happiness and freedom. Coasting through life gets you nowhere. Learn to dream big and chase your dreams.

Taking no risk is risking everything. Being out of your comfort zone makes you grow. Be fearless, do things that others fear. You enjoy public speaking and being asked to take part in interviews or lively discussions. From interviewing a certain President's ex right-hand man in front of a 1500+ audience in the US, to being a 'winning red tomato' on a well-known UK television cooking show.

You must constantly stretch yourself to move forward.

Never stop going to events or networking in your fields of interest.

Don't ever underestimate the power of your own network. Whether you are an entrepreneur or in the corporate world your 'net-work' is your 'net-worth'.

Invest the time to create one. It can change your life – opportunities can arise that you would never believe possible. Make great connections and nurture them. The possibilities abound when you have the courage to get out there and share your voice, ideas, opinions and views. Just this very week, you have been invited to be interviewed and filmed at several events.

Continue to learn and develop your knowledge and skills.

Never stop being curious and inquisitive – brain feed, read and listen to successful people. No one can ever take away two things: your 'love' and your 'wisdom'.

Be a good listener and always listen to Mum and Dad – they do know best!

Welcome 'change', the world is moving at such a fast pace. Don't get left behind. How you change is how you succeed. Embrace technology, it drives everything.

Gone are the days where you could be known as an expert in your field, in just your city. If you choose to be, you can now be globally recognised. Social media is powerful and it's here to stay. It is designed to be addictive but can be a real game changer if you use it wisely.

It is OK to fail and make mistakes. Pick yourself up, look at what went wrong and learn from it. You will come out stronger – remember hard stuff takes time, keep trying and evolving. Nothing ever worth having is easy – if so, everyone would be doing it. Be bold, believe you are credible. Look for opportunities where others see challenges.

Always trust your instincts and listen to your gut. If something doesn't feel right or you have doubt in it, even a little, it's probably not for you.

Learn not to worry what others think of your actions and decisions. It genuinely holds you back. You don't have to fit in.

It is good to be different and you don't need other people's approval. Just be you.

You will never please everyone, it's impossible. Don't waste time trying.

Throughout your life you will meet some amazing people but, unfortunately, it's a given that you will meet some negative ones too – avoid them, do not listen to them, they judge you by their own success. Don't beat yourself up over their issues.

There will be people who let you down, but you have to move on. Not everyone has the best interest of others at heart. So, choose your friends wisely. You don't need hundreds of friends. If you find true friendship, grab it and cherish it. Hang out with people with whom you can be your 'authentic true self' around.

Never break someone's confidence – being loyal, honest and trustworthy are the best qualities you can have.

Find people who will challenge and support you and do the same for them. Always be kind and make the time to help others, especially supporting others when bad stuff happens – be that person that sends a message or makes a call. Many people don't know what to say and just do nothing. Be the decent one.

Hard times reveal true friends, and you will need those true loyal people around.

When life is tough, be brave and remember that you are resilient.

Living a life of wellbeing is essential. Without good health everything is insignificant. Health truly is wealth. Get fit and stay fit – your body will love you for it.

Be mindful – listen to your body, know when to relax and learn to switch off.

Don't sweat the small stuff – 99% of things people worry about won't happen.

Implement the power of Positivity; you will be more productive, less stressed and more likely to live a longer, fuller life.

Always think of the future environment and have our planet's best interests at heart.

Live with Gratitude – it is an essential precursor to happiness; you must appreciate what you have.

Laugh until you cry – there can never be too much laughter in the world.

Try to do something every day that your future self will thank you for.

It's the small things that make a difference, the little things that are easy to do and easy not to do.

We will all die with a 'to do' list; just do as much as you can of the things that count.

Life is not a competition, be the best version of yourself.

Be comfortable in your own skin and enjoy your own company.

Look after the people that you love and keep them close.

Most of all, be kind to yourself on the journey ahead and never settle for second best.

RYAN CARRUTHERS

Don't get caught up by the sexy stuff

'Life is 70% events and 30% how you handle them'

Anon

ABOUT THE CHAPTER AUTHOR

Ryan Carruthers, from Lincoln. Physiotherapist by trade, property developer by choice.

What do I do? I work very hard and enjoy myself through buying property, playing golf and spending my time away from working.

The difference I make – I treat everybody the same. I will laugh and joke with everybody.

Website: www.venturepropertylincoln.co.uk

MY CHAPTER

I've been in business all my life; the biggest lesson I can teach you is don't get caught up by the sexy stuff.

Let me start by saying that we all like the sexy stuff don't we? But when it comes to business it is, and will be, a massive distraction. When I talk about the sexy stuff I am not talking about what you think – I am talking about having a focus that's so laser targeted that you don't get carried away with the next buzz word in any industry because a lot of the time these businesses are fads that will die out, they will not build you a business that can provide the life you want.

I have had many businesses in my life and looking back over them, while writing this chapter, has been an eye-opening experience and I have learnt a lot about myself through this process. The main point I want to get across is that unsexy businesses are great – they are like tugboats in the water that just keep going and building slowly, but they are dependable. You need to have a laser targeted focus, make yourself accountable and never ever believe your own hype.

What has led me to think this way?

It's really not rocket science; it's years of trying things, failing, making a lot of mistakes and then finally seeing what has worked for me and the people around me – and then just doing it better. I used to sell make-up at university and was training to be a physiotherapist (definitely not a sexy world to be in!). Then my father was sick and I stepped in to run his window cleaning business, cleaning windows is a real unsexy business – yet this business had staff, gave my dad a great work-life balance, the ability to provide well for his family and have many trips away every year. It was also one of the most dependable businesses I have ever run – it was built on a solid base and could be easily managed; it had the ability to scale at a manageable pace. I see so many businesses these days blowing up and then a year later they are gone, owners stressed because they grew too big too quick. Cash flow, which is king, got stripped from them and they spent more time firefighting the issues of the business than growing it.

When I left my dad's business, I moved into the property world and have been involved in some amazing property experiences all the way from the standard buy-to-let to development, through to commercial – guess what it all comes back to? The unsexy works. When I first started out it was as simple as buying run-down properties, adding value by selling them on or keeping them for the good yields. What this also does is produce cash flow which enables the business to grow, but it builds the right base. A lot of people want to start a business in any niche and have success straight away – it doesn't work like that. It takes time and you need to accept that and know every day what you are working towards. My property business has moved on steadily over the last seven years to a point where I have built it up in an unsexy way every single day. Following the game-plan and having a filter means that any opportunity that doesn't fit the criteria, I don't waste any time on – I only focus on the things I need to focus on. You have to know what your business does and when an opportunity that does not fit that criteria comes along, you just politely decline because it doesn't fit what your business is about and it pulls your attention away.

If you are then truly working on what your business aims to achieve and have reversed engineered this, then every day is easier because you are following the plan you have created and you will just flow through the days.

You need to be able to engage with people, the right people, in any niche – build a connection with them as people really are the key to business and life. They will teach you things that will not only make your business life better, but also your personal life, which when you are in business, is very much a case of blurred lines. You can learn from everybody around you – make sure you take advantage of that.

My life has been one hell of a ride so far. I'd like to sum up my chapter by giving words of advice to my younger self:

- Don't get caught up in the sexy – I know it looks great but it really isn't all it is cracked up to be

- Enjoy the unsexy strong business or businesses and build your business that way

- Remember that people are key to anything in life, not just business

- Don't stay on the phone all the time, don't work every hour, don't think you need to be 'hustling' all the time – work smarter and make sure that you spend the time with the people that mean the most to you

- When you are with these people, be present in the moment – the downtime is where you will be most relaxed and also you might strike onto a creative flow that enables you to break a barrier

Enjoy the ride – it only happens once.

DAVID CLOUTER

The long and winding path to the top of the mountain

"The time to hesitate is through"

Jim Morrison, 1966

ABOUT THE CHAPTER AUTHOR

Over the course of a long and varied life, David Clouter has been lucky enough to have done many of the things that would feature on his bucket list if he had one (he doesn't!).

From an early age he learned how ordinary people can provide themselves with a passive income through investing in property and other assets. This allowed him to 'retire' at the age of 35 and pursue other interests, some of which have involved what a few folk might think of as work, but as far as he is concerned, if you follow your passion with your whole heart and soul, then this is not work at all.

David founded a number of radio stations which are still going strong today (and a few that are not). He worked alongside some of his childhood heroes, including the late Tommy Vance from BBC Radio One. A lifelong music fan, he partied with Iron Maiden vocalist Bruce Dickinson at his West London home to mark his 40th birthday, and he's been backstage with Metallica. He's had an access-all-areas invitation to the Olympics and dinner with a former British ambassador who told him about his unique window on some very memorable historical events. He spent the night in the captain's cabin on the 'pirate' ship Radio Caroline and visited the fascinating top secret complex in the middle of a forest, from which "Operation Barbarossa" was launched during the Second World War. And so on.

David is a firm believer that everyone should make a difference in life and his way of giving back is to share as widely as possible the steps he took to achieve financial financial freedom. People often ask him, "Why don't they teach this stuff in school?". The reason is that society wants you to stay on the unproductive 9 to 5 treadmill for the rest of your life. But there is another way and he's always happy to share what he knows, as his own mentor once did for him. It's David's way of 'paying it forward'.

facebook.com/david.clouter

MY CHAPTER

Suppose you could write a message in a bottle, throw it far out to sea, and then your younger self, strolling along the beach, would pick it up and start to read it.

What would you write?

What lessons have you learned?

What mistakes did you make that could have been avoided?

What are the most important nuggets that you would pass on?

Well, here's my list. A few home truths that I have learned during a long and varied life. After you've read it, perhaps you'd like to sit down and write yours. I would be very interested to read what you have to say. Find me on social media at facebook.com/david.clouter

GOALS

1. Don't put off until tomorrow what you can do today. If you have a good idea, act on it immediately, or you risk losing it. Knowledge without action doesn't really count as knowledge at all, since it benefits nobody, not even you.

2. Seize the day and make the most of every opportunity that comes your way. Wherever possible say "Yes" to every invitation, but learn to say "No" as well if something takes you out of your comfort zone, or too far away from your chosen path.

3. Take chances. My father used to say: "Nothing ventured, nothing gained" and he was right. Never be afraid to take (measured) risks, for if you live your life in a comfortable bubble or cocoon, you will never achieve greatness. If you risk nothing, as the saying goes, then you almost certainly risk everything.

4. Be aware of your own self-worth. Don't be afraid, and don't let the people you meet put you down. You are totally unique, and if the people in your life don't recognise your value as an individual, then you need to know that this is their problem, not yours.

5. Never settle for second best. People compromise and lose their

dreams along the way. We all remember the hopes we had when we were younger. The world was ours and we could achieve anything we set our mind to. Then, day-to-day concerns came along and we had to compromise; something we'll always regret because it's nearly impossible to press the 'reset' button and start afresh.

6. Don't follow the crowd. Follow your own star. You will never meet anyone rich, famous or successful on your morning commute to work because nobody ever achieved greatness by working 9 to 5. So watch what everyone else is doing and saying, then look for opportunities to profit from doing the opposite.

7. "Never give up, never surrender" as the saying goes. Do whatever it takes (within reason!) to achieve your goals. Successful people sometimes fail, but they always pick themselves up and carry on, stronger than before. You may fall down seven times, but you should stand up eight times.

8. We are all standing on the shoulders of giants. There are always talented people who have gone before us in our chosen field, and who have achieved great things. The best starting point in life is the combined experience of those who have done something similar before. Make yourself totally familiar with the achievements of others, then build on them and make big improvements.

LIFESTYLE

9. Follow your passion, even if it doesn't make you rich. A life unfulfilled is a life wasted.

10. Work smart, not hard. Working for a boss, for 40 hours a week, spanning 40 years so as to eventually retire on 40% of what you couldn't afford to live on in the first place, is not the answer. Make

smart, passive investments that will compound and soon allow you to escape the 'rat race' altogether.

11. Time is the greatest asset we have. We each have a strictly limited supply. You cannot add to the 'bank of time', not even for as little as a single second to extend your lifespan, though your lifestyle choices can shorten it. So, make the most of the amazing opportunities that every day brings.

12. There is so much in life to discover, so be on the lookout and never stop learning. It is our sense of wonder about the world that keeps us young.

13. Live your life as if you have cancer, heart disease and diabetes and there's a fair chance you'll reduce the likelihood of getting any of them. This means eating healthy food and getting enough regular exercise, which doesn't have to be at the gym.

14. Remember that stress is a major killer. So find what makes you relaxed, whether it's yoga, flying a kite, or just sitting on the sofa with a glass of wine watching the telly. And do more of it. Set aside at least half an hour a day for 'me' time.

15. As the saying goes, "Don't worry, be happy". We can't make things better by worrying about them, but we can make them far worse. Don't forget that mistakes are all a vital part of the University of Life. Learn the lessons and move forward. This will make you stronger in the long run.

16. Don't make excuses. Admit to your mistakes and try to make things right with anyone who may have suffered as a result.

17. Listen to the quiet voice; this may come from within you, or

from an external source. Empty vessels make the most noise, but wisdom has no need to shout and is usually a quiet partner.

MINDSET

18. Be more open with your feelings. Tell your grandparents (and parents) that you love them, since they won't always be there for you. So, make every moment you spend together count.

19. Never be afraid to help others. Give your time freely. One day, you will be grateful when someone helps you, without seeking anything in return. The combined effect of a lot of small good deeds is to make significant improvements to everyone's quality of life. Does karma exist? There's only one way to find out.

20. Strive to make the world a better place. Put yourself in the other person's shoes and be slow to judge. Ask yourself: "What would the world be like if everyone did this?". If the answer is "better", then you should commit yourself to doing it without hesitation.

21. Recognise your true friends, the people who will be there for you in bad times as well as good. Be totally loyal to them and expect the same in return. Everyone needs a rock or an anchor to help them weather the inevitable storms that life throws our way.

22. It's all too easy to remember the bad things that people say, but we tend to forget their good deeds and sayings all too quickly. Strive hard to reverse this. The world will take on a whole new significance for you if you do.

23. Try not to be jealous. Celebrate the achievements of your friends and they will come together to celebrate yours in a totally positive way.

GUIDING PRINCIPLES

24. Never be afraid to make a stand for what you believe in, and to fight for what is right. Our firmly held principles should guide everything we do, every single decision we make.

25. Always hold our leaders to account. It is so easy to make promises when you're on the road to a position of power, telling everyone you meet what you think they want to hear. But once you arrive at the top, the campaign trail soon becomes a distant memory, and all such promises are swiftly forgotten by the new government.

26. Remember that we've only got one beautiful blue planet, teeming with life in a universe full of vast emptiness and the devastating forces of nature. It is our responsibility to ensure that our leaders never forget this because if we mess it all up, whether by war, climate change, fracking, pollution or whatever, the inevitable outcome will be a medium-sized lifeless rock floating aimlessly through space for all eternity, alongside billions of others. The physicist Stephen Hawking recognised this.

SAFEGUARDS

27. Cut out unnecessary expenses and put the money you save to good use. For example, think what you could do with a lump sum of £10,000. Do you really need that daily coffee in the local café? Save £3 a day for 10 years and you will have nearly £11,000 saved up.

28. Don't leave your savings in the bank. The value will either be eroded by inflation and tax, so that it loses its purchasing power over time, or in extreme cases you may lose some (or all) of your

money – and valuables stored in their vaults – if the bank itself fails. Remember that the purpose of a bank is to make money for their shareholders, and not to protect your savings or assets. My grandfather lost his entire life's savings in this way and lived the rest of his life in poverty, working 16 hours a day as a baker.

29. Expect the best, but plan for the worst. It is almost inevitable that many of our carefully laid plans will simply not turn out as expected, which is why it is important to always have a backup plan – and not just a plan 'B' but a plan 'C' as well. Try to think what you would do, and how you would react, in a variety of different situations.

LEGACY

30. Dear 'past self', please remember that there is a light at the end of the tunnel and the fact that you are able to read this list today proves that many years from now, you did make it safely through to the other side. 'Future self' is standing there now, with that light shining brightly all around.

At the end of the day, it is our words and ideas that survive us. A legacy for future generations and a helping hand for each and every one of us to reach our goals, hopes and aspirations as easily and as effortlessly as possible.

EDDIE COLLMAN

Don't believe that your bubble won't burst

"Life is a series of highs and lows. The trick is to tip the balance in your favour by following your heart and taking some risks"

John Avery

ABOUT THE CHAPTER AUTHOR

I was raised in the leafy suburb of Hersham in Surrey and now live in South-West London with my partner Sahra, our twin boys and dog. Family is a big deal to me; it's a very important lesson to value your family while you can, they often give you the best advice and they (or you) won't be around forever.

I was 16 when I left school in the year 1988. I found a job at a design company where I learnt how to use various Computer Aided Design (CAD) systems. My CAD skills took me into the telecoms industry 25 years ago. I still work in telecoms, although there have been a few diversions along the way including three years at university, plus I was lucky enough to end up working across Asia for 18 months and spent 5 valuable years (part-time) within the NHS.

I'm also a property investor and part time children's author. I've been a TV script writer, radio presenter and stand-up comic. I've also had a 'BBC TV room makeover', drummed on stage a few times in a band and performed the lead role in Bugsy Malone back in the eighties, all the above with varying degrees of success!

The Difference I Make: *I often 'Dad Dance' when out with my children which makes quite a difference to their social standing.*

MY CHAPTER

I'm Eddie Collman and this chapter centres on my journey into property investing which began over twenty years ago now. I think the majority of the lessons I learnt can be applied not only to property investment, but to broader life principles.

The year was 1997 and I was a student in my second year of university when I purchased my first property. It was funded by a student mortgage requiring a 10% deposit and a guarantor. The house cost me £116k and just three years later I sold this house for £210k. This was a lot of money to me (and most people at that age) and I hasten to add it was more luck than judgement that I purchased when I did.

When I left university I used these profits to start my own property portfolio. My thinking was to invest in a collection of cheaper properties to minimise my financial impact if there were any long vacant periods between tenancy agreements. Lending restrictions at this time were quite relaxed and if you were able to find a relatively small (circa 15%) deposit, then buy-to-let mortgages were very easy to come by. I decided to spread the risk around different localities and so I spent most of the year 2000 touring around the country, buying property and building relationships with various estate/letting agents and buy-to-let mortgage advisors. I still own most of the properties I purchased at this time and rent them out to private tenants across the UK.

By the time the year 2001 arrived, I had begun buying properties at auction. My thinking was to tap into the knowledge of the local property agents I had met along my travels to get an idea on where the next 'property hot spot' might be. I would then purchase at a local auction, wait a few months and sell (or 'Flip') at the same auction for profit. Of course, this wasn't an exact science and after a time the market became saturated, which meant I retained and 'rented-out' my latter purchases which had failed to exceed my price reserve at auction.

These strategies served me well back then and I was very fortunate that the housing market was so buoyant at the time I was investing.

I can't over emphasize how important it was to build relationships with the various agents and advisors at that time. It is so important to meet people face to face, let them know who you are and build the trust.

I also believe that it's a very English trait not to talk about money. I would advise my younger self to ignore convention and speak openly and honestly about it. Ask the questions, ask someone who has made it work.

There are plenty of very successful people featured in this book who are in a far better position to offer advice than me, and I would listen to every single one of them. So there's another piece of advice: read this book!

A few years later, a colleague of mine asked if I was interested in a property investment in the Philippines, on an island called Boracay. I had holidayed on this most beautiful of islands when I was working in Asia and I was very tempted. A seemingly small (at the time) £15k initial investment was all that was needed from me to build this dream house overlooking a beautiful award winning white sandy beach and the South China Sea. The property would have low management fees and high rental returns all year around – it was all too good to be true!

Initially all was going well, I was sending monthly instalments to my contact and she was sending back regular progress reports.

It was about six months into the project when the problems began and I started to sense that something wasn't quite right. Construction had stopped and more worryingly my contact had gone eerily quiet. I was informed by my work colleague (who incidentally was my contact's uncle) that the person in charge of construction was spending my money gambling on cockfighting, a legal 'sport' in the Philippines. I was also informed that the build team had not been paid because the project manager was also using my funds as stake money for the cockfights.

So began the most painful, stressful, money-sapping process of my life. Requests for funds were constantly arriving into my inbox. I had to take the builders to court because they were gambling my money away – roads suddenly needed to be dug-up to allow for services to be run-in to my property. I was getting deeper and deeper into a situation that was spiralling out of my control, but I couldn't stop chasing my losses.

Every month the demands were growing exponentially. Astronomical charges for pumped water, electricity supply and now local taxation were cropping up by the day. I have since found out from a good friend of mine that my charges were around ten times the amount they should have been.

Tens of thousands of pounds later the property was finally on the market and finally I felt the end was in sight. But worse was to come as it just wouldn't sell – month after month more charges would arrive, but month after month still no sale. Everyone around me was telling me to walk away, but just one more month, I thought; I couldn't walk away from all this money that I'd lost. I wasn't sleeping, I was worrying about everything and there seemed to be no end in sight. It felt like I had no escape route.

Eventually I had no other choice than to pull the plug and walk away. It was the toughest decision of my life. I looked into the possibility of trying to reclaim my losses but by then I'd had enough.

For many years I was not sure who to blame; I now accept my naivety and perhaps ultimately my own stubbornness and blame myself.

Maybe I believed that everything to do with property investment was gold plated because of my early successes.

When you are within a situation like this where so much is at stake (including your own pride), you don't always see what's right in front of your eyes. Yes, it's important to grasp opportunity but be bold enough to take control and change or pull out it if it's not right.

In spite of this rather harrowing experience, I still firmly believe that you should be less cautious at a younger age – just make sure you get plenty of trusted advice from the people around you and carry out your due diligence.

The most important thing I would mention to my younger self is that when you get older you will be fortunate enough to find love and be the proud father of two wonderful sons. Make sure you spend as much time as you can with these boys. Their perspective on life is pure and untainted, whereas I'm writing this at a stage of life when I'm becoming rather glum and cynical which I'm afraid means you've got all that to look forward to!

When I finished writing this, I sat down with my boys and spoke about how the advice I had for my younger self could benefit them. They looked at me when I had finished talking, looked at each other, and uttered these sincere words: "Dad, can we play Fortnite now?" (Incidentally Fortnite is a computer game you'll grow to hate). It's therefore also worth considering that advice is worthless unless the recipients are willing to accept it.

I'd like to end with this:

A good friend of mine died when he was just twenty-one years old. We'd been friends since nursery school. He was first diagnosed with cancer at the age of eleven and was in remission for a number of years until sadly his illness returned. I remember my mum telling me he wasn't very well, so I took the film Karate Kid (original version obviously), to his house and we watched it together over and over again. As I left his house I asked him whether he was OK. He looked at me and said, "I'm fine". His mum was in the background, she looked over to me with tears welling in her eyes. It was very sad.

I will never forget just how much he did in the short time he had. He travelled the world; wrote a play that he directed in the months before he died, watched by his close family and friends. He experienced so much in his twenty-one years, probably more than most achieve over their much longer lifetime.

So younger me:

1. Don't waste time.

2. Learn from your successes in life and learn even more from your mistakes.

3. Self-reflect, be confident, dust yourself down and go again.

4. Repeat numbers 1 to 3.

5. I can only assume you didn't get the advice regarding the property in the Philippines!

JOHN B. COREY JR

Being different

"Only when the tide goes out do you discover
who's been swimming naked"
Warren Buffett

ABOUT THE CHAPTER AUTHOR

30+ years of experience with creative finance as it applies to real estate. All phases in the residential (1-4 unit) and residential-related (5+ units) commercial sector.

Direct experience with real estate transactions in 4 countries. A portfolio that extends across 11 time zones.

Capital raising for real estate transactions. Conventional and creative financing techniques for funding your real estate deals or for the purchase of the home you want to move into now. A special focus on UK crowdfunding and USA syndication for investment.

Deep technology background with years of professional experience.

Executive management experience with international firms.

Specialties: Structured finance, loan packaging, trading of notes and other debt instruments secured by real estate. Team management in cross-functional projects. Global deployment of cross-border solutions.

www.propertyfortress.com

MY CHAPTER

When I was young, around six or seven, I found out that I had a learning disability. Not that I would use that phrase or that I would know what it meant. It was the abuse from the teacher which told me there was an issue. A bible across the face while standing in front of the class sticks out in my mind. A year or two later, I was in remedial reading classes. Myself with two or three others. I do not remember the other students or the teacher. I just remember sweating through the book cover. We used brown paper bags from the supermarket to cover books. My book cover became soaked and started to come apart where my hands were positioned.

One message to my younger self is that being different is OK. It will not always be fun. You are what you are so make the best of it. Being 'different' helps you see things from a unique perspective. You learn to spot things. Mostly because you cannot count on the usual viewpoint working.

Some informal studies of Silicon Valley entrepreneurs, the successful ones, show a high occurrence of dyslexia and other learning disabilities. People who are not the most successful in traditional educational environments.

I also learned that I was not good at certain sports because I have a depth perception problem. Games involving 'catching a ball' were a challenge. Baseball was a big deal as a boy growing up in the USA. Failing to catch a ball, or hitting a ball with a bat, made you less likely to be picked for the team. Pick-up games started with picking folks to be on each side. I would be picked last. It makes sense when you think about it logically. It just did not feel very good at the time. You learn to find other sports like cycling or running.

I learned that my path would not be 'normal.' That it was OK to be a bit different. After enough disappointments, you get over it.

A big message to my younger self is to accept the defects without throwing in the towel. There were times when I could have done more, I could have had more success if I had pushed on rather than remember that I was destined to fail given the 'defects.' Be slow to accept defeat.

Later in life, I could see patterns where my unique perspective brought an advantage. As Steve Jobs said during his Stanford Commencement speech, "it is when you look back that you can connect the dots". Having worked for Steve, I also learned that you are shaping how your story is told. You get to pick and choose the dots – the ones to leave out and the ones to highlight – when you 'connect the dots' in your life.

A related lesson to pass on to my younger self is to focus more. Being really good at seeing alternatives and coming up with ideas can be a curse. You are prone to move on to the next observation or insight. Many times, real success comes from continuous improvement, from repeated execution. Figure something out, get really good at it, and scale it, then move on. Be a bit slower to move on to the next 'new' idea.

My Wealth Dynamics profile says I am strong at creating product solutions. I have learned that given my talent for creating solutions, I am more financially successful when I work with others. People who can take a product idea and drive it to the next level. The quirks in my biology that made me weak at some things resulted in a more individual style. Working in teams is not the first thing I want to do. While I am fine as a team player, emotionally, I was not used to being in a team. Message to younger self: focus a bit more on building teams who can scale a business. When there are more ideas than time, write down the ideas and then get back to work on the team's project.

Wealth has come easily for me. I started out 'lower middle class,' and I am smart. So, I did well in school. I found ways to compensate for the defects. My curiosity leads me in specific directions. My younger self did pretty well by focusing on where I had natural interests. It helped that the choices I made turned out to be in demand. That people would pay good money for someone who had a degree in computer science. Being prepared to relocate or take on new adventures contributed to my success. There are places of groups doing things which will be seminal to your future success. Be open to a change. Oh, it will not be all that obvious beforehand that the move/change is a tipping point.

What my younger self would have benefited from was a bit more strategic thinking in terms of a career progression. Stumbling forward is fine when you want to maximize the serendipity. It is not the best way to reach a high level of success. Note to a younger self: think about how the choices line up. There is no right answer, yet you can tip the scales towards a more likely outcome if you put in a bit of thought. Do you want success by standard measures (wealth, impact etc) or just a new adventure?

I saved the best for last. The one key piece of advice to my younger self is to focus more on scaling the real estate business. There is limited downside compared to the technology sector. Nothing is being invented which has not been done before. That said, the real estate investment opportunities are there for someone who focuses and plays the long game. Focus on demographic trends. The value in the sector is created when people use the property. If you buy cheap in areas where people do not want to live and where there are few employment prospects, the real estate will never be valuable. If you focus on areas where there is always someone new who wants to move in, where there is suitable employment, the future will take care of itself.

In summary, my younger self needs to experiment to increase what can be learned in the least amount of time (Minimum Viable Product: MVP), focus on business opportunities which scale (Traction) and collaborate with others who have complementary skills. Along the way enjoy your life as it is the stories you remember later, which will tell you if you had a good life.

ROSS CRAWFORD

Dreams can come true

"Because it's not failure itself that constrains us.
The path to truly new, never-been-done-before
things always has failure along the way"

Regina Dugan

ABOUT THE CHAPTER AUTHOR

With over 10 years' experience in online marketing, Ross is an expert in helping businesses generate more sales through effective digital marketing. Ross runs multiple businesses, including a results-driven digital marketing agency, Mr Digital, which offers affordable digital marketing packages to business owners. As well as that, Mr Digital himself, Ross, also runs a software company that develops and operates a leading Customer Relationship Management (CRM) system for the direct sales industry.

www.mr-digital.co.uk

MY CHAPTER

When it comes to giving advice to my younger self, there's so much I could say. After 32 years of living, I've made lots of mistakes, but I learned from them. I spent a few hours contemplating the different bits of advice I would give my younger self and decided that there is one bit of advice I wish I'd known when I was younger that would have made the biggest difference to my life. That piece of advice would be that 'everything starts and evolves with a thought'.

The concept that your mind is *'THE most powerful tool'* we each have available to us is not a new one, but it's still not wildly accepted or taught, which I find crazy when it's so heavily promoted by some of the most successful people in the world, including many who started with very little in life such as Oprah Winfrey, Jim Carrey and Arnold Schwarzenegger.

I still have lots of friends and family members who have seen me grow my businesses, and achieve lots of my goals, and they know I do daily mindset training and I stress how big a part that is in my success to date, but I'm not quite sure they 'get' it. It can be a hard concept to 'get' and I understand that. It took time for me to understand and appreciate it. It's easy to think that success is a result of hard work – and it is – but that hard work will only achieve the success you are aiming for, so you need to believe you will achieve more before you even begin. If you open your mind up to the possibility of achieving more, and continue to work hard, then you will see your success comes faster and reaches new levels that you have never even dreamed of.

I was first introduced to the power of the mind through the book *'The Secret'* by Rhonda Byrne, which talks all about the *'law of attraction*' and how you attract what you think about. I was about 28/29 years old at the time, but I soon realised the *'law of attraction'* was not something new to my life – it has always been there and is the real reason for all these 'lucky' moments throughout my life so far.

Anyone who has met me knows I'm quite an excitable person and this excitement was amplified when there was something I really wanted, whether it was a moped when I was turning 16 years old, a house I saw when I was 'just seeing what was available on the market' or starting my own business when I was £20k in debt and had just got a mortgage. In each of these scenarios, my excitement was driven by my vision – I could see myself driving that moped to school every day, living in that beautiful townhouse and starting my own digital marketing agency so I could work for myself and get rewarded for achieving great results for my clients. I didn't see that I had no money at the age of 16 and my parents could not afford to buy me a moped, or that this stunning house was more than I've ever dreamed of so would be unaffordable to me or that starting a business was too much of a risk as I was already in debt and had just taken out a mortgage. Because I chose to believe and was willing to work hard to achieve these things, I got all three of them – and each time that just raised the bar for me and made me believe I could achieve even more. These are just three examples of how the mind drove my successes.

If I'd have known to raise the bar, and my vision, for what I could achieve when I was even younger, I have no doubt I will have achieved even more success and at a younger age. It's certainly something I will be teaching my children when I have them; little daily habits that open the mind to the possibility of achieving anything you want.

One of the things I find really interesting is that the older we get the more scared we get of taking risks and, as a result, we start limiting our goals. You would think it would be the reserve but it's not. As children we all have huge aspirations and goals; when I grow up, I want to be an astronaut, or a popstar, or a footballer – and these dreams are supported by our friends of the same age regardless of how challenging they might be to achieve. As adults this changes so much. If your friend came up to you and said they wanted to be an astronaut you would probably laugh and tell them all the reasons why they couldn't do it – you would not be in the mindset of your 3 year old self who would support your friend in their vision to visit the moon. As children we are fearless, but as adults we often over-think things and let fear take over. When really, in the words of author Susan Jeffers, we should '*feel the fear and do it anyway*'.

There are many ways in which we can all improve our mindsets and support our goals, even as adults. I have a few daily habits that work for me, but they will not be for everyone as we are all different so it's about understanding what works for you – what dreams turn up the fire in your belly and fuel your vision with excitement.

For me, I find watching a couple of specific motivational YouTube videos every morning gets my mind in the zone for the day. I particularly like speeches from Friends' star Lisa Kudrow, Harry Potter author and self-made billionaire, JK Rowling, and the very own 'Fresh Prince of Bel Air', Will Smith. They each have a unique story that I find motivating and inspiring and it helps me stay positive and focused when faced with the day-to-day challenges of running my own businesses. I find this morning routine sets me up for the day perfectly.

Another thing I find that works for me is reading books on self-development, with my favourite being 'Attitude is Everything' by Jeff Keller. This book really resonated with me and I 'just got it' – it hit me that my attitude determines the outcome of almost all situations, even situations that arise which are outside of our control. We each still have the choice of how we deal with that situation, regardless of how we 'want' to deal with it. For example, a customer is rude to a staff member. The staff member had no control over the behaviour of customer to stop them being rude in the first place, but they have the responsibility to control how they respond – and that's driven by their attitude to the situation and them understanding that they need to rise above it and handle it appropriately.

I am also a big supporter of visualisation and I practice this by having a vision board on my wall, which has images of things I want in life, from the evolution of my relationships to the growth in my business or materialistic things. I change my vision board every couple of years as I achieve the things that are on the board, or my goals change. Now I'm getting married, Toby and I do the goal board together as our vision for the life we want to build together. I also have the wallpaper on my phone as something I want to achieve – currently my mobile app as the number 1 app in the app store. This keeps me super focused on this goal and keeps it at the forefront of my mind, reinforcing it.

I'm not saying that having a positive mindset or by practising daily mindset habits will remove all stress or negativity from your life or make life all go perfectly. That's not how it works. What it will do is make you approach challenges differently, stay positive and achieve more success than you have before, providing you are willing to put the hard work in.

There are many great resources out there that can help improve the mindset. By investing your time in them and discovering what works for you, and committing to it for at least 30 days, you will notice a positive difference in how you approach every day. This will have a positive impact in both your personal life and career/business. I truly believe there is no better habit that will generate such a great return-on-investment (ROI) than investing in your mind.

JUSTIN DAVIS

Injury, mindset and resilience in the face of adversity

"Circumstance does not make the man; it reveals him to himself"

James Allan

ABOUT THE CHAPTER AUTHOR

My name is Justin Davis, I'm 31 and a positive, hard-working, passionate, driven and completely motivated individual. I enjoy seeing others work hard, push their personal boundaries, succeed and grow through the process, but it didn't come in a completely natural way to me. I have had to, and continue to, fight for the privilege both physically and mentally on a daily basis. I was born and raised in a small town in the very South-East of the Cotswolds, England, UK. Looking back, an absolutely beautiful location to enjoy the freedom that any young child should be able to do so. Climbing trees, making dens, and playing soldiers in the fields was a favourite past time. I used to borrow my dad's tools and head out into the fields to saw and chop-up wood to construct my latest hiding place/observation post. Looking back, I was always destined to be a soldier. It was my calling. My mother told me that anytime I needed a new set of trousers or trainers it would be army fatigues and black combat boots instead. I fondly look back and now realise just how simple and easy life was compared to this very moment, as I write this. I never thought that some 20-25 years later I'd have been to the places and done some of the things that I have done. Nor could I imagine my life to be so different due to my actions on one day in my early 20s, and I now sit here and wonder what life might be like in a further 25 years. I'm fully aware that plenty of challenges await me but it's nothing that hard work and commitment won't fix.

www.justinoliverdavis.com

MY CHAPTER

December 15th, 2011. Tasking: Quick Reaction Force. I'm point-man of a patrol that was tasked to close-with, cut off and engage a group of enemy Taliban fighters who had ambushed another group of British soldiers within our Area of Operation – my primary role was as a search team member. I was to guide our call-sign safely to the location of the enemy, searching the ground for hidden improvised explosive devices as we patrolled, observing the ground in front of my feet and beyond for any signs of disturbance that could be suspected of containing hidden explosives – all the while utilising every piece of equipment and human sense possible. Crossing open ground, through tree-lines, between compounds with high, hard-compacted mud walls and over, or through, irrigation ditches filled with water.

The day had already begun with a fluster of activity. A large explosion in the distance followed by the sounds of gunfire. It came over the radio that one of our senior commanders from a sister platoon, a Platoon Sergeant, had been severely injured by a projectile fired from a directionally fired improvised explosive device (DFCIED). The piece of shrapnel – likely to be a nut or bolt, bullet or random fragment of metal – entering and exiting his lower leg causing significant damage. The device was simple, hastily assembled, and was constructed from only a very few basic components: a metal drainpipe about 4-6 inches in diameter that was packed with shrapnel and explosive material, then laid in a favourable position to cause the most damage. The device would be initiated by a single wire connected to a small power source. It was as simple as that. A range of emotions instantly arose – shock, fear, anxiety and excitement, all within milliseconds of each other. The senior commander was a man whom many respected, a small and slight figure in stature but the complete opposite in tenacious attitude towards fulfilling his role as a senior non-commissioned officer. His fight was over. He was extracted back to the UK where he would then go on to make a full recovery. With another 4 months of our tour left to complete, I had no idea that I would be seeing him again so soon.

There is smoke all around, I am alone in the checkpoint super-sangar. A bright flash followed by debris and smoke closely rushing past my face in an upwards vertical motion. A constant overpoweringly loud and metallic high-pitched ringing is in my ears, my mouth is moving but no sound is coming out, the smell of burning flesh, fertiliser and the distinct metallic iron scent of fresh blood is in the air. My nostrils and mouth have been force fed and lined with dry dirt, debris and secondary fragmentation from the explosion. My helmet chin strap is inside my mouth and being forced down my throat. In a full state of panic, I pull at it and begin to cough and choke violently, my personal weapon ripped from my grasp and violently flung out of sight. The metal detector in my right-hand evaporating before my eyes like the special affects you expect to see in a five-star blockbuster movie screening. My eyelids now flickering, I pulled harder and harder until I choked even more, my vision blurry and all my senses in shock. In an attempt to escape my impending fate, I notice all movement is restricted by an unseen force. Then, I wake up.

I noticed that my feet felt strange and there was nothing but what felt like a powerful electrical current running through them. I can only describe it as extreme pins and needles. With my left hand I lifted the thin white bedsheet that was covering the lower part of my body and I was presented with what can only be described as an utterly heart-wrenching horrendous sight. This was not a dream. Seeing the absence of both of my legs for the first time, I have never been so genuinely surprised and astonished in my entire life. For that split second I felt every single possible human emotion.

A quick visual check over my body to scan for any further injury; first an oxygen mask over my face, a medical intravenous line in every remaining limb providing essential life-saving support; drains in both of the stumps to remove any fluid build-up, reduce swelling and take away any foreign bacteria and dirt; a feeding tube up my nostrils, down my throat and into my stomach; Intravenous drips in my forearm and neck; a catheter in my penis; an epidural in my spine; my right arm is contained inside a pressure bandage to keep my forearm together whilst it healed from the injuries it sustained during the blast. It was hell on earth. So much pain, discomfort and uncertainty. So many fluids being pumped into my system. I was a mess. Take me back to Afghanistan, throw me into a field or irrigation ditch laden with IEDs, I'll be happy to take the chance and spin the wheel of Afghan-roulette once again. Anything, but this.

It later transpired that en-route to the ambushing site I had missed a device with my search equipment, stood on it, and in doing so, initiated an explosion under my right foot that ultimately resulted in a life-changing injury. Both of my legs were amputated through the knee. I was devastated. Truly heartbroken. Life as I knew it was over. But I must fight on. This is truly where the 'Circumstance revealed the man'.

It has taken extreme effort to maintain and fight this injury for the last 8 years. I have suffered both physically and mentally the hardships of becoming "Disabled". It is simply all-encompassing. Every single step I take, every time I stand up, sit down. Every prosthetic appointment I attend, I am aware that I am different. As the years have passed, and with multiple further surgeries to recover from, I have had to put my life on hold and focus all my attention on my recovery – never really having a chance to progress. But, looking back, each one has been a blessing in disguise as it has incrementally instilled mental resilience of the highest order, and thus enables me to push harder in my everyday existence and pursue the challenges I desire.

I now accept that I have been set on a completely different pathway – one of learning, adapting, discovering, enlightening, sharing and challenging. I now aim to continually push my personal and physical limits to summit the highest peaks in the world, and in doing so, raise awareness for the disabled and less fortunate in the world. I will turn what seems like a wholly negative experience into something much more powerful. All for the greater good. It's now my purpose in life.

At the time of writing I am currently in training for a summit attempt of Mt. Blanc. Hopefully, when reading this, you will find that it was successful and I will then be hunting the next challenge!

MATHIEU EVERSON

Now is the time, wait for perfect and you'll be waiting forever

"Have no fear of perfection – you'll never reach it"
Salvador Dali

ABOUT THE CHAPTER AUTHOR

Being born with parents from different nationalities – Mother being French from a little Island called Corsica and Father, British from the Northern Powerhouse that is Manchester – I didn't have an ordinary childhood. I'd spend 3 or 4 months in summer in Corsica and the rest of the time in England.

I started traveling to Corsica on my own at around 4 years old – well I was always with ground staff or the airhostesses, however at such a young age I felt brave, independent and could take on the world and any challenges it gave me. I spent my summers exploring nature, building dens in the forests and only ever having to come home to eat.

This feeling of freedom, confidence and making my own decisions on what my day entailed, engrained a strong self-belief and sense of independence in me and I believe it's what has made me into the success I am today.

My name is Mathieu Everson, I am an investor in property and business. I am currently in a transition period of my life where I am increasing my personal wealth via property developments but also holding down a full-time job as well.

Not many people can say this, but I'm in a fortunate position where I love my 'Day Job', been promoted many times and get paid well for the experience I bring to the business.

I've always been comfortable in my life. I realised a few years ago that being comfortable is dangerous, as you remain still, you don't grow as fast as you should do. Not analysing where you are in your life constantly, we always default toward a more comfortable journey. Your comfortable zone provides a state of mental security and you can appreciate why being in this zone for too long, is so hard to get out of.

This is when I started my journey into property development.

The motto of my company is 'Creating Communities Together'. In everything I do I look to instil that motto, be it a collaborative approach with other investors and entrepreneurs or adding value to the local community – again, adding value via property, be it by increasing the average value in the local area, or making a run-down property a fantastic new family home for someone. The pride this gives me is powerful, especially when you, the local community, take time out of their day to thank me for making their street look welcoming again.

Let's be honest, we do this for wealth creation to live a better life for ourselves and family. However, the bi-product is making other people's lives better also.

What a perfect combination this is.

www.zalanaholdingsco.com

MY CHAPTER

Rarely is there a perfect scenario in life for you to take action. I'd go as far as to say there is never a perfect time to do anything – stopping a bad habit, getting healthy, speaking to the girl/boy you like, getting into a better routine, learning new skills to develop yourself as person.

Once this is acknowledged, you will get a lot more profound work done a lot quicker every day.

Too many times have I stopped myself, when I was younger, waiting until things are perfect. I waited and I waited for so long, that when I look back now, I realise that I was paralysed by fear. The fear of not being perfect and judged by others, worried about any failings I could have.

In my early 20s I was very much into electronic music. I bought my first pair of decks in 2000 and started to DJ in some of the biggest clubs and festivals in the UK. This led me to producing music, which even though I was great at DJ-ing, I wasn't great at producing. So many times I've been sat by my Mac, with a finished track, but wasting time trying to make it better, adding other elements into it, editing it further, putting in extra vocals. In the end I had wasted so much time and effort and the outcome didn't make the track any better. In reality, it made it worse. I didn't want to release a track that wasn't the best I could do.

I acknowledged that this is the best I could do right now and I would get better with every new track I made. I released the track and was happy. Now, when you listen to the first track I did, compared to the last one, there is a world of difference in quality and sound. I had perfected my skills, however still never perfect, as you are always learning.

I got over that fear of perfection and the outcome was I had a few of my tracks played on Radio One and by superstar DJs all over the world. What if I had started earlier and released my music sooner than I had, could I have had more success? Could more music have been broadcast?

Now I am in the property and business world, I know there is no perfect time. However, when I am analysing property deals or working on cashflow models for new businesses, I'll look at where I stand right at that moment in time.

Is it the perfect time to do business? The property market is stagnant, some high street businesses are failing, people are spending less – is this the right time? YES IT IS.

As long as your business model stacks up, you've perfected your numbers as best you can to suit your business needs, then go for it. Yes, you could get a better margin in a few months if you wait, but what if you wait too long and things get worse and the deal that did stack up, doesn't anymore?

Don't let the fear of perfection stop you. If your numbers stack up for where you are on your journey right now, have the courage and go for it. In time your skills and knowledge will expand and better projects will come your way.

We're in an era where people are craving information, where information is readily available at our fingertips. There are mentors in every vocation, courses in everything you can think of, someone else you can learn from who was in the same position you were in a few years ago. You have everything you need to make it in your life's goals -you don't need it to be perfect. All that matters is that you overcome your fear and get the courage to start now.

Let me tell you this: right now I am doing a business plan for a new venture I am looking at starting, with a new business partner. I have been working on a cashflow model and forecasting the first year, speaking to designers and construction companies etc.

I'm constantly meeting/emailing commercial agents, looking for projects for me to develop. Going to networking events, looking for likeminded people to potentially joint venture with. Traveling up and down the country in my day job, presenting in front of a Board of Directors of big companies to win business with.

All this whilst making time for my health and staying on top of my fitness.

When Mark Stokes asked me to write a chapter in his book, I asked myself: is now the right time for me to take on something else? Have I ever written a chapter in a book which is going to be read by thousands? Do I know what I am going to write about? Do I know how to structure what I am going to write about?

The answer to all those questions was No.

However, what an opportunity this was – will this come about again? Probably not. Now isn't the perfect time, but when is? So, here I am, almost finished my first ever chapter. I am happy with the opportunity and I've made time to take advantage of this situation.

"I learned that courage was not the absence of fear, but the triumph over it. The brave man is not he who does not feel afraid, but he who conquers that fear".
Nelson Mandela

DR. STEVEN FAWKES

Beware of fulfilling other people's expectations

"Never play to the gallery.... Never work for other people in what you do. Always remember that the reason that you initially started working was that there was something inside yourself that you felt that if you could manifest in some way, you would understand more about yourself and how you co-exist with the rest of society.... I think it's terribly dangerous for an artist to *fulfill other people's expectations*"

David Bowie, advice to artists, 1997

ABOUT THE CHAPTER AUTHOR

Dr Steven Fawkes is an internationally recognised, award-winning energy efficiency and clean technology expert with more than 30 years' experience of advising companies, investors and governments on policy, strategy, projects and capital raising. He has worked in Europe, Asia, the Middle East and America, built a number of energy services businesses from start-up and advised governments including the European Commission, UK, Romania, India and Saudi

Arabia. He has been a pioneer in energy efficiency throughout his career and over the last five years has been closely involved in the development of the energy efficiency financing market in Europe.

Steven is committed to building platforms for investment at scale into companies that support the Sustainable Development Goals. He is the founder and Managing Partner of EnergyPro (energyproltd. com), a group of companies that is committed to accelerating the energy transition and our shift to a more sustainable global economy by providing advice, asset management and capital raising services for companies supporting the SDGs. Steven is the independent member of the Investment Committee of the London Energy Efficiency Fund, an adviser to three other funds in Europe and a Director and board adviser for several companies at the leading edge of energy and smart materials.

Steven is an experienced public speaker and has undertaken engagements in Europe, the USA, the Middle East, Asia and Africa. He has more than 300 publications and writes an influential blog: Only Eleven Percent (www.onlyelevenpercent.com). In November 2012 he was awarded the Energy Institute's Individual Achievement Award; in August 2017 the American Council for an Energy Efficient Future awarded Steven a "Champion of Energy Efficiency in Industry" and in 2018 the Indian Business Group awarded EnergyPro its SME of the Year Award.

www.onlyelevenpercent.com

MY CHAPTER

The quote from David Bowie, who was the favourite musician of my younger self from when he first became famous in the early 1970s, and still is my all-time favourite musician, sums up much of my advice to my younger self. Even though it is from the perspective of an artist to other artists, it definitely applies to work and in general.

Growing up you have an idea of what you want to do, perhaps even a dream like becoming an astronaut or working in the space programme which, like many children of my generation who grew up watching the magnificent Apollo programme unfold, was mine. Of course, in the Britain of the late 1960s and 1970s that truly seemed an impossible dream – first of all, back then, only the US and the Soviet Union had manned space programmes and to be a US astronaut you had to be an American citizen. Even without that barrier, of course becoming an astronaut was incredibly competitive – the vast majority of them were test pilots who had come out of the US military flying fast jets, a career path that certainly was never going to be open to a short-sighted Brit. It is easy to forget that in those days even visiting the US was a dream not open to most people.

What I have learnt since is that three of my contemporaries growing up in 1960s Britain and watching the space programme – admittedly amongst the thousands who had the same dream – actually made the grade and became US astronauts and got to fly in space: Michael Foale, Piers Sellars and Nicholas Patrick. The lesson here is that dreams can come true, but you have to hold onto them and work towards achieving them every day. Many astronauts who get selected including Michael and Piers certainly applied to the astronaut programme multiple times – never giving up on their dream. Of course, I am sure there are plenty of others who did that but never made the grade to be selected as astronauts – the criteria are incredibly exacting and many equally qualified candidates apply at every opening; not everyone can make it. Perhaps many of the others got jobs connected with the space programme but even if they didn't, at least they gave it their best shot. The important thing is to make the best possible effort and keep moving towards the dream. As depression era self-help author Napoleon Hill said, "whatever the mind of man can conceive and believe, it can achieve" and Walt Disney allegedly modified this to "if you can dream it, you can do it".

I think David Bowie, in the quote, was saying that you should not listen to other people when they try to limit your dreams or ambition. Parents and teachers say – or used to say – things like "work hard and get a safe job", typically they didn't say "follow your dreams". We are influenced by others, particularly parents, teachers, friends and spouses to meet their expectations of us and this leads us to making compromises about what we want to do, or even what we can talk about. Listening to that influence can lead to burying the dream, the real desire that deeply motivates us and lead us to look for the 'safe' route or job rather than working on the things that really 'turn us on' – the things that come from deep inside us. It is right to listen to the advice of others, but it is not right to make this kind of life changing decisions based on the expectations of others. Practical advice should be sought on how to achieve the big dreams but you should discount any negativity or attempts to dissuade you from following them. When you are young, other people – and you – literally have no idea what you can actually do or about the world you will grow up into.

Another aspect of this advice is that once you make decisions, doors close and new doors open. New dreams and ideas can be conceived and actioned. Opportunities to move towards your dreams and objectives appear every day– make sure you recognise them and take them. Often they are disguised in things that appear unconnected or buried in the busy-ness of everyday living.

Another part of the lesson is that you only regret things that you didn't do or attempt to do – very rarely the things you did. Therefore, make sure you take action and do something in every situation that could lead to a desired outcome – doing nothing can only lead to regret. Usually doing nothing results from the fears that you have – fears of failure – and you have to recognise them, park them away somewhere and still take action. As the master David Bowie said in "Fill Your Heart" from the brilliant Hunky Dory album:

Fill your heart with love today
Don't play the game of time
Things that happened in the past
Only happened in your mind, only in your mind
Oh, forget your mind, and you'll be free, yeah.

Taking action in the face of fear is the definition of bravery and therefore you should always seek to be braver. Say what is on your mind. When you have an idea about what to do, work out a plan of action that starts today and take the first step. The old saying about a journey of a thousand miles starts with the first step is so true. If you don't take the first step you will never get there – you can achieve anything. It may appear contradictory but although taking action is essential, major life decisions need to be taken only after a lot of thought and consideration. It is sometimes easy to get carried away in the momentum of a relationship or a project for example and not consider whether it is the right thing. Getting married or having children is a decision – or non-decision in some cases – with long lasting and massive consequences. Think carefully about whether moving to the next step is the right thing and then take clear decisive action – one way or the other.

The other big lesson is that there really is no time like the present and time disappears very quickly as you get older. Ten years seems like an age when you are 20 but by the time you are 50, it seems like a short while. It may seem that you have time to make decisions, to settle down, to have children and start on the things you want to do but you really don't have much time at all. Get on with it today! If you put something off other things may happen, or get in the way, that make it impossible later on. Also, health is precious and illnesses and accidents can take people away far too young – make sure you tell people how you feel about them often, you never know when they won't be there.

My other piece of advice, which is related again to the David Bowie quote, is not to give up those things that give you, or could give you, satisfaction even when it is easier to do so or when they seem childish. I am thinking here of past times like drawing, painting and making things from models to houses to cars. Those are part of the things inside you that you are driven to manifest in some way. By letting them slip you miss out on the opportunity to express yourself and also the opportunity to become a master in them. Only by practicing relentlessly can you master a skill. Also, by practicing them, new opportunities to create a more satisfying career or a second income may come about. In your dying days you won't take satisfaction from how many TV shows you watched or how many films you saw, or even how many books you read – satisfaction will have come from what you have created.

My final piece of advice is that those dreams that you have when you are young do come true – maybe not all of them, and maybe not always in the exact form that you envisaged them – but they do come true. Stick with them.

NIGEL GREENE

Push yourself!!

"In order to succeed, your desire for success should be greater than your fear of failure"

Anon

ABOUT THE CHAPTER AUTHOR

My name is Nigel Greene and I am a devoted Husband to my wonderful and supportive Wife Annette, and Father to four amazing children: Dan, Hannah, Caitlin and Josh. It is my family who planted those seeds of desire many years ago, to create significant wealth through business and property; to seek a lifetime's ambition of creating a multi-generational legacy. Derby is my place of birth where I spent the first 30 years of my life before relocating to the Essex area through my work in 1998.

I have always had a firm belief that if you cannot directly input into something then you will have very little control of the outcome, which very early on made me opposed to the concept of the stock market and particularly UK Pension schemes.

With 29 years board level business and property expertise in engineering, construction, energy and telecoms industries, I have co-founded and operated within many national and international businesses, deploying complex projects of values between £5million – £500million.

As previously mentioned, I wanted to create wealth in my life and that all important multi-generational legacy. However, a pension today effectively halves in value on death and disappears totally when your next of kin/beneficiary departs, reducing the wealth and that legacy to zero. Therefore, my approach was to never invest in the Stock Market and to find an alternative/supplementary route to pension, and to invest in an asset class that would generate a passive monthly income throughout my lifetime and beyond. The answer for me was residential and commercial rental property. Over the past 20+ years, my Wife and I have invested heavily and we have built an impressive multi-million-pound international property portfolio. This continues to grow both in property numbers, valuation and provides a monthly income that is impactful to our lives now.

I left the corporate world for the last time in March 2015. My business partners and I established a property development company, EquaGroup (www.equagroup.co.uk). As a company, we focus on our combined passion for creating shared and sustainable value through property and building a powerful and enduring legacy for future generations. I am passionate about helping others to succeed in their lives and sharing the knowledge that I have gained over the years. Our training and mentoring business EquaSSAS has created a wonderful platform for us to help others to achieve great things in their lives and for us to achieve our passion. Despite my personal views on pensions, over the years the corporate world has contributed to a significant personal pension value, through a combination of final salary and stakeholder schemes. In 2016, I transferred this into a Small Self-Administered Scheme (SSAS) Pension, where myself and fellow trustees now actively invest this money into commercial property, or other HMRC approved investments.

I retain a low profile, by choice, and looking back have quietly and consistently achieved over the years through lots of hard work, my love of detailed analysis, being creative and being decisive when it matters. I have always given more than I take and I remain determined and passionate about achieving my life's goals.

This is me: Husband, Dad, multiple Business Owner, successful Property Investor, Pension Trustee, Trainer, Mentor and multi-generational Legacy Creator.

MY CHAPTER

I want YOU to be (as I am) a firm believer that anyone can achieve their dreams and experience amazing things in life if they apply themselves with focus, have personal drive and passion, be agile and surround themselves with likeminded people. If YOU can be this person then YOU can (and will) achieve your goals and have a very fulfilling life.

I have set out below a summary of my early career and how being significantly pushed by others, and by pushing myself, broadened my mind, my personal experiences and attitude to achieving personal goals.

When I left school, I entered the workplace and started a 5-year apprenticeship scheme which was an absolute eye opener. This route was not my first choice as my career plan was to follow in my Father's footsteps into the Police force. Having passed interviews, medicals and been shortlisted for a place in the Police as a cadet, at the very last-minute government policy changed and I could no longer join the force at 16 years old, as the entry age had now been lifted to 18 years old. My plan B was to start an apprenticeship, train for two years and look to jump ship into the Police Force at 18 – but the reality was very different!

The first few years as an apprentice were tough and pushed my boundaries, both physically and mentally. The guys that I worked with were my trainers and mentors and they were very tough individuals who would only accept the very best outputs from themselves and from the team around them. This manifested into their training methods of driving levels of quality and attention to detail beyond anything I had ever seen, which explained why the company at the time was in a league of its own in the industry, when compared to its peers. To this day, I hold a huge amount of respect for my trainers, and I am very thankful to them for pushing me to levels of detail and quality standards that I have taken with me through my life. They taught me respect, the importance of a great team, how quality should flow down into the smallest detail and when the going gets tough, you have to keep going.

As I approached 18 years old, I was learning so much (and also earning quite a bit), and the thought of taking a pay cut to go into the Police Force was not an option for me. That being said I also knew that I did not want to spend the rest of my working life on the tools as a tradesman. That year, just by chance, I was put forward by my senior management for the National Apprentice of the Year awards and won it – and the following year I won the regional award. The company I worked for was then taken over by a multi-national, and I quickly fell into the spotlight of their senior board who promoted me onto a Junior Engineer programme with a place in the office to help run projects, as opposed to working on them. My new manager, a senior engineer, was in his mid-60s, smoked endlessly and liked a few drinks in the evening; he again was a stickler for detail. He was a task master, but a great engineer and he taught me engineering design, estimating and methods of project management to a level whereby my college lecturers struggled to keep up. His teaching methods were tough, but then again, I was now used to these methods from my time on the tools.

Being promoted onto the Junior Engineer programme meant that I was now earning less than when I was on the tools as I was now on a fixed salary, rather than being paid an hourly rate. Yes, I had a company car and was being paid through college but my take home pay was significantly less than the guys on the tools. This inspired me to earn more through working out of hours on private jobs to gain a secondary income.

The Senior Engineer then became ill and could not work and the Manager of the branch left, and the other Engineer became the Manager, so I was then promoted in short order to Project Engineer and became responsible for estimating, designing, purchasing, quantity surveying/cost management and project management for pretty much all of the projects in the business. I was now working all hours, being the first in and the last to leave, and had to dig very deep to keep up with everything that was going on. I was physically fit due to my martial arts training which helped to combat some of the fatigue, but life was definitely all work and no play and all on a fixed salary!!

One day I took a call at home from one of my old lecturers who had moved away from the college scene and was now working for a local business and wanted support in its growth. After a few meetings, I was offered a new job with a further promotion and pay rise – and I jumped at the chance for a fresh start. Workload was no different, but I was now earning a lot more and together with my old lecturer, we expanded the business very quickly.

After a few years, I was approached by another company – got promoted again, but unfortunately, despite being successful, this company went under due to a large non-payment by one of its clients. At the time I was working on a major project in London. We quickly set up a new company, employed all of the trades and we were contracted to complete the project which was very lucrative. I decided that I no longer wanted to work too far down the food chain, due to the uncertainty of payment and business survival, and received an offer to work for a US based global telecommunications company based out of its London office. The company wanted me to move to London from the Midlands, but I was not prepared to do this during the 6 months' probation period, so I travelled from Derby to London every day for 6 months which was exhausting. After the six months' probation period had passed, I relocated to the South with my wife and family and my first significant project was in Glasgow, so off I went again!!

I could go on giving you further experiences and examples of how I pushed myself, (and was pushed) created and took new opportunity in all parts of my life as and when it was presented, but it would need multiple chapters and I've only been given this one to write, so my advice to YOU is:

1. Push yourself and accept with open arms being pushed by people who are more experienced than yourself.

2. To always accept advice with thanks (it's up to you whether you use it or not).

3. Accept that from time to time it's going to get tough and when it does, keep moving forward a step at a time.

4. Share your challenges with the people around you.

I hope that the above helps YOU to accept the importance of having personal drive and determination and sharing and accepting advice from the people around you.

"In order to succeed, your desire for success should be greater than your fear of failure"

Understand your personal strengths and weaknesses and see if you can find others who have opposing but complimentary skills.

As human beings, it is fair to say we are all different. We like doing different things and have different strengths and weaknesses. Ask yourself a few questions:

- *What do I enjoy doing?*
- *What things do I dislike doing?*
- *What are my strengths?*
- *What are my weaknesses?*

The responses to the questions have no right or wrong answer as they are unique to you. However, by thinking these questions through you will get to know yourself a lot better and as you progress through life, and maybe into future business enterprises, it would be great if you could find business partners with some opposing likes, dislikes, strengths and weaknesses. This is how great teams are created, essentially by filling in all of the skill gaps needed and collectively achieve amazing outcomes.

I personally have had the honour and privilege of meeting and working with some of the best people in the industry. Together in business we have achieved incredible, life changing results and some of these people I am proud to say I still have as great friends and colleagues. Knowing the strengths and weaknesses in a team of people, and more importantly knowing when you have skill gaps in a team, can be the difference between success and failure. I have seen so many different personalities in some of the great teams that I have run and accepted sometimes that the management of the difference of opinions and viewpoints can be as challenging as getting the project done.

Personally, my management style is one of mutual respect, with a friendly and supportive tone but with clear objectives and direction. This approach has worked for me personally throughout my career and when the chips are down, I have had my colleagues in the trenches with me working through the problem and overcoming it. I am very aware that there are more abrasive methods of management and leadership which I have seen, but it's about finding YOUR style and fine tuning that style to achieve the results that are needed.

My upbringing, my early career and moreover my martial arts training established mutual respect as one of my highest values, and I have always adopted this value in everything that I have done, both personally and in my career. Unfortunately, from time to time, I have come across and worked with individuals who have not been respectful to me or others around me and therefore our parting was necessary, and I wish them well.

In summary, know yourself and the people around you, build great teams, support groups and relationships and always be respectful.

"If you do what you have always done, you will get what you have always got."

Personally, I like the phrase "If you do what you have always done, you will get what you have always got" which is a true statement for a lot of people, and this is absolutely fine. However, if you want more from your life then some things will have to change.

The breakaway from the norm requires lots of courage and change which occurs when personal boundaries are pushed and accept that you will be well outside of your comfort zone. Being outside of your comfort zone will enable you to grow and learn, which is very exciting, but equally the mind can translate this as feeling scared, nervous and overwhelmed.

Your support structure is key here, make sure that you have great people around you (friends, family, colleagues) who you can talk to and confide in – the phrase 'a problem shared is a problem halved' is a very true statement. Speak to people who are on a similar journey as well as people who have previously trod the same path.

Take offered advice with thanks from everyone and learn from their challenges which may help you avoid experiencing the same ones. If you speak to as many people as you can and hear their challenges and experiences on how they navigated their problems, it will help you to get up the learning curve much quicker than if you don't speak to anyone.

"Start with the end in mind."

Always, but always, start with the end in mind.

What do you want to achieve in your life and in what timescale?

Having practiced martial arts for many years and attaining many levels of success, the art itself taught me many things. When I progressed through the black belt programme, I faced a number of situations where I would be in a full contact environment with multiple opponents (from memory seven was the maximum I have competed against at the same time). In this moment you enter a heightened state of awareness and considering the task ahead, it would not be uncommon to be overwhelmed by the challenge. However, by starting with the end in mind and working back, it is clear that the objective is to defeat all the opponents and to minimise injury to yourself, and the most effective route to achieving success is to pick off one person at a time. So, by moving or herding the pack this way and that to expose one person at a time, and then onto the next, is the way to achieve success in this situation.

Life is very similar so whatever you want to do with it, I would suggest that you set your main goal and then break it down into achievable sub-sections and pick off one at a time. If you were to start with your whole life goal you may find it too overwhelming and your plans may stall.

A few years ago, with a group, I rode across Borneo in Asia on a mountain bike for Charity and we raised £25,000 for that charity which was great. The ride itself was over 350 miles, climbing over Mount Kinabalu which in itself was slightly over 4,000 meters high, in temperatures of up to 45oC and humidity levels nearing 90-95%.

The mountain climb was the most gruelling. Starting with the end in mind and then breaking it down into bite-sized chunks was very relevant here. In actual fact the bite-sized chunks were putting one pedal in front of the other and keeping the wheels turning.

We experienced such intense conditions that the tarmac on the roads was melting and if for any reason the wheels stopped turning, the bike tyres would sink into the tarmac and the bike would stop.

Towards the top of the climb we rode through the clouds and out the other side. Our first night in our treehouse accommodation had views similar to those out of an aeroplane when it has flown through the cloud base and out the other side. The next day was downhill on a high-speed decent traversing across dry riverbeds, dodgy suspension bridges into the lowlands of Borneo and the paddy field areas.

This went on for seven days and every day was different with different terrain and challenges, not forgetting a bout of heat stroke on the sixth day which was unfortunate. Here drive and determination took over to get over the finish line on the seventh day!!

This pursuit taught me a lot about myself and the techniques of achieving amazing things.

The message here is to break everything down into achievable parts, which in my case were daily challenges and, furthermore, where required into pedal strokes.

A couple of quotes that I hear from time to time:

- *Try not to boil the ocean – it's impossible to boil the ocean due to its size, so start with a cup of water and repeat this as many times as necessary until you achieve the objective.*

- *How do you eat an elephant? One bite at a time!*

Once you have reached your first milestone, celebrate your achievements, reset your objectives and actions and go again to the next level.

Map out your plans, starting with the end point and work back to today. Keep yourself accountable to time scales and avoid excuses for non-achievement.

Review your plans on a regular basis with your support structure and take feedback (good and bad), revisit the plan and reset if necessary.

"Many of life's failures are people who did not realise how close they were to success when they gave up."

YOU will get many bumps in the road – this is life – accept it and embrace it as there is no better learning; it is really important that you experience these challenges as they are part of your personal growth and experience building.

Keep looking back and reflecting on what you have achieved and how you have pushed your boundaries. You will be very surprised on how far you have come and how your confidence has grown and indeed what your new norm now looks like.

"Never, ever, give up!!"

Always keep moving forward. You may have played a game called *'Whack-a-Mole'* as a child – it's a mechanical game that when a mole pops up out of his hole you need to whack it on the head with a plastic hammer. The thing is, there are multiple moles and multiple holes! Having chartered a new course and being on that course, you will encounter problems and issues – as the problems come up, deal with them and keep moving forward. Try not to feel down when times get rough – talk and share and find ways to lift your positivity; go for a walk, play football, go to the gym. Find the thing that works for you to keep you positive and in the best shape to work the problem and whack that mole!!

Be aware that the people around you who do not have the courage to push themselves, will be very keen to give you opinion-based advice and they will tell you every reason under the sun why you should not be doing it. Just thank them for their comments and move on. Always seek sound advice either from people who are more experienced than yourself or chartered professionals.

Hopefully most things go well but it is fair to say that from time to time there will be challenges (Whack-a-Mole time!!). Embrace the challenges and deal with them positively, but more importantly learn from them and put measures in place to avoid re-occurrence if you can.

Detail, detail, detail – this will be the difference between success and failure, make sure you drive down into detail at every level. If you don't do this, there is a high probability that you will hit some problems and retrospectively you will be dragged into the detail to resolve the problems, so better to be at this level from the outset.

"Opportunities don't happen. You create them."

I hope that YOU will find that my personal experiences and learnings (good and bad), will help you to map out your goals and achieve whatever you desire in your life.

I would ask you to be very mindful of the people around you – family, friends, colleagues – and to make sure that your goals are not all consuming without regard to your nearest and dearest. It's your family and friends who will be there for you when times get tough, it's your children who need you present in the moment when they are growing up, so please if you can (and I know it can be very hard) from time to time think why you are doing what you are doing and commit your time appropriately across your personal and business life. Please do not compromise one for the other!

Remember, you are only competing with yourself, so off you go now and achieve amazing things – make a difference and make yourself proud!

Live life with passion!

ANDREW GREENHALGH

Guidance to my younger self

"As soon as something stops being fun, I think it's time to move on. Life is too short to be unhappy. Waking up stressed and miserable is not a good way to live"

Richard Branson

ABOUT THE CHAPTER AUTHOR

I'm Andrew, 40 years old, from Leek, Staffordshire. I'm from a loving, middle class family and had a good private school education.

I am a business and property investor. More importantly, I am a parent. I live in a great house near the Peak District with my better half and our crazy dog. I don't work a 9-5 or have a boss to report to and I earn mostly passive income. To many this may sound ideal, and it is fantastic, but my path to this point has not been straightforward. I have changed career three times and have weathered the breakdown of three previous relationships. There have been times of stress, strain and self-doubt but also lots of fun, and many successes along the way. I started my career as a civil engineer before moving into corporate law. I am now financially stable as an entrepreneur in the property sector. To many this may seem successful. However, my personal barometer does not register this as such. Why? When I reflect, it's not what I truly wanted to do with my life.

When I was asked to write this chapter, I jumped at the chance. It's a poignant time for me. I have a one-year-old son and I feel it's my fatherly duty to dispel what I have learned about life so far. There are so many lessons that it would be impossible to compose a finite, concise guide. I hope the reader finds this snippet helpful; it is not a dictatorial list of the do's and don'ts. Ultimately you will learn the most valuable lessons for yourself. My aim here is to give you an insight into what I feel are the most valuable lessons from my own experiences. I hope you find them useful and can apply them to your own lives.

MY CHAPTER

1. Do what makes _you_ happy – following your dreams

At 13, all I ever wanted to be was a professional golfer. I dreamt about it, I was good at it and I practised every day come wind, rain or shine. It is fair to say I was obsessed by it. However, I did not follow this dream. I was afraid to go against the grain. Looking back, I was embarrassed about doing something different and lacked the confidence to speak up. My parents had worked hard to afford my private school education and I did not want to disappoint them. They expected me to go to university. Education was the priority; sports were just a hobby and consequently my dreams faded away.

What I have learned:

Reflecting on this experience, I have realised the importance of asking yourself as early as possible in life: what do you really enjoy? What is really important to you? What do you, deep down, want to do with your life? Once this is clear, you then need to build the confidence to pursue your goal. Don't be afraid to have a go. What's the worst that could happen? Failure? Failure is nothing to be afraid of. It is part of life and to be embraced. I've learnt my most valuable lessons from it and I still do. True success is personal and unique to you.

2. Have fun and be happy

I have tried hard throughout my life. I've set myself ambitious goals. Whether it be completing a sub 10-hour Ironman, achieving a +1 golf handicap or earning a certain income. I have always worked hard to realise my ambitions. In spite of the successes, on reflection, I can see that at times I have tried so hard that I stopped enjoying the journey.

What I have learned:

Trying your best and being driven to succeed is admirable. But box-ticking goals is not the measure of success. Enjoyment is also a factor, and if you are enjoying what you are doing, there is also more chance of success. It is also important to maintain a healthy perspective. Some goals are optional and nice to achieve, others are more critical. As in the example above, work out which goals are important to you. In setting about achieving them, try to have realistic expectations too. Putting yourself under pressure to achieve all the time may result in feeling like a failure. In achieving your goal, you will endure the process rather than enjoy it. You should always strive to do your best. However, you are human, you have limitations and sometimes, things are simply beyond your control. If you know you've done your best, then you have been successful whether you achieved your goal or not.

3. Look after yourself

I have always enjoyed sport. As a consequence, I have led an active and fit lifestyle and fortunately not had any unforeseen health issues.

What I have learned:

Your body is the best instrument you have. It should not be taken for granted – enjoy it but don't abuse or neglect it. You don't have to wrap it up in cotton wool or behave like a saint to have the best chance of it serving you well. There are certain things that may happen outside your control, but there are many within it. I realise how fortunate I am to be healthy, it's allowed me to enjoy so many experiences with few limitations. But it's not a constant and you get out what you put in. Take care of yourself and it will see you through.

4. Getting to know your family and friends

I'm 40 and luckily still have both parents. My family has always been there for me but at times we have drifted apart. I also have many friends from different stages of my life.

What I have learned:

I've learned just how precious family are and how fragile life is. The harsh truth is we are not around forever. Recently, my father survived a heart attack. Others I know have not been so lucky. It is an awful feeling when you face the possibility of losing someone close to you. You quickly realise how much you may have taken their presence for granted. Your family and friends are very important so it is worth making an extra effort to spend quality time with them. Accept their differences, cherish their quirks and don't hold grudges. It's never too late unless you wait until it is.

You will have many friends in your lifetime. Most you won't stay in touch with. For those friends you have stayed close to, you will have to constantly work to prevent them drifting away over time. Be proactive, call them, arrange to meet and go out of your way to make this happen. The rewards from the friendship outweigh the effort. I've always been my happiest when in company with close friends.

In summary:

What's important to you at any given time will inevitably change throughout your life. Nonetheless, there are constants you should not forget about. Your dreams, your health and well-being, your family and friends are the priority. If you have those, you are luckier than you realise. Keep things in perspective and don't sweat the small stuff.

I hope you have found my learnings useful. Good luck, enjoy the journey and remember:

"As soon as something stops being fun, I think it's time to move on. Life is too short to be unhappy. Waking up stressed and miserable is not a good way to live".
Richard Branson.

DARREN GRIGAS

Car crash to Buckingham Palace via the Sahara

"One day you will wake up and there won't be any more time to do the things you always wanted to do. Do it now"

Paulo Coelho

ABOUT THE CHAPTER AUTHOR

I consider myself a pretty average forty-two-year-old guy, living in my quaint little cottage on the outskirts of my hometown of Peterborough. Wow, forty-two came around quick, I'm sure I was still pratting about at university just a few weeks ago! Now I have a sixteen and eighteen-year-old reminding me that I'm a dorky old dad with thinning hair and terrible jokes. I'm proud of the dad-jokes but not so thrilled about the hair.

I was stuck in the corporate life and desperate to make a break for it, to take the chance that many people dream of, but also fear to do. I feared the uncertainty too, but this is what I eventually did, and so far, so good! (Fingers crossed!).

I'm not mega-rich, I don't have a huge house or drive a supercar, but I'm having a bloody good time, on my terms, not dreading Mondays or living for the weekend. It's taken me a lot of work to get here but it's so worth the leap.

In recent years, I've struggled to give a short answer to the common question "What do you do?". I don't have a 'job' as such, but instead a mixed bag of ventures ranging from property investments and development projects, and online ventures, to my real passion of running around the world, across deserts, jungles and giant frozen lakes in Outer Mongolia. These adventures started as a fun hobby, but to make them sustainable I made them pay me back. So, now I'm subsequently writing and talking about these experiences, becoming a paid speaker to share stories of these adventures, also training and coaching others to achieve similar epic goals. No two days are the same, it's overwhelming at times, but totally beats the old desk job, building websites from 9-5.

www.darrengrigas.com

MY CHAPTER

As I sat still in traffic on my way to work, I looked up into my rear-view mirror to see a beast of a car speeding towards me, then skidding about five car lengths before the bull bars of the Land Rover Defender slammed into the back of me, shunting me through the next two cars, leaving a four-car pile-up scattered in the road. This was a game changing moment for me, and I didn't know at the time where it would lead but looking back, it set the seed for a lot of changes. Fortunately, there were no serious injuries, but my back took a big hit – there was tissue damage around my lower spine where my vertebrae got knocked around. I underwent around twelve months of physiotherapy, cortisone injections, acupuncture and MRI scans to do the best we could with the damage and pain; there were a lot of sleepless nights in that first year.

Due to the nature of the damage, it was recommended I stay active, so I turned to running as I had done in my teens. It took me a while to even get past that first mile, not only was I not as fit as I used to be, but the injury had a knock-on effect, causing all sorts of issues in my back, hips, legs and knees. I stuck with it, huffing and puffing, stretching and walking at times, but I eventually passed that mile, then another, and another, until I was eventually running half-marathons and obstacle races and it was getting quite addictive. The injuries could have easily been so much worse, that could have been game over, or loss of the use of my legs and who's to say there won't be another accident on any given day? That moment was the stark reminder that tomorrow is never guaranteed to go how you expect, so I'm making the most of every single day. I promised myself to stay ahead of hindsight, make the most of my fully functional body whilst I could, and to create some amazing memories in the process. I had no doubt I owed it to myself to make the most of this one fragile life whilst I'm fortunate enough to have that opportunity. On my website, I have the little strapline: 'I run because I can'. What other reason do we need?

I looked for the biggest running challenge I could find and came across the Marathon des Sables, dubbed as 'The Toughest Footrace on Earth', 156 miles across the Sahara, carrying all your food and belongings on your back, effectively running six back-to-back marathons over undulating dunes in temperatures topping fifty degrees. That should do the trick right? Sign me up! Ten months later, I'd not only completed the race, but it turned out I was pretty good at it too, finishing somewhere in around the top ten percent of racers that year.

The greater things that came from the experience was that in fundraising for a local charity – Anna's Hope – I not only raised around £20,000 for them and the children they help battle brain cancer, but also greatly raised their profile as they used my challenge to make many press releases for the exposure. This led to me sharing my story in magazines, newspapers, BBC and Heart radio, BBC news and even being invited to speak at local schools and businesses.

What started off as a personal challenge just for me, had become way bigger than me – responses were amazing and the rewards of being able to inspire and motivate others were greater than the rewards of achieving the goals for myself. You could say I'd found my purpose, to push my limits and set an example to others; in short, to run a really long way in amazing places and then to share stories about it.

The most common two questions I get now are, "have you recovered yet?" and then "so what's next?". I'm now somewhat obliged to deliver the next chapter, the next big adventure, and share more stories to show people that if this dorky dad from Peterborough with his screwed up back can do these things, then imagine what others can achieve when they step out of their comfort zones.

I've since achieved three world-first crossings of Namibia and Panama (there will be at least a fourth by the time you're reading this book, check out the glaciers of Patagonia!), I've competed in some of the toughest races on the planet, meeting incredible and inspirational people along the way, including my Sahara tentmate,

Sir Ranulph Fiennes, an amazing man who snores like a trooper but is a humble legend in my experience.

I have spoken at schools and businesses across the country and have twice been invited to speak and present at both St James' and Buckingham Palace at the Duke of Edinburgh Gold Awards alongside royalty and a bunch of 'celebs'. The best part about going to Buckingham Palace was that it was my mum's birthday and I took her as my plus-one. It was brilliant to see my little mum in the Palace, drinking tea with Alan Titchmarsh, chatting and joking with Gabi Roslin and Alexandra Burke, whilst me and David Mitchell got told off for taking a cheeky selfie not realising we weren't allowed. Oops! But yes, of course I still posted it online – me and David Mitchell messing about in Buckingham Palace, that's not something that happens every day! Well not to me anyway.

So, would this all have happened if that fool hadn't ploughed his car into me on that random Tuesday morning? Who knows?

It's funny how you look back on key moments and choices that led you down paths you may not otherwise have taken. But now I'm here, in this position, would I do anything different if I could? Knowing what I know now about what my body and mind is capable of, I do wonder how far I would have come if I had set myself these epic challenges earlier in life. I would urge my younger self to think bigger, to aim higher, and not just settle for average. Life so far has been good to me, from being a party-boy at university, to being a young dad to two incredible children, to having great family and friends around me.

An interesting thing I've noticed is the amount of people who appear to have it all – money, cars, success – but are still looking for that something else. I gave a talk at one of Mark's Property Networking events to 150 or so successful business folk, some already property millionaires. I wasn't sure how my talk would be received as I didn't mention a word about property or business, but instead shared my adventures, highlighting the mindset, goalsetting and the overcoming of adversity that it takes to complete these amazing endurance feats. These processes can be applied to all areas of life, business, health and fitness. At the end of the talk Mark asked if there were any questions – a load of hands went up and we talked for another 20 minutes.

At the end of the evening, I had a circle of people around me asking questions, each person excited to learn more and telling me how they'd love to do such things. This kind of response from people who seem to have it all worked out reassures me that I'm doing something right with my time, for it to be envied and admired is reassuring for me as I usually feel like I'm winging it all the way. It shows that chasing all the money and nice 'stuff' isn't the only way to success and happiness but finding your passion and purpose needs to be explored and embraced.

You may not know what your purpose is until later in life, I'm still working out what I want to be when I grow up. I've been many things from Barman, Graphic Designer and Landlord to Personal Trainer and all of those things have led to the unique bag of tricks that I am today.

I once received an email from something I'd subscribed to – it was signed off by the guy's name and below that it simply read 'Adventurer'. I thought to myself I'd like that as my job title one day. I still don't know exactly what my 'job' is, but I think I could now justify having 'Adventurer' on a name badge if I had one.

If you have a passion and dream goals of your own, then no matter how big, just take action to make them happen – keep chipping away at them, don't worry about getting it wrong as you'll always learn something new and fail forwards. But ultimately put your heart and soul into being the best version of you; share your experiences to help others learn along the way, say yes to new adventures and enjoy everything you do, because tomorrow is never guaranteed.

MO HAYKIR

The 3 Ps – positivity, pro-activity and people

"If your dreams don't scare you, they aren't big enough"

Anon

ABOUT THE CHAPTER AUTHOR

Mo Haykir is a full-time property investor and developer, author and podcast host.

After attending a well-respected local Grammar school, Mo's grades started to slip after GCSEs and with a C, E and U at AS-level, he was politely asked to consider other options for A2.

This took him to Falmouth Marine School to study for a BTEC in Outdoor Education (Watersports) which enabled him to get a double distinction (same UCAS points as 2 'A's at A-level) and get in to Plymouth University to study BSc (Hons) Business Economics with Accounting, graduating with a 2:1 honours in 2011.

Whilst at university Mo bought his first property with his friend and now business partner James Yorke.

Since 2010 Mo and James have grown a sizeable personal property portfolio. As well as an HMO lettings business managing over 150 rooms, a property sourcing and refurbishment business and a development business (KHP Group), they work with three other business partners to develop unloved historic, and often listed buildings, and bring them back into use as high-end residential properties.

Mo is also a podcast host (Your Success Podcast) where he interviews successful people from all walks of life to get under the skin of success and understand what makes successful people tick. This podcast led Mo and Angelos to write their best-selling book 'Your Success: Hidden Traits of Successful People and How You Can Become a Success Too'.

www.mohaykir.com

MY CHAPTER

The 3 Ps – Positivity, Pro-activity and People

If I were to go back and give some words of wisdom to my younger self, they would be: "Be positive, be pro-active and life is all about people". Now, I'm not saying that because I don't think I've done well in those three areas, but I think an earlier appreciation of just how important they were would have helped me and (as all entrepreneurs lust for) would have sped up my journey.

Positivity

"I'd rather be optimistic and wrong some of the time than pessimistic and right all of the time".

Life is what you make it, and what you look for you invariably get. If you are looking for the risks, if you are looking for the negative traits in people, if you are looking for all of the ways it could go wrong, that's what you'll find.

Do you really want a life of moping around being pessimistic about everything? Giving out (and receiving) negative energy all of the time?

Now, it needs to be said that in the context of business, entrepreneurship and especially property investing, blindly waltzing into new ventures and ignoring any potential risks with people that may not be aligned to your values or have your best interests at heart, is quite clearly a recipe for disaster.

What I'm advocating is an overall approach of 'there are going to be bumps in the road, there are going to be people that don't want me to succeed, but I am going to exhaust all possible avenues and approach these potential pitfalls with a positive, can-do attitude'. The reason this stuff works, anatomically speaking, is way above me in terms of scientific understanding.

All I know is that asking your brain/subconscious specific questions, framed in a positive way, unlocks new ways of thinking and new problem-solving abilities. Ask your brain: 'How can I overcome this issue?' and don't be disheartened if attempts 1-99 don't work out. Keep going, keep chipping away at the problem/issue you are facing and eventually it will all fall into place.

Another massive advantage of being positive is that you become a magnet. People (who are like-minded) are attracted to you as a positive, action taker. This opens up more opportunities for you to cherry pick from.

Pro-activity

Closely aligned to positivity is pro-activity. We all know the classic phrase 'be pro-active, not re-active', but what does it actually mean?

Well, I like to think of pro-activity as 'taking ownership'. A very simple example would be following up on a sales call. Don't be mad that the customer hasn't called you back after you left a message. It's your fault. Maybe you didn't sell the product well enough, maybe they are busy and need to re-schedule with you. Maybe they would prefer a face to face meeting to explain your proposition rather than a phone call. Maybe they are not the decision maker.

Whatever the reason, if you sit there and complain about the person not calling you back, you are not taking ownership and you are not in control of the outcome.

Follow up, call back, re-arrange for a better time, present your information differently/more clearly, tailor your proposition to the client, arrange a visit on site, find out who the decision maker is in the business and schedule time with them.

There are SO many action steps that could be taken in this (very simplified) example. But we encounter things like this every day. Got a speeding ticket or a parking ticket? YOU were in control of the car.

Got fired? Take control of the outcome and start applying for new jobs. Understand the reason you were fired. Is there something you can change? Is there a training course you could attend to up-skill?

Not getting any interviews? Don't mope around. Ask employers WHY they are not inviting you for interview, apply for more roles. If you think you need to apply for 10 to get an interview, change your goal and activity level and apply for 100.

When we fail to be proactive and take ownership, we lose control of the outcome. We lose control of our destiny.

Of course, things aren't always going to go exactly to plan. If you are taking ownership for things, if you hit difficulties, you can learn, alter course if required, adjust and move on. No dwelling, no down time. Just action – be pro-active.

People

Life is about people – plain and simple.

Even if you are a business that is supplying another business, the ACTUAL relationship is between two or more humans that work within the two organisations.

If you want to make sales, you need to be a people person.

If you want to impress in an interview, you need to be a people person.

If you want to grow a multi-million-pound business, you need people.

Everything you want in life is accessed through other people.

Don't blame lack of people skills on being an 'introvert'. That's a label that people use to excuse themselves from not LEARNING the SKILLS of communication. In reality, people are more or less extroverted relative to each other, but you don't need to be the centre of attention, life of the party for people to like you – what else do you have to offer in conversation? People often like quieter people that listen rather than talk and are often put off by

'Alpha' type loud personalities. Be authentically you, but genuinely interested in other people and you will succeed.

As we move into an era when EQ (Emotional Quotient: the ability to have empathy and understanding for other people and an ability to identify, evaluate, control and express emotions) is becoming more important than IQ (Intelligent Quotient: what has historically been assessed through various maths and problem-solving tests to score 'intelligence'). PEOPLE are even more so at the forefront of a successful career/life.

As computing becomes more powerful and AI and machine learning becomes more prevalent – and as old labour-intensive jobs are being replaced by automation, systems, robots and machinery – roles like being a taxi/bus driver, a manual labourer or even solicitors and accountants are becoming redundant.

This is putting increased focus on the importance of people-to-people relationships, having a vision and a strategy for your business and life; being able to lead teams with empathy, passion and understanding and, ultimately, being a people person with a magnetic influence on others.

If you help others, the mysterious forces of karma will make sure this comes back around, but even if it doesn't (and you shouldn't help others with any level of expectation of return), don't you want to get that warm fuzzy feeling and for people at your funeral to say "what a nice person and didn't he help other people out a lot"?

People can give you everything you want in life, but you have to give before you can receive.

CHRIS HENRY

4,000 weeks

"Time and health are two precious assets that we don't recognize and appreciate until they have been depleted"
Denis Waitley

ABOUT YOUR CHAPTER AUTHOR

Born and brought up in beautiful Yorkshire and just about to fulfil our dream move to Ilkley (with a hat), I am married to my amazing wife and Business Partner Tracy and between us we have three inspirational children: Ben, Alex and Owen. Both our backgrounds are in banking which we left in 2012 to create our two businesses, a business coaching and a property business. The property business is fuelled by pensions which we transferred from the bank into a SSAS Pension. It is ironic that we left a bank to become our own bank, but for us and our family a complete game changer.

www.chrishenryactioncoach.co.uk

MY CHAPTER

As children we have a special place, a place where dreams are formed, and imagination is allowed to meander. My conversation with the young Chris Henry starts here at a sports field (Beck Lane) close to our childhood home, where school summer holidays and evenings were spent practising being the next big football superstar – this was our Wembley.

Looking back isn't something I've spent much time doing. I've been so focused on moving forwards, meeting the challenges that life has brought, so when I meet myself in my memory, that young man of twenty, his whole life ahead of him, I can't help but feel a strong desire to impart to him an understanding of the one thing that lies at the heart of everything – the precious gift of time.

The average person lives 4,000 weeks, I tell young twenty-year old Chris as we sit in the goal mouth, looking across the well-manicured Beck Lane pitch in Liversedge, West Yorkshire, a place I have known all of my life. Back then the days were long, the memories short and time seemed endless. This area is where I grew up, where I went to school, where I had my children, and where I finally learned what truly mattered. Interesting I say to Chris, that as children we dream but then as adults sadly, we stop as reality kicks in.

Time, I tell him, is your most precious asset. It's the one thing you cannot halt or get back once it's gone. That perception was never more acute than in 2005, after suffering a pulmonary embolism in Madeira at the age of 44, when time very nearly ran out. What followed was two weeks in intensive care, followed by six months recuperation. I'd been forced to stop, literally, and after being handed my life back, I slowly, over a period of years, began making changes to bring my one precious life back into alignment with who I really was. It made me focus on what I really wanted and though we can't halt time, I tell young Chris, we can start to use the knowledge and insights gained to make the absolute most of the life we have been given.

We were so busy, I tell him, in our twenties, thirties and forties – life went by in a bit of a blur. It was all about earning a living, bringing up a family and not stopping to question. It was only in my 50s, when I'd reached a level of financial comfort, that I started to appreciate the importance of developing who I was as a person. I discovered that the only way to develop and grow personally was to really get comfortable with being uncomfortable. It was not something I found easy at first but key to this was finding and discovering people further ahead on the journey than you are – inspiring people, with clear plans and goals, mentors, coaches and people who keep questioning you to discover your limitless potential. The key to this is to focus on what brings you joy – 'follow your bliss'. When you find what you enjoy doing, throw yourself into it wholeheartedly. Don't be afraid to reach out for help either – we learn not just from our life experiences but from those around us too.

I look back at Chris again and reflect more sadly on the things I didn't do or say to the people who really mattered. Time eats everything, it leaves nothing in its wake, and when time runs out for people you love, that's when you regret all the things left unsaid. I wished I'd spent more time with the older people in my family, especially my parents. I know you think they don't know much – well, you think like that when you're 20 – but ask them more questions, take their advice, and listen. You won't regret a moment of that once they're gone.

Young Chris and I make the short walk up the hill to my childhood home, the garden of which was the meeting point for most of the local kids, at the time a large grassed area with a swing and make-shift football goal. We had an amazing upbringing; we weren't short on laughs/or love/or whatever it is you appreciated most, but with four children in the family, things were financially very tight. We were the children on the free school meals and the hand-me-down clothes and my limiting beliefs about money, set the stage for my earlier work experiences. These beliefs have since being rooted out and challenged and now my thinking around money and wealth has created a freedom I never knew existed. Young Chris looks at me and smiles. Good times ahead maybe, but money isn't the answer to everything.

As a father now myself, it's become easy to overcompensate with my own children and smother them with the things I wished for as a child, but never had. But the risk is always that they don't grow themselves, that they lose sight of the journey and every step that brought us here. In February 1995, my beautiful daughter Alexandra was born with a disease called Cystic Fibrosis – a genetic disorder that affects mostly the lungs but also the pancreas, liver, kidneys, and intestine. Life expectancy for Alex, when she was born, was just 40 years. Her appreciation of time and life and her drive and positivity astounds me. As Alex would say, we will all face challenges in life, but don't ever take your health for granted because some people do not have a choice.

Swimming was a big feature of our childhood and the open-air swimming pool in Morecambe was where all our summer holidays were spent. Summers seemed to be hotter then, the outdoor life served us well as children. Eat well and exercise well and just as you take your car in for a service and check up, get your body checked at regular intervals and act on the advice given. Don't underestimate how important fitness and health are in creating a successful and happy business and personal life.

Have an understanding that although money and wealth aren't everything, learning how money works is the key to creating personal freedom. Having enough money dropping into your bank account whilst you are asleep, enough to cover your basic and luxury needs, is a life-changing concept. What this gives you is choices and options – it gives you back the time you sold for over 30 years making someone else rich. Own a business rather than have a job and make sure that this becomes an asset that can operate without you giving your time and freedom but still reap the financial rewards. Learning this became a game changer.

We take a longer walk to the beautiful cemetery in Robertown where my dear parents are buried, an oasis of tranquillity, a place where reflection is easy. There's something comforting when you visit about having the place to yourself.

I explain to young Chris that my parents both died in 2012 within exactly 6 months of each other. Now we are left with the memories. One of the best things I ever did was voice record my father in general day to day conversation, a treasure on my phone that I will keep forever. We also converted some reel tapes to CD for my father shortly before he died and I managed to give him the pleasure of listening to his mother's voice, a voice he had not heard for 34 years. He listened in private, but I can only imagine the emotion that he felt from the experience. What has this taught me? Start from an early age thinking about how you want to be remembered and what legacy you want to leave behind. What recording of your life do you want future generations to listen to? What do you want people to say at your funeral? This will give you a focus and help you with your road map for your life. As you get older, you do start to look back and reflect more and ask more questions.

As I take in the words on my parent's graves, I think back to my life before Madeira. My life was matter of fact, on autopilot and possibly devoid of any emotion. I remind young Chris of his desire to please others all the time and tell him eventually it will come at the expense of his own happiness. Be true to who you are, I say, without that you will be lost for a very long time. Be yourself, follow your passion, don't compare your life to others and don't live by others' rules either. Be the best version of you possible.

As we leave my parents grave behind, I am mindful yet again of the preciousness of time and am reminded of a brilliant poem often read at funerals: 'The Dash by Linda Ellis'. The Dash is the squiggle on your headstone between your date of birth and your date of death. That's your life – it's short, it's a blip and it's over in no time. So don't waste a day of it, I tell my younger self. Savour it all and when it comes to your eulogy, be proud of the things they say about you and how you lived your dash.

ANDY HUBBARD

Lessons I teach my twin boys that I wish I'd known

"If someone offers you an opportunity but you are not sure if you can do it, say Yes – then learn how to do it later"

Richard Branson

ABOUT THE CHAPTER AUTHOR

My name is Andy Hubbard, a 46-year-old bricklayer from Peterborough, who in my opinion has always thought a little differently to most people. I've never been one for following the masses, being told what I can or can't do or abide by the rules that are instilled in us from an early age by parents and school, but I do have a clean driving licence and no criminal record which is quite amazing considering some of the things I've done ;)

Looking back on my life I have seen and learnt a huge amount, usually down to experiences and lessons learnt by just going for it, committing first and figuring it out later – just like the Marathon Des Sables I've signed up to do next year even though I've never ran anything in my life. This philosophy has allowed me to take control of my life and experience some incredible things in amazing places throughout the world, but if I'd just said no, I would have most likely just plodded through life in a job I hate, being told what to do like most people are, and that is clearly not me.

MY CHAPTER

My parents brought me up to get a job, work hard, pay my taxes, save money, retire at 65 with a pension and then die. I got myself an apprenticeship at Peterborough City Council which was seen as a huge success as the Hubbard's are hardly academics with none of us going to university. Within weeks of starting my apprenticeship I soon realised employment wasn't for me. I had parents telling me what I could and couldn't do and I didn't need multiple bosses telling me also, so at 19, after completing my apprenticeship, I quit and said I would never work for anyone again – ever! I noticed people who worked at the council for 50 years, walk out with a cheap gold watch as a thank you, then die, or make do on a pittance of a pension – a path I clearly didn't want to follow.

Around the same time as this, my dad didn't like his job at the Royal Mail working nights as a lorry driver. I said to him "Why don't you quit and get another job?" at which point he said "I only have 15 years left until I get my pension". He also said "you just can't walk out of a job" but never could he give me an explanation why. I was shocked that someone could keep doing something they didn't like for as long as I'd been on the planet.

Lesson 1 – Figure out what you really want to do, what/who inspires you, look at others and see who is really happy in their work. Don't trade time for money (unless you really enjoy it),

think long term – unfortunately school doesn't help with this very much.

After walking out of my 'Job for Life' at the council I realised I didn't want to wait 46 years until I retired to start doing all the things I wanted to do, so I thought I would go traveling for a while – 13 years to be exact. I travelled around Europe in a motorhome for a ski season, worked on dozens of campsites all over Europe, climbed the highest mountains around in Europe, Africa, Australasia, America, South America and Asia including the 6th highest Cho-Oyu at 26,906 ft. I cycled all over Europe, Morocco, Turkey and New Zealand. Getting severe altitude sickness, frost bite, avalanched, falling off mountains, hit by rock fall, food poisoning, bitten by dogs, broken bikes, exploding plane engines, two-inch hail stones all added to the adventures. Whenever I returned back to the UK, I would pick up the trowel and lay bricks, usually 7 days a week on a huge variety of projects from building many houses to large supermarkets to industrial units in order to fund my next adventure. A big thing I noticed was nothing had changed when I returned, even after being away up to 9 months – everyone was still just doing the same old thing, day in and day out. Life was very good to me, having the freedom to do what I wanted whenever I wanted without much stress.

Lesson 2 – You only get one life, don't waste any of it wishing; only you can make things happen – go out and do the things you want to do as one day you won't be able to. Write down your goals regularly – don't be limited by what you think you can achieve but anything you want to achieve, and as young as possible, then go tick them off one by one. Go travel the world, it's an amazing place that will create memories for life. Life seems to last forever, travelling, whereas life speeds by

when you're dreading Mondays and wishing it was Friday. Don't live life regretting or wishing you had done things sooner or when you had the chance – the life clock will tick by regardless.

Most summers I would head down to the Alps climbing for a few months. While I was in Italy I received a text message from a girl called Sam, that I used to date when I was 21, saying she was splitting up from her husband and taking her twin boys and mum to Malta for a couple of weeks to get away from the stress. Now this girl made a big impact on me when I was 21 but it wasn't the right time for her, so we split up not long after meeting. We had always kept in contact and I knew that if I didn't take the opportunity to get back with her now, then I would miss my chance and regret it all my life. But I had made plans to climb Everest the very next year, I had spent years building my fitness and experience up for the biggest mountain on Earth and what would be my biggest achievement so far. I had to make a decision, and fast. Everest would always be there, wouldn't it, so I texted her back and said, "I'll be in Malta tomorrow as I want to be with you and the boys". Sam thought I was joking as she knew I was in Italy – "how could he possibly get to Malta by tomorrow anyway?" she asked herself. I threw my tent and some pretty stinky climbing gear in my van, sped home, booked the first Ryanair flight out of Stanstead, grabbed a bath, packed a bag of clean clothes and drove to the airport and flew straight to Malta. Now Sam said she didn't believe I would turn up, but she was at the airport so she must have had a little faith in me. Fast forward now and we have been together ever since for the past 15 years and just celebrating our 8th wedding anniversary.

Lesson 3 – If an opportunity arises then go for it; don't over think it as the little voice in your head will start throwing all

the 'what ifs' and doubts at you and you will find some excuse to justify why you shouldn't do it. Just say "yes" and figure it out later. Life can be completely different depending on what you say yes or no to, so think before saying no to things. Everest is still there – and so are all of my toes. ; -)

Now I had responsibilities with four mouths to feed. I had to have consistent income coming in as I had just self-certified a £200,000 mortgage for our first house. How easy was that – go find a house, tick the box to say you can afford it and you're away. In fact, it was that easy I went and bought another three that month plus a brand-new truck as I'd noticed property prices accelerating while I was travelling. But then the recession hit in 2008 and self-certified mortgages were gone overnight – and so was all the construction work. It was New Year's Eve and we had family over to celebrate – I wasn't sure how I was going to do that as we only had £30 in the bank and didn't know what we were going to do for money as I had no work. I started converting garages into usable rooms, the first time I'd realised that doing a niche means less competition and it can demand a higher price. It was also 'recession proof' as people could afford a garage conversion but not the re-mortgaging to fund loft conversions or extensions. This turned things around financially but I ended up working 100+ hours a week – before I read 'Rich Dad Poor Dad'.

Lesson 4 – I wish I had read 'Rich Dad Poor Dad' when it was first published and learnt to put money into assets and not liabilities.

After falling asleep at the wheel several times on my way home from work in the dark and ending up in a field (I live in the fens), something had to change. I was on burnout, not seeing my family, and when I did, I was too tired to do anything anyway, so I reached out to find a mentor. That's when things really changed – my mindset, the clarity, the reason I did anything, making decisions etc. The first thing was to build a portfolio to replace my income. Once this was achieved it freed up my time to start developing for myself – after all I had more skills than most. I've been mentoring others for a while now and more recently my kids, guiding them through on their first few developments so they can learn hands on.

Lesson 5 – I wish I'd known about mentors sooner, how they can help you reach your potential, and then go on to help others which is very rewarding. Find your purpose. Be clear on your values. Have a vision. Give back and help people, the law of reciprocity is amazing. Create a legacy. What do you want to leave behind when you've gone?

ALEX IMPEY

The humble square

"The things you think about determine the quality of your mind. Your soul takes on the colour of your thoughts"

Marcus Aurelius

ABOUT THE CHAPTER AUTHOR

Alex Impey is from Hartlepool, England along with over 100,000 others who bear the affectionate title of 'monkey hangers' (a reference to the town's maritime past). He is the founder and head of property operations for XUSA Properties Ltd. This is a property development company which specialises in mixed use mixed tenure property. XUSA's sole aim is to make living affordable and enjoyable for everyone in the world.

Alex had a previous life as a chartered Mechanical Engineer (CENG). He has travelled around the world working in a professional integrity and assurance role across highly resilient global infrastructure. His role has always been simple: to mitigate risk and provide steadfast assurance at all stages of a project's life cycle. He has achieved this whilst visiting some of the most challenging and extreme locations in the Middle East i.e. Iraq. Other locations include the notorious city of Aberdeen. He has personally delivered over £250M of CAPEX projects during his time in that profession.

Alex loves all things related to his personal development so he has committed himself to a process of continual learning. Thus, he has dedicated the last 11 years of his life to researching the best ways to improve and evolve personally, whilst mapping what he has learned and distilling it into a single repeatable system for others to use.

Alex has also studied Astronautics and Space Engineering at Cranfield University. Not only is he a massive geek but is also a closet Star Trek fan too.

His ultimate ambition is to build a collective alliance which develops mankind through space exploration and scientific development. His aim is to send humans on the first ever return mission to explore Jupiter and its moons before 2060.

www.aleximpey.com

MY CHAPTER

"Space: the final frontier. These are the voyages of the Starship Enterprise. Its continuing mission: to explore strange new worlds. To seek out new life and new civilizations. To boldly go where no-one has gone before!"

As a young child I vividly remember watching Captain Kirk, Picard and their galivants across the galaxy with some very questionable make-up. I was always fascinated by the huge potential for mankind in the universe. It was probably this love of science which guided me on my path towards an engineering career from an early age. School and college passed by in a blur and before I knew it, I was walking into Newcastle University's Mechanical Engineering Faculty to attend my first lecture on the principles of thermodynamics. In general, university was a fantastic experience but it was in this exact moment that I donned my sports gear, sweat band and jumped head first into the race of rodents.

During university, my priorities shifted quickly; I started to worry about the need to find a secure job, buying cars and suits. Like many other graduates we are often forced into the notion that our level of education defines our career requirements and that after university we should all be pushing into high paid corporate positions. Rather than focusing on those things that once excited me and fired up my passion, I began pursuing what society told me I needed. Success is not something that is defined by possessions or experiences but rather it's something that should be defined by you, your values and your purpose. At this point, if I had a time machine, I would go back and offer up advice to a younger Alex. This advice comes in the form of four carefully defined actions which conveniently create the 'humble square'.

A square derives its strength and form from four simple right angles, which we will call cornerstones, as well as four sides of equal length and proportion, which we will call pillars. Without these cornerstones and pillars of equal proportion, a square has no definition or purpose, which is what we need to develop in our own lives. The cornerstones are the attributes we need to move us towards a fulfilling and purposeful life. The pillars represent the work needed to support each attribute. The devotion of equal amounts of time and continual work will help provide a well-balanced life and happiness.

1) Define your values	**HARMONISED LIFE**	**2) Frame your own version of success**
3) Be your authentic self		**4) Create your life vision**

What are your values and why define them?

Values and your own internal value system represent the first cornerstone and pillar of the humble square and journey towards a brighter personal future. However, what exactly are values? Dr De Martini suggests that values arise from conscious or unconscious voids, which are the things you perceive as most missing in your life. It's the desire to attain these areas which brings you to attach personal importance and turns these voids into your values. Values are those things which give you joy, ambition and help guide you when things become difficult. One of the main ways which helped me create a fantastic set of values was discovering the principle of Ikigai. Ikigai is a methodology which can simply be interpreted as 'the reason for living'. This Japanese ethos of life is made up of four key principles: Passion, Mission, Profession and Vocation. When you get synergy and balance between these, you are able to live a fulfilled and happy life. We will use these four principles to develop our own values.

Looking at each area individually, simply open your eyes and look around at everything in your life up to this moment. Your values are built on the actions you choose to take every day. It's the people and hobbies you choose to spend your time with. It's the thoughts of a future life that fill the empty moments in your head. It's the decisions you consistently make. Go back through both painful and happy moments in your life. What created these moments? Were they linked to an attribute or area of your life which succeeded or failed and how has this moulded your life from that point onwards?

Try and avoid society driven values such as 'hard working, honesty or integrity' – many people live the values that their culture dictates. Each one of my own values is uniquely personal and has helped guide every decision I have made. They have helped maintain my focus, my drive, my vision and my pursuit of a balanced and successful life.

Why frame your own version of life success?

If we were to frame a picture, for example, we would do this in order to enhance its already natural beauty, to give it context and provide a focal point to the piece of art. More importantly, it's there to protect the art from damage and to ensure future generations can continue to enjoy it.

If only I could have told my younger self that success is not measured by how many cars, houses or watches I owned. That's why it's so important to define your own version of success first, rather than seeing success as an achievement in one area. It is more important to look at your life holistically and divide it into multiple balanced facets. I call these Life Key Result Areas (LKRA) – this is the second cornerstone and pillar of our humble Square.

We know from Ikigai that we can attain a harmonised life using four key principles. Taking this one step further, we can break these facets down into more personal areas of our own lives. There are many different categories which you can base your version of success around: business, relationships, finance, health, spiritual well-being, pleasure and career. How many you select and how you define these areas is not the important aspect. The aim is about selecting what matters to you. This will be borne out of the values you identified earlier and the things you want to achieve in your life. By making sure that your values and Life Key Result Areas are aligned, then you will constantly be working on those areas most important to you and not living an imposed life like the majority of others.

It is important to remember the model of the 'humble square'. Without four equal sides (the pillars) the square isn't a square. You need to devote equal amounts of time and effort to each area to keep your life defined and balanced.

Why define your life's purpose and how do you go about doing this?

The next cornerstone and pillar serve to create the bigger picture concerning your personal vision and legacy. This will be the central constant which defines your life and inspires not only you, but motivates countless others to get up every morning and work towards a vision of betterment.

Just like Victorian sailors would have used sextants and the stars to guide them on their own voyages, we too need our own vision and purpose to help navigate our lives in the right direction. This leads directly into the third cornerstone and advice for my younger self "Alex, you need to start with why?".

Although this task may sound daunting, you should already start to see the commonalities between your values and your Life Key

Result Areas. These are already pointing you towards what your mission should be. If it's still not clear there are a few things we can do to help tease it out. The first piece of advice is to go back to the dreams you had as a child, along with the moments which defined your life to this date. Make sure to look at both the happy and painful memories, as it is often out of pain that we find the motivations to change ourselves. What were the things you always had passion for, the constants which motivated you when you had difficult periods? Who did you think about becoming? There will be common themes and thoughts which have re-occurred throughout your entire life. I call these 'life crystallisation moments' and it is these points which help define what your purpose is right now. To ensure you have an epic vision, instead of a mildly motivating one, you can ask yourself three important questions:

- Will the journey this vision takes me on provide happiness and fulfilment?
- Will my life vision challenge me constantly to improve as a person?
- Am I prepared to work at all costs to achieve this vision?

If the answer to any of these is 'No' and you don't get goose bumps from reading it, then you need to start this again until it does.

Be your Authentic Self

This final cornerstone and pillar of the humble square is the single most important feature and without it the square lacks stability and, more importantly, identity. This is a direct analogy to our own lives and even if you manage to master all three other areas, if you are not your authentic self then there is no meaning. You will never have your own identity or the ability to stay resolute to your vision, to yourself and those around you. It's this ultimate part of the square that provides the stability to continue. But who and what is your authentic self? There are many possibilities to this answer and it is highly personal, but I have tried to summarise these into a number of key statements:

- It's the person who has clear values in life and uses these to guide their own decisions and actions.
- It's the person who strives for happiness in accordance with their own version of success, underpinned by their balanced personal KLRAs.
- It's the person who has a clear vision and a plan to attain this.
- It's the person who believes in their own identity and is not afraid to act in spite of fear, inconvenience and uncertainty to protect this.
- It's the person who understands that continual introspection, conscious objection and course correction are needed in order to succeed.

I lived many years battling, trying to find my authentic self and often projected myself as the character others wanted me to be. However, once I was content with myself and my identity, I was able to set myself on a path for stability and fulfilment to complete the journey of a humble square.

To summarise, I would say it's important to remember through all of this that we do not know what life will bring and therefore which other defining events are yet to occur. The humble square which you create around your life now, will not be the same in 10 or 20 years from now but if you live your life in accordance with the cornerstones and pillars at each stage of life, you will get that fulfilment and happiness and provide continuity to each passing phase. Much like a photograph, it represents only a specific instant of our every changing timeline. This is the beauty of life and why, as individuals, we need to constantly monitor and complete correction and critical updates to our life journey.

Finally, remember that success and pursuit of a vision isn't the most important thing but rather it's the journey which this takes us on – this is what you must savour and I truly hope that this adventure allows you *"To boldly go where no-one has gone before!"*.

DOUG JAMES

The advice I would give to my younger self

"Surround yourself with people that are better than you, they will make you rich"

Doug James

ABOUT THE CHAPTER AUTHOR

Hi, my name is Doug James and I am on a mission to help the next generation learn from the five secrets to my success – to enable them to copy my results, the proven learnings from 30 years in business.

I am fortunate to have been mentored all my life by people who have achieved what I wanted to achieve. I founded, from my kitchen table, what was to become a top five independent branding and marketing company called 'Honey Creative', which was based in London. In 2015, I sold this company, retiring at the age of 42. My ultimate goal was to have financial and time freedom, to live life on my own terms.

I brought my first property in November 1999. Fast forward and by accident, I learnt the power and importance of an asset-based income. I believe that assets and the income they generate is the most important financial lesson everyone should learn. I still own that first flat in London. It has grown fivefold in capital value and the rental income has paid for me to travel the world. It has bought me many more investment properties so that I am able to enjoy an asset-based income from the rental income. It has also bought and paid the running costs for the beautiful beach house we live in today.

Today I am an investor and property developer leveraging my skills, not my time. I continue to grow our asset-based property portfolio, which continues to grow our wealth and cash flow. I am able to do this from anywhere in the world, from the mountains or the beach.

I left school at 15 with few qualifications and hardly able to read and write due to being dyslexic. If I can achieve what I have achieved, then you can too.

www.joindougjames.com/gap

MY CHAPTER

The 5 Secrets to My Success:

1. Dream Big
2. Mentor
3. Asset based income
4. Strategy and growth plan
5. Accountability partner

1. Dream Big - have a clear why

This will get you out of bed every morning and drive you to take action daily to get to your dream.

Purpose:

My #postcard tool is a simple tool to capture your why, your dream and your vision. You need to know what and where you are aiming for, to be able to get there.

Process:

Writing your postcard only takes five minutes. Enjoy the process, make a cup of coffee or tea, close your eyes and dream.

Think where you would love to be in five years' time. Why five years? Because you need a big hairy-ass goal to aim for. Through my five key steps to freedom you can potentially collapse the time frame to three years. Aim big and you will get there.

Here are some prompts to help. Fill in the blanks.

Start your postcard with:

Hi *blank* I am – (the 'I am' kicks your belief system into action) example below:

Hi Doug, I am sitting here in *blank*, I have a *blank* bed house, with *blank* cars etc, my kids are at *blank* school, we have just got back from *blank* holiday – we go on *blank* holidays a year. Life is amazing; my *blank* business/property investments have delivered me *blank*. Thanks to my fab property assets (or other assets) and the monthly residual income from them, it has enabled me and my family to live the life of our dreams.
We can't wait for you to get here and enjoy all this freedom with us. Love always, Doug.

After this, work out what it costs you per month to live your dream postcard life. What cash flow and what capital? Write this at the bottom of the postcard.

The second key part of the postcard is cementing it into your belief system. Find two or three pictures to support the words, then print this out and put in a picture frame by your bed. Read it every morning and evening when you wake and before you go to sleep. Do this every day for at least 21 days in a row. This will give you brain/muscle memory. I recommend doing it for 18 months! This will turn your belief into a deep-seated habit!!

2. Mentor – copy your way to freedom

Get yourself a mentor and copy everything they do. Don't challenge them until you hit your first level of asset-based income that you require. A mentor will collapse your timeframe to your freedom.

Purpose:

A mentor will share their secrets to their success. They will give you extra confidence and belief; they will be there for you.

Process:

It's important to find a mentor who has achieved what you want to achieve, their lifestyle and wealth.

How do you find one?

Use the contacts you are going to learn from in the next heading 'Asset-based income – educate yourself'. Think of the people you have been listening to in podcasts, or reading their books, watching them on YouTube, on Facebook, interacting within Facebook groups,

Instagram or LinkedIn, going to their seminars or networks or conferences. Ask them directly if they will mentor you! If you don't ask you won't get!!

Do your due diligence on them – if they are very famous you may believe they have achieved what you want too. Always check their back story – ask them to share their story and if needs be, ask them to prove they have got to where they say they have.

Some may mentor you for no cost, some will charge. I have done both – paid and what people call free. In actual fact, it's not free! It's their time, your time, energy, their IP (intellectual property) – therefore if you get one that does not charge, please treat it with as much respect as if you were paying £50,000.

From personal experience, paying makes one focus more, probably respect more and I believe, delivers results more quickly for you.

Whatever happens, get yourself a mentor. It will be the best thing and investment you have ever made – I promise!!

3. Asset-based income - educate yourself

An asset-based income is where you get paid daily or monthly from assets like property rental income. We call it 'lying-on-the-beach' money or 'it pays you whilst asleep'. The rich are rich because they do not swap their time for money as most do in a JOB (Just Over Broke!!!).

Don't believe, or mix up, the above with the traditional education system. Yes, it has its place to learn the basics – reading, writing, maths and to expose people to the sciences. However, it is also built to get you into massive debt, drive you to believe success is a

JOB, switching your time for money!!! This is a con and what the establishment wants you to think is success!

Purpose:

Educate yourself in what an asset-based income is. Become financially minded on how wealth is created, grown and preserved.

Process:

Tip your wallet into your brain and it will fill your wallet up many times.

Where to get started?

Find your heroes who have achieved what you dream of achieving. One of these people could become your Mentor!

A good place to start is by reading or listening to Robert Kiyosaki's 'Rich Dad, Poor Dad' and then his book on the 'Cash Flow Quadrant'.

Learn how important systems, processes, delegation and leverage are to wealth creation – how the smartest business people use them.

You have so many resources at your fingertips which are free or very affordable. Start listening, watching and following people via podcasts, audio books, YouTube videos, Facebook groups and live videos etc.

Paid Education

'Surround yourself with people that are better than you, they will make you money!'

I went to Cranfield Business School and did their BGP (Business

Growth Programme) in 2008. Cranfield is one of the top Entrepreneurial schools in the world. BGP is a vocational programme where they taught us the importance of 'Working on your business' rather than 'in your business' to getting to your postcard.

Whilst at Cranfield, I was mentored by people like Angus Thirlwell, founder of Hotel Chocolate and Tristram Mayhew, founder of Go Ape. I, like many over the 30 years the programme has been running, put their accelerated growth of themselves and their business down to the smart tool kit and processes that Cranfield taught them.

Don't mix up education at one of the property education businesses with learning how to create wealth and cash flow. These companies focus on selling you a course or courses as it is their business model! However, they can be good at teaching you specific 'How To' within property when you have created your personal strategy to freedom.

4. Strategy and growth plan - create yours

With your mentor and new education on asset-based income, create your personal strategy, growth plan and your DMO (Daily Method Operation). The three key actions you make today, that affect your business or life goals today and tomorrow are direct, focused actions with measurable results.

Purpose:

With a clear strategy, plan and DMO, you will stay focused and avoid distractions. With your DMO you will take little steps often and get to your dream. As my Dad said to me "little and often and you will get there in the end!".

Process:

The detail to my well-trodden process to explore and deliver your strategy and growth plan can be found on my website, see the below diagram:

Start by undertaking Wealth Dynamics (WD) – it's an amazing tool that gives you a very accurate snapshot of your strengths to focus on how, and who, you are best working with. On the WD site there is a fantastic video by the founder Roger Hamilton, explaining all.

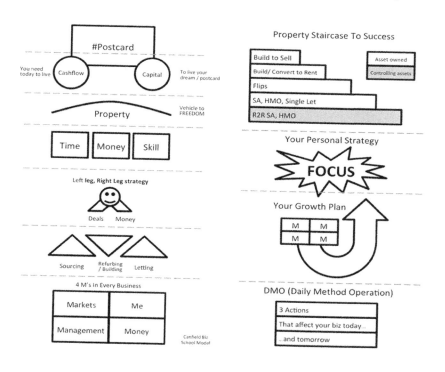

5. Accountability partner - deliver consistently

Get yourself an accountability partner. This could be your mentor or business partner. This, and the above, will cost you a huge investment in time, energy, emotions and a small amount of money.

Purpose:

You need an accountability partner to help keep you on track. When I ran my agency, Honey Creative, we had a board, an external Chairman and two Non-executives. They were mentors and accountability partners to us who ran the business and we met every month for a board meeting. This should be the same for you, even if it is only you wanting to get to an asset-based income of £3k, £5k or £10k per month.

Process:

First think about your mentor – are they right? Will they want to be your accountability partner?

It could be a friend, your business partner or a family member. They need to be strict and willing to ask you every time you have agreed to update them on your results against your DMO (Daily Method Operation).

Remember: if your accountability partner isn't your mentor then you will likely just be sharing your results and targets with them, asking you how you are doing and if anything, motivating you to focus and stay on track.

Your mentor is the one to ask for help if you miss your targets, not your accountability partner. Don't confuse yourself with other people's opinions, especially if they haven't reached their own dream of financial and time freedom!

Remember Dream Big and follow my advice above and you too will reach your dream by taking focused, mentored action daily.

Enjoy and reach out to me to share your personal journey.

KAL KANDOLA

True happiness comes when you realise your own worth

"When you start seeing your worth, you'll find it harder to stay around people who don't"

Anon

"Follow your heart, listen to your inner voice, stop caring about what others think"

Jimi Hendrix

ABOUT THE CHAPTER AUTHOR

My name is Kal Kandola and I was born in India in 1970. I came to the UK when I was five and I had a thirst for knowledge and education. I spent my youth with my head stuck in books – I am proud to say that I was the first in my family to go to University and I have a BA (Hons), MBA and a PhD. Education was everything to my father, especially for his little girl. I worked hard over the years and as a Mortgage Broker I was in a predominately male-orientated industry. I am now a Property Developer as well with my husband. I started running my own networking events to help other people and to encourage and inspire more women to come into property and business.

The difference I want to make is with the Eco Homes Build system that we are bringing to the market. We want to provide more homes that are not only affordable to buy, but also to run. I do charity work to help young girls in India who would not be able to afford an education. I want to do more in this country to make a change to homelessness.

www.kalkandola.com

MY CHAPTER

At some point or another in our lives, we all wish we could go back in time and often think about what changes we would make if we could do it all over again, knowing what we know now.

Unfortunately, I don't have a time machine to do this for myself so I hope that my words here will help my children and anyone else reading this today.

Growing up I was advised to treat people how I would like them to treat me. This was my father's motto and I lived with it until just a few years ago. In my younger years I was very shy and I would mask that by resorting to comedy. I wanted to fit in so I would try to be everything I could be to everyone around me. I tried to be the perfect daughter, sister (although my brothers may disagree with this), niece, aunt, friend and then when I got married, wife (yes Pete, I am the perfect wife), mother, daughter-in-law and so on. The word NO was not in my vocabulary and I would go out of my way to do everything I could to keep everyone happy. For my mum, family was everything and if you know any Indian families you will know that's a lot of people, because everyone is family. So, I focused all my energies on my extended family which included almost everyone in the village.

In everything I did I forgot one person – ME.

I treated everyone how I wanted them to treat me, but I never took stock of how they were actually treating me. So, when people upset me or took me for granted, I would feel hurt by their actions and would spend a lot of time wondering why, and what I had done wrong to make them do that to me. I never realised that I was to blame for this because I was allowing them to treat me this way and that was because I did not see my own worth.

In the last few years since my father passed away, I have looked at things differently and realised that this attitude has affected my physical and emotional well-being. None of us can ever be perfect or be everything to everyone without causing more damage in the long term.

Once I started to see my worth, I found it harder to stay around people who didn't.

I stopped going to functions and occasions that didn't serve me and stopped spending time with people that did not share my values – I have never been happier. I realised that family is not a bond that should be defined by blood relationships but by how people treat you. So, focus your love and energy on the right people. Recognise people who are negative or toxic and cut them out of your life. Never try to fit in when you were born to stand out. People will try to derail you and influence you. Remember just because your path is different it does not mean that you are lost, so don't let anyone tell you that you are.

There will be tough days in your life so make sure you look for something positive in each day, even if some days you have to look harder. Remember reality is malleable and there is no one fixed reality for everyone. Your reality is your perception and you can create your own reality. Don't let the past define you or your future. We all make mistakes and I know I have made many over the years, but I didn't realise that they were mistakes until much later.

Looking back now I can see where I went wrong; I didn't talk to anyone about my feelings and just accepted everything for what it was. If I had sought advice and guidance maybe I would have done things differently, maybe I would have been happier. I now know the value of mentors in my life but that came through from my property career and training, and the people that I have met over the past four years. The mentoring I have had in my business has helped me to focus on things in my personal life.

I no longer feel like I have to please everyone around me. I have the courage to say NO and I do not feel guilty when putting myself and my needs first. I have learnt that unless I feel good about myself and my life, I cannot really be what I need to be for the people that I truly love. My advice would be to seek mentors who will listen to you and guide you to focus on what course of action will be best suited to you. A mentor doesn't have to be a paid professional; it could be a parent, family member or a peer. I was speaking to someone who I have always seen as a sister over the years and she said that I had changed her perception on life and those around her. She said that I had been a mentor to her with the guidance that I had given her in the past year, which was heart-warming for me. I love helping people and I want everyone I know to be truly happy. So always be the best version of you that you can be. You don't have to be perfect, but you do have to be true to your values. If in doubt call me, you know I know everything!

Always be kind to the people that genuinely love you. If you are having a bad day, don't take it out on anyone else – it's not their fault but if you let them, they will try to help you. Don't stay with someone who treats you badly just because you are scared of being lonely or on your own. That will only hurt them and you in the long term. Time spent on your own is valuable.

If you are having a bad day call your Dad – he will probably tell you some crazy story about something daft he and his mates did when he was your age or crack some daft joke, but you know he will make you laugh and forget your worries.

If you're unsure of anything, call your Mum – she knows everything.

Cherish the time you have with your siblings – it doesn't matter how old they are, they look up to you, whether they show it or not.

Hug your parents, give them a high five, spend quality time with them to share your thoughts, dreams, challenges and above all laugh with them. It will keep them young and keep you connected as a family. Don't take life too seriously, after all none of us are getting out alive.

Now this one is more for the kids of today. Don't spend your life looking down at your phone, lift your head and look at the world around you. Take the time to make memories, they will stay with you forever. Read something every day. Invest in your self-development by reading, listening and attending events with people that will inspire you. Explore who you are and what you really want out of life and live the life of your dreams every day. Travel as often as you can and see the world with your loved ones. When you have a life partner, don't forget your family and friends – make sure you still spend quality time with them. Don't let your busy life get in the way of your relationships. Allocate time in your day for yourself and for others – work will still be there tomorrow. Tell your loved ones that you love them – don't just expect them to know.

Focus on your health and always look for holistic and natural remedies before you take any medication. Don't compromise on your body, it's the only one you have. The Universe will give you what you need so make sure you are in tune and sending out the right signals. Take time out each day to clear your mind, focus on your breathing and meditate – this will give you so much clarity.

Be good to those around you but first be good to yourself. Know when to stay and when to walk away and if in doubt call your mum – you know she knows everything. When you are unsure of what course of action to take, it will help to talk to someone you trust about it, sound it out, do some brainstorming and then sleep on it. The answers will come to you – just be ready to receive.

In conclusion I would like to leave you with the following thought:

From today forget what's gone, appreciate what still remains, and look forward to what's coming next.

IAN KAVANAGH

Making it happen

"Whether you think you can, or you can't, you're right"
Henry Ford

ABOUT THE CHAPTER AUTHOR

Ian Kavanagh – I was born in 1961 and brought up in Bedford where I continue to live today. I have been married to my wife, Alison for 38 years and we have two sons and four grandsons.

I left school at the age of sixteen to join the family book binding and print-finishing business, which was started by my father in 1968. The business expanded to provide a wide range of mailing, fulfilment and distribution services to publishers, auction houses and large corporates. While the business was growing, we created a family SSAS in 1988, which we used at the time to build a new warehouse and office premises for the business in Bedford.

I led the company as Managing Director for more than 20 years and achieved our family goal of selling the business in 2008, when the business was acquired by the French Post Office.

I briefly retired in 2013 when I left the business and took time out with my wife, travelling around New Zealand and Australia, where my son Mike and his family live. In 2015 my other son Matt and I formed a new property investment company to expand our property portfolio. We bought and converted 12 properties into HMOs over a period of 18 months. We then undertook our first property development in 2017, which was the conversion of a former doctor's surgery into seven apartments. We currently have two further building projects under development and are actively seeking additional similar projects.

My focus is to grow our property businesses to provide shared value and financial freedom for generations to come.

www.frdevelopments.com

MY CHAPTER

Having run several businesses for over more than 30 years, I would like to share what I believe are some fundamental learnings from my experience:

1. Be confident in your own ability

I have always thought of myself as being very lucky in that as children, my brother, two sisters and I always had it ingrained in us by our Dad, that we could achieve whatever we wanted in life, so long as we were focused and wanted it badly enough. I therefore went through life with great confidence, truly believing, knowing I would be successful along my chosen path.

How many times have you put someone up on a pedestal, thinking they are far better than you, only to find out when you get close to that person, that they are not so special and indeed you can compete on a par with them? This certainly happened to me many times over the years and taught me to approach life with more confidence, self-belief and a positive can-do attitude.

2. Create a powerful reason why!

Having a powerful reason 'why' is key to achieving your dreams and clearly defined goals is a hugely important part of the planning process. Defining a clear vision of what you want to achieve, by when, and committing to these goals in writing is vital. Producing vision boards containing pictures and statements of all you desire, that can be viewed and reflected upon daily, will help you keep focused and on track to achieve the goals you have committed to.

Follow your passion as you search for direction in your life. If you aim to get involved with something you love doing and are passionate about, you will most likely be good at it – which will help you to succeed.

3. Running your own business

Being in control of your own destiny by running your own business can bring huge rewards, both financially and emotionally, as you develop and grow your business in a sector that excites you. Like-minded people will be drawn to you and your passion for your business will play a powerful role in helping to drive your business forward to greater success.

The production of a well-considered, detailed business plan, with specific timelines and ownership responsibilities agreed, is essential, so you and your team can regularly report upon and review progress being achieved against the plans.

One of the most important skills is to surround yourself with super talented people in your team. Don't skimp and settle for second best and make sure your team is made up of positive people, appropriately qualified to succeed in their area of expertise. Building a strong element of trust within your team is critical and, over time, each team member must prove themselves in their areas of expertise.

Having complete trust and confidence in the financial information being provided by your Financial Controller is critical for any business. You and your team are making key decisions daily that affect not only the performance of your business, but also the livelihoods of everyone working within your business. If financial reporting is incorrect for any reason, the wellbeing of your business is jeopardised and the business is at risk. Make sure you build complete trust and confidence with the person providing the financials within your business.

Your job is to inspire and lead your team to successfully deliver the plans and goals for your business and this certainly does not involve micro-managing and being a control freak. Supporting and nurturing your team to deliver successful outcomes is a hugely enjoyable and rewarding experience.

Holding regular one-to-one meetings with each member of your management team will allow you to monitor, support and steer each member to ensure the collective success of the management team. Regular monthly management meetings should be used to track the performance of the business and review progress against the plans and budgets agreed for the business.

4. Be an action taker

It always amazes me to see how few people take positive action to achieve a goal to be successful. In 2015 I attended an excellent property investment education programme where all two hundred plus people in attendance had each paid over £20,000 to attend a series of three-day courses, covering a range of different property investment strategies. I was staggered to find out later that despite the high cost paid, only ten percent of people moved forward to take positive action, implementing what they had been taught. Many people had attended all the courses, done all the theory but failed to take the next step to put into practise what they had learnt – what a waste of money and opportunity.

Taking positive action towards achieving your goals, targets and dreams is, in my opinion, the most important attribute anyone can possess, and procrastination and non-action is a killer of the achievement of many dreams.

Surrounding yourself with experts with proven track records in your chosen path is critical to provide you with the confidence to move forward positively with any project you undertake. Do your due diligence – talk to your peers, ask for help and advice but once you have thoroughly worked through everything in your plan, you must move forward positively to execute your plan. Goals simply cannot be achieved without positive action being taken.

Attendance at regular industry networking events provides a never-ending source of contacts and experts to help and guide you along your journey. If this means getting out of your comfort zone, then get over it and remember the more you give, the more you receive in return.

5. Keep fit and healthy in body and mind

I have no doubt that staying fit and healthy is important for any individual's success. Building regular exercise into your week helps ensure you stay fit and healthy with a positive mental attitude. Your exercise time will also provide an opportunity to reflect on where you are on your journey, challenges ahead and daily issues that arise in all businesses. There is no better feeling than having just completed your workout, feeling fit, positive and ready to take on any challenge put before you.

We are all so lucky today that there are so many books, audiobooks, webinars and online education opportunities available, covering every industry and market. Make sure you take full advantage of continual learning opportunities to ensure your own continuous improvement and development, both in your business and personal life.

There are many amazing books I have read to broaden my education but a book that really struck a chord for me was 'Rich Dad Poor Dad' written by Robert Kiyosaki. This book changed the way I look at money and taught me about good debt, bad debt and the true difference between assets and liabilities. It also taught me how rewarding and tax efficient running your own business can be and I would recommend this book to anyone.

Throughout my working lifetime I always operated using a daybook for meeting notes, daily plans, etc. Current mobile devices provide instant access to a range of suitable apps, but I strongly believe daily action plans, updated and reviewed on the previous evening are the best way to ensure you achieve success and get through the daily tasks that form part of any day. Reviewing your plan on the evening before doesn't take long but can be a great help, as I have often found that issues I considered and thought about would be resolved in my subconscious mind overnight – I'd have the answer in my mind when waking up and thinking about the issue the next morning.

Owning and running businesses has presented me with many challenges but leading teams to overcome and achieve success has been a hugely motivating, enjoyable and rewarding experience, providing me with direction, purpose and great fulfilment in my life.

I would encourage you to follow your passion, develop an ambitious plan and take positive action to move forward. Inspire your team, track your progress and never give up until you succeed in achieving your goals and dreams.

I wish you good luck and great success with all that you strive for in life.

Ian

RICHARD KENNEDY

Lessons from wisdom

"Our deepest fear is not that we are weak. Our deepest fear is that we are powerful beyond measure. It is our light, not our darkness that most frightens us.

We ask ourselves, who am I to be brilliant, gorgeous, talented, fabulous? Actually, who are you not to be?

You are a child of God. Your playing small does not serve the world ... As we are liberated from our own fear, our presence automatically liberates others"

Nelson Mandela

ABOUT THE CHAPTER AUTHOR

Richard has never sought the easy over the difficult where the outcome is for greater good.

His first career was running multimillion-pound turnover restaurants, often engaged to turn around under-performing sites. Seeking something with a greater social impact, he moved to Cape Town with his wife and 6-month-old baby to study for an MBA with a focus on social enterprise. After completing his MBA at London Business School, he joined a pioneering social enterprise providing strategic capital and support to leading UK social enterprises.

After six years he moved to The Young Foundation as Interim Director of Ventures supporting early stage social enterprises and, shortly after, became Managing Director at FINCA UK, part of the global FINCA micro-finance network. Richard then spent four years at a global strategy and marketing consultancy leading, project managing and delivering global strategy, purpose, sustainability and human-centred design projects with clients such as Unilever, Danone, Coca Cola and the UN in Europe, Africa, the Middle East and Asia. Richard is also chair of Social Value UK and co-chair of Social Value International which are dedicated to changing the way society accounts for value. Guided by his faith and grounded by his wife and four children, through his new business and social enterprise – Cornerstone Place – he strives to address inequality in a practical and sustainable way by providing supported accommodation in partnership with the social sector.

www.cornerstoneplace.co.uk

MY CHAPTER

On a blustery day in July 2018 at the foot of Helvellyn in England's Lake District, three of my children and I began a four-hour climb talking along the way about the wonder of the world around us.

If there is ever a time to hear wisdom, it is all the time! We are never too old and should never be too busy for wisdom. Three of her (wisdom's) greatest lessons to me over the decades have been gratefulness, wonder and our connectedness.

1. Gratefulness

In 2015 I met a lady in the 18th century town of Bagamoyo just north of Dar es Salaam, Tanzania. She undoubtedly lived a materially impoverished life. She was blind in one eye and the sole carer of her three children with very little income. Business was tough because the bridge on the main road leading into her town had been recently broken and so there was much less passing traffic for her modest charcoal selling business. Despite the battles she was facing daily, she was very vocal about her gratefulness for what she had – her children were relatively healthy and she had just managed to build a second room onto her house so her 12 year old could have his own space to sleep. She was an inspiring woman who humbled me and made me realise just how grateful we should all be.

No matter the differences in our personal circumstances we all have something to be grateful for daily. Being grateful elevates the mind and soul. Every morning I begin my day by thanking God for all that it will contain – good and bad – and for all I have. It diverts my attention away from self-absorption. There is a tangible outward-facing feeling to beginning my day this way. For others this exercise in gratefulness may take a different form. Of course, the subjects of our gratitude will differ also. For some, material possessions such as a nice house or car or a well-paid job; for others this might be good health, a supportive and loving family or spiritual well-being; for some it might be having food on the table that day or a roof over their head.

A grateful mindset, I find, leads to a heightened sensitivity to the good things in the world and in people. This becomes wonder.

2. Wonder

"A capacity for wonder ... takes us to a deeper understanding of life ... it asks us to take time to reflect on our lifestyle and our ideals ..." Pope Francis, 2015.

To be able to marvel at the wings of a fly or 'see within the seed a tree' as the Victorian poet, Christina Rosetti puts it, is for everyone – young and old – and draws us into something bigger than ourselves. We are deeply connected to creation and each other and MORE than this we need each other. On a certain level we all know this. Therefore, it must follow that we are connected to the needs of others and have a duty to work together in realising the needs of our world.

This might sound too abstract but when you are fortunate enough to experience cultures outside your own, this is made very clear. I have come across extraordinary people from very different backgrounds already working for the needs of our world on a large scale. Just in my field of work, as an example, I have experienced the simplicity of various villages in some of the remotest parts of Africa (from one I contracted Typhus and while still undiagnosed in the UK, was given the last rites by my priest!). I have had the privilege of spending time with the Maori and speaking at a Maori conference in Auckland where family is rooted in every fibre of their being. I have had a small taste of the life of the cowboys in Calgary which transports you back to the Canadian Wild West in all its natural glory.

In these very human experiences, I have found the most authentic people to be those who are most open and allow themselves to be vulnerable. I find when I embrace my own weaknesses, I can better understand those of others and then find ways to serve their needs better. This is connectedness.

3. Connectedness

As I have said, the capacity for wonder leads naturally to our desire for connectedness.

Newton's third law states: "For every action, there is an equal and opposite reaction" and while physics doesn't directly translate to our globally intertwined social world, I believe we can learn something from the great physicist which is still relevant today. I believe that every choice we make, and action we take, has an impact beyond our individual reasons for that choice or action. Whether we are running a multimillion-pound business or selecting which groceries to buy, this truth is the same.

Last weekend I opted for the 'imperfectly perfect' strawberries in the supermarket sending a small message that to discard this fruit is wasteful, given the shortages of food around the world. I use a steel refillable bottle for water and my family and I recycle and compost wherever we can to minimise our use of plastic.

In my work (as a non-executive) with Social Value UK[1] we often talk about positive and negative 'externalities'. By that we mean that businesses and programmes may have a clear set of positive goals, such as making a profit or helping a disadvantaged person to get a job, but we also need to consider if our activities have any negative outcomes. It might be that the profit we aim to make might reduce profit for someone else in the supply chain or have a negative environmental impact.

---

1. Social Value UK is the national network for anyone interested in social value and social impact. We work with our members to increase the accounting, measuring and managing of social value from the perspective of those affected by an organisation's activities, through our Social Value Principles. We believe in a world where a broader definition of value will change decision making and ultimately decrease inequality and environmental degradation. www.socialvalueuk.org.

So, in our connectedness to others in our choices and actions (whether these are for a business or us as individuals), we should always consider if there is a way to maximise positive impacts while minimising negative ones. We no longer have the excuse of being naive to the impact our choices make and as the connection economy[2] goes from strength to strength and transparency increases, I hope that we will all be held accountable for the choices we make and actions we take.

While my connectedness ramblings may seem depressing, I am hopeful for the future because our children, the next generation, are growing up in the connection economy and they have a strong moral compass. I believe some of the actions we have taken, sometimes

---

2. The **connection economy** is a term coined by entrepreneur Seth Godin. It rewards value created by building relationships and fostering **connections**, rather than assets and 'stuff' like the industrial **economy**.

through naivety and thoughtlessness, will become harder and harder to justify in the near future. In 2017 my, then, 10-year-old son decided to raise money for the 'Vision 4 Children' charity instead of receiving birthday presents. Last year he did the same for charity, 'Street Child'. This year his 13-year-old and 9-year-old sisters did the same for charities of their choice. A very proud father seeing connectedness in action!

Back on Helvellyn, we battled through some quite tricky weather and the knife edge contours of part of the mountain – but we made it to the top. I was reminded in a small way of the gift of perseverance. No matter how hard or impossible things appear, we should persevere in realising our common human goals.

There is tremendous richness in our wonder-full(!) world and we are incredibly lucky to be living during the connection economy where we can understand, like never before, the richness and abundance which we are surrounded by. It allows us to better understand the impact of our actions and choices. With knowledge comes responsibility towards the next generation to whom we must pass the baton as caretakers of our world and all who live in it.

Gratefulness > Wonder > Connectedness

RON LI

Son of a chinese immigrant – humble beginnings

"Your past and experiences will shape you, but don't let that define you!"

Ron Li

ABOUT THE CHAPTER AUTHOR

My name is Waldron Li, most people know me as Ron Li. I grew up all over the UK and now live on the South Coast in Chichester, West Sussex.

I've had a ton of different jobs: waiter, cook, sign maker, builder and account manager in Print/Design and sales to name a few.

I'm now a full-time property investor alongside running a Design Studio & Ecommerce business. I teach children to create wealth through entrepreneurship while allowing them the freedom to choose to work on the things they are passionate about.

www.noxproperties.com
www.redpocket.co.uk
www.elixifit.com

MY CHAPTER

Growing up in the 1970s and 80s was hard for us second generation Chinese immigrants. My father came over to Britain in the 1960s as an 18-year-old. Like many of his friends and family they looked for a better life; he'd tell us stories of walking to school in bare feet from the top of the mountain down the hill several miles to go to school in Hong Kong.

I was born in Cheltenham, Gloucestershire in 1970 and grew up mostly in Bristol. My parents owned a Fish & Chip shop and a laundrette. English wasn't their first language so I guess they had to be entrepreneurs. We were pretty comfortable with a nice house, nice cars etc.

My parents divorced in the early 1980s – it was unusual in our culture. We moved to a tiny village called Dursley in Gloucestershire and noticed my father was not with us. My brother and I would spend the school holidays at my father's in Bristol. He didn't cope with the divorce very well; he eventually had a mental break down and spent some time in hospital. My mother was absent quite a lot of the time, she would not be around overnight or in the mornings as she had gained an addiction to gambling at casinos. So, at the age of around twelve, I woke up one morning, got myself and my younger brother up to get ready for school. There wasn't anything to eat – all we could find were potatoes! My brother was upset and hungry, so all I could do was chop up some potatoes to make some chips. In the process I managed to chop the top of my middle finger to the bone. Of course, I couldn't find any plasters so I fashioned one from tape and tissues. Meanwhile, in the kitchen, the chip pan had caught fire – I ran in to discover the blaze, ran back out to grab the fire extinguisher and told my brother to call 999. He just burst out crying saying, "I don't know how to!". So, I told him to raise the alarm with our next-door neighbours. By the time I ran back to the kitchen with a wet towel around my face, I tried to tackle the fire with a tiny extinguisher whilst in my mind all I could think about was my mother was going to kill us! The extinguisher ran out and it hadn't made any difference – all I could do was get out! The fire brigade didn't take long to come, they kicked down the side door and it was soon out – the whole kitchen was gutted. The police were called as my mother was not around. Opposite was a local newspaper called Dursley Gazette. A reporter came over and I remember a photo being taken of me and my brother with the firemen's helmets on, which made the front page. We were taken to school in the police car – I guess they couldn't leave us there on our own. I remember going in late, late and smelling of smoke. My mother didn't say a word when we got home; I suppose she knew she was in the wrong and not us, 12 and 10-year-old boys.

We were shipped off to stay with my father who was staying with his older brother and his family in Surrey. So, a new school with new bullies to deal with – being the only non-whites we received plenty of abuse. Our Aunt really resented us being there, she made the Witch of Eastwick look more like a fairy godmother. I came off my bike and managed to graze my left side; covered in blood I dragged myself home only to be greeted by my Aunt with Chinese words equivalent to 'Good, you deserve it'. Later that evening the pain in my arm grew much worse – a trip to A&E with X-rays confirmed a broken arm.

Even with my arm in a cast, the abuse at school didn't let up. One day a six-former decided to have a go at me and that was like a red flag to a bull and I retaliated. I grew up learning martial arts from a young age; I was always taught never to use it to attack, only to defend myself, but as a 12-year-old taking on a 16-year-old, I thought that was fair game! It wasn't long after the cast came off that my father had his second mental breakdown and was taken to hospital. Pretty much as soon as he was admitted my Aunt demanded we call our mother to take us away. Back to Dursley we went, now the house was repaired. A few months later, we moved yet again – this time back to Bristol! New school, new bullies, same shit, same abuse. I was getting into trouble at school, with relentless racial abuse. Eventually I was suspended for fighting. It wasn't unusual not seeing my mother for several days, her gambling addiction controlled her. It wasn't until we had not seen her for a few days and there was no food about or money that I had to call my father. He had spent some time in hospital and was now better. He had moved to London to help my Aunt, his younger sister. My father picked us up from Bristol and we moved to London, we could only take whatever we could fit in the car.

We lived above a small restaurant where my father and Aunt worked. Space was tight – I shared a tiny room with my father and brother with just enough room for a single bed, a bunk bed and a chest of drawers. My Aunt and grandmother were in the other bedroom. There was a bathroom, which only had a bath, there wasn't a sink or a toilet. The only toilet we had was in the basement of the restaurant which we had to share with the customers. A new school yet again, we braced ourselves for a new round of racial abuse – but it never came. Holloway Boy's School was an inner-city London school which was very multicultural.

My brother and I helped in the restaurant, taking turns to do our homework and working. Things were stable for a while – until one day. I was working front of house and had to wash my hair as I had something sticky in it. Whilst I was upstairs I heard a bit of shouting – my Aunt shouted for me to call the police and to come down. When I did come down, I saw some of the customers holding someone down and others helping my father. He had been stabbed in the leg – there was blood everywhere; we were terrified! The police and ambulance came, my father was taken to hospital and a woman was handcuffed and taken away. It transpired the woman had mental issues – she had come in crying and my father had asked what was wrong, handing her a napkin – she pulled out a large knife and lunged at dad. He managed to block the attack to his stomach by grabbing her hand, but it had cut his thigh which required eleven stitches. It was some kind of intervention that I had to go upstairs – that could have been me, I couldn't have blocked a knife attack. It took a while for my father to recover physically, but it affected his mental health.

I remember one day my Aunt telling me to follow my father to keep an eye on him. He took the underground to Leicester Square and London's Chinatown. I watched him stare into the restaurants' windows, banging on the glass and making faces, people shouting at him "Crazy Guy!". I tried to drag him away – this was so embarrassing for a young teenager to go through. We ended up in a record store where he picked up a few CDs. He didn't have enough money to pay for them but refused to put some back or leave the store. Shortly afterwards the police were called. He still refused to move when they arrived, and they promptly arrested him. He still wouldn't move! He wasn't a small man and very strong with decades of martial arts training – it took six officers to take him down. There was shouting and screaming – I just wanted the ground to open up and swallow me. He was bundled into the back of a police van. I managed to contact an Uncle who happened to be the Chairman of Chinatown; he managed to get my father out. He was admitted to a mental hospital where he did get better eventually.

I finished school and did a year at an art college before dropping out and going to work for a small sign maker and helping out in the restaurant.

To date I have managed to buy my own house and several investment properties in excess of over £2 million. I'm happily married to an amazing wife, with my son, daughter and Cookie the Cockapoo. We live on the South Coast and are semi-financially free.

So, what is the story, what would I have told my younger self?

"Your past and experiences will shape you,
but don't let that define you!"

RICHARD LIDDLE

A life less ordinary

"If somebody offers you an amazing opportunity but you are not sure you can do it, say yes – then learn how to do it later!"

Richard Branson

ABOUT THE CHAPTER AUTHOR

Richard has been a Military Officer, helicopter and jet pilot for the past 21 years; he is also a successful property investor and skydiving instructor. Graduating from Newcastle University in 1998, Richard joined the Royal Navy as a Commando Helicopter pilot. Following training he joined 846 Naval Air Squadron and saw combat around the globe, including the invasion of Iraq in 2003 where he was part of the advanced force through the Al Faw Peninsula up to Basrah. He has also been on operations in Libya, Syria and multiple times to Afghanistan where he was involved in many multi-national operations including the largest helicopter assault British Forces have ever been involved in.

Three years flying Search and Rescue helicopters covering the West

Coast of Scotland and the highlands proved some of the most exciting, dangerous and challenging conditions ever seen. Two hundred and twelve live rescues during this period saw him rescue fallen climbers from Ben Nevis, sailors from sinking boats and even the swift movement of premature babies in incubators between remote Scottish locations in order to save lives.

All the while, alongside globally flying on Military Operations, Richard was growing his property portfolio and business. He even bought a development building while deployed to Afghanistan using only a satellite phone to secure the deal. This took remote and challenging investing to a new level, as not only were the communications bad but also the deal was not as vanilla as many, requiring extensive due diligence.

Richard enjoys living on the more adventurous side of life. He loves travelling and spending time with his family as well as falling from 15,000 feet doing his other passion which is skydiving as a sport. He has been involved in multiple world records as well as teaching it to the next generation. His lasting claim to fame however still lies in his role as an X-Wing pilot in the 'Rogue One' Disney movie, which is part of the recent Star Wars series.

www.Richardliddle.co.uk

MY CHAPTER

I debated the contents of this chapter for quite some time, as I wanted to fully honour the value that people would place upon it when they opened this book. I felt an obligation to give real value to my younger self. I debated back and forth to really search for the most valuable lesson I could find from my past experiences, one from business, the military or an opportunity missed that I wish I had taken. What would people expect me to say? However, the one thought I returned to again and again was the concept of time. As adults, we place value on many things in life but as children what we often valued the most, was the time people invested in us, the time our loved ones spent with us. Research has shown that children need time with their parents and that relationships can become strained when hard working parents appear to be too busy, in the eyes of their children, chasing a dream or working rather than spending time with their family. In many cases a simple answer for parents is to replace 'time' with 'objects', to give our children what we wished for, what we wanted to be able to afford for them. This can create its own problems, when a young person's innate understanding changes over time to value material things, whether that be toys, computers, cars or Lego sets, more than the presence of the person who provides them. Hindsight is often tinged with regret when we realise it is too late to change the balance of our choices or decisions, to create a balance between dreams, goals, loved ones, health and time. I have a passion for watches and maybe this passion is born from the value which I place on time.

Time genuinely waits for no one. It is an abstract measure of who we are and is the one thing we will never be able to recreate or buy. Technically, we have all been given a terminal diagnosis from the moment of our birth. We simply don't know if we have 60 years or six months. Few of us take notice of this until the time period becomes finite and the reality of our human fragility is thrust into our faces, in its raw emotional state.

Born in Bahrain in the 1970s, I have been surrounded by driven and motivated individuals from an early age, people who valued and enjoyed every minute of their time. My father worked in the oil industry in the Middle East, and his thirst to succeed was always apparent in the air – something I feel shaped my attitude, my views and desires as I grew.

In school I always wanted a little more, something a little different, something a little less ordinary. I would regularly ask my parents to drive me to events that other children in my school had little interest in – learning to snowboard by myself while my father sat in the car park or dragging him out on a Wednesday evening to practice clay pigeon shooting, going to Scouts or the numerous other things I tried in a quest for something more. I was always striving to better myself or learn something new and this has continued throughout my adulthood and has been taken into my career.

A chance sequence of events while at university led my own quest for adventure to include skydiving. I really wanted to push myself and experience the ultimate and I felt that this might be the way to achieve it. The day arrived and I found myself sitting in an old Cessna aircraft – there was no door and a bitter wind blew as we took off and I watched the ground fall further away from me. Having had a full day of training I felt invincible, confident with my new knowledge, right until the moment I was told to move into the doorway and prepare to exit. At a moment like that your mind clears, no thoughts, just true clarity and focus. The wind was blowing down the side of the aircraft, I felt its cold bitterness, my mind focused on the training and processes I had received. I sat twisted in the door, gripping the frame as if my life depended on it, my legs blowing backwards in the wind, my eyes looking to the ground and the small houses below. A voice shouted at me "Get your head up!" and all of a sudden, I was out of the aircraft. I fell away from that plane with not a thing in my mind except heart wrenching fear until, with a sudden crack, a parachute opened above my head. The second that big red and blue parachute opened, the fear rushed from my mind and was replaced with elation – elation I had never felt before, a feeling I could not describe other than I needed to feel it again. From that moment on I knew I would always want to be in the air. Leonardo da Vinci, who actually sketched the first parachute design in the 15th century, once said, "For once you have tasted flight you will walk the earth with your eyes turned skywards, for there you have been and there you will long to return".

From this very first exposure of expanding and stepping out of my comfort zone, one thing stuck with me – the voice telling me to 'get your head up'. Wherever we are in life and whatever hardships, tasks, obstacles, challenges or seemingly insurmountable feats lay before us, simply 'get your head up'. Focus on the training and the process and keep going. The fear maybe overwhelming but the elation on the other side will be worth every ounce of hardship.

In joining the military, my thirst for adventure continued. I became a pilot in the Royal Navy, a Naval Aviator within the Fleet Air Arm, flying and operating all over the world, from the deserts of Iraq and Afghanistan to the waters of the Atlantic and the frozen waste lands of Norway. I saw and witnessed events which confirmed to me the need to value time, to be happy and content in my life. Many of us strive for happiness. We may spend a lifetime looking for it without ever feeling that we have attained it. Happiness can be as elusive as an orgasm – if you think about it too much it goes away! It needs to be lived; it is a decision, a choice. Make your own choice to live happily in your busy life and, more importantly, aim to add value to another's life, to make someone else happy. Serve others and you will rapidly find that you get back as much as you give; a happy side effect. We did not evolve as humans to be constantly content, however that is what society now seems to expect. In reality, it is the contrasts in life that allow us to experience true happiness. The struggle to achieve, the living 'without' showing us the beauty of appreciating what we now have.

Sometimes it takes a major change or event to happen in life before you truly know yourself. I had seen, experienced and achieved a lot before I felt I knew who I was; at times I still question if I truly know myself, even now. You will not discover your purpose simply through making one choice, which University to go to or what you want to do for your career. You will continue to search for your purpose, convincing yourself that you will find it at your next achievement, only to find that it's not there. It is easy for life to pass you by in an endless search for something special that never seems to materialise. The answer to this is to simply stop focusing on what you want and spend more time focusing on what you already have inside you. In this way you will discover your passion, and therefore your true purpose, by listening to your inner voice. I once spent ten days in the isolated wilderness of Peru, ten days on a river that had only been navigated a few times before. There was me, on the other side of the world, in a canyon with four others for ten days trying to navigate the length of an unknown river with rapids so vicious, that if we got them wrong we would instantly be fighting for our lives in the icy water, having been flung from our canoes. The contrasts of fear and elation traversed all of our minds on multiple occasions during this journey, but I found that my mind was clearer without the influences of the outside world pressing in. Knowing yourself is the beginning of all wisdom, a phrase coined by Aristotle centuries ago, 'the happiest people are those who are evaluating and improving their own self and the unhappy people are those who usually indulged in evaluating and judging others'. This still seems to hold true in today's society. We are so busy comparing ourselves to others that we forget to look deeper into our own true self. Take time to learn who you really are, not what others expect or what you think you should be, but who you truly are. This gift to yourself, of time taken to evaluate and value yourself, is the real investment and will lead you to the discovery of what makes you happy, bringing a new light into your world.

Think big, dream big, make goals so big they seem unachievable and unattainable to the average person – but have a goal or you will forever drift around. There is no rush to reach an end point. You don't need to know what you're going to do with the rest of your life, few people do. I'm not saying sit around with no ambition but also don't panic! Our life path changes, our desires mature and evolve and what we wanted at twenty is not likely to remain the same by the time we are forty. I know people who were sure of their career path at twenty but are now re-evaluating, having their 'midlife crisis'. However, they still have goals in other areas of their life. If you aim for an achievable target you will no doubt achieve it, but it will never challenge you and allow you to grow. Grow as a person, leave a legacy, and value your time every day that you are here as you never know when that terminal diagnosis will come to fruition. You will fail along the way but learn to be comfortable with failure – failure helps you to recognise the areas that require development, use it to mould your success. Never getting things wrong means that you will never truly get things right. Embrace failure; let it drive you to success.

But above all else, never stop valuing time and those around you. 'Get your head up' and walk with your eyes turned skywards because life is precious – never forget that.

KUNAL MAKWANA

A game of two halves

"There is no talent here, this is hard work, this is an obsession"
Conor McGregor

ABOUT THE CHAPTER AUTHOR

Hi everyone, by way of introduction my name is Kunal Makwana. I'm from London, England, in a small area in Harrow. I was born in Kenya and lived in Tanzania until the age of eight when family life took a turn for the worst and I lost my dad at the age of 37 to lung cancer. It was devastating and a numbing experience. For a number of years we spent time bouncing back and forth from Kenya to Tanzania. With no real direction for us, we uprooted and moved to London, England. This wasn't easy either, not having a place to stay for the first nine months, moving into different neighbourhoods, new environments and new schools was tough – however, as the great Conor McGregor says "you overcome and adapt" and I certainly did. If it wasn't for my challenging upbringing, I certainly wouldn't be the man I am today.

With the first half of my life growing up in East Africa, my brother and I were always pushed towards the law/doctor route and we didn't know any better either. After living in this country for a couple of years, I realised that being a doctor, dentist, accountant or being in finance wasn't the only option. Try telling that to an Asian parent. Sports were constantly shown everywhere, and it caught my eye. The thrill of last-minute winners and nailing-biting matches was a drug for me. I was constantly picked for my school teams, from middle school all the way to high school. I knew I would be involved in sports/fitness somehow, regardless of the social norms and barriers the Asian community has.

After graduating from Sports Psychology, my goal was to work with people and help them change their lives from a physical and mental perspective through the form of body transformation. I currently work for RNT Fitness where I get to live this dream. This has been my lifelong passion and one which was introduced to me from the age of 13. Sport has always been part of my life and ever since my dad's death, I wanted to make health a top priority. After all, health is wealth.

www.rntfitness.com/transformations

MY CHAPTER

The quote I have chosen is one of my favorite quotes from one of my favorite athletes in the world – THE Conor McGregor. After gaining popularity overnight after his KO of Jose Aldo in December 2015, I went back and watched his documentaries and interviews to see what he was all about, and this quote from him stuck out to me the most. Essentially, none of us have talent; we will have to put in our 10,000 hours in order to succeed in our chosen field.

Every year I reflect on how my year has gone, and some of the important and life changing lessons I've learned. I've done this from the age of 16 onwards. I had some really bad habits when I was younger which led to lessons and, in turn, allowed me to be the person I am today. Many of you may be able to relate to my story – if not, I hope you can take away some of the lessons learned so far in my life and journey.

Today, I'll be writing a post to my younger self. Below you'll see me writing to my younger self at different stages of my life so far.

Before the teenage years:

Relax. You're in a different environment, learn to relax, you'll meet new friends, your accent will change, and you'll meet friends for life!

Be Playful. Don't mature too quickly, still be good and enjoy the new environment around you. Take part in new activities, you'll surprise yourself.

Sports. Carry on using sport as an outlet, play as many sports as you can, go and excel in cricket, football and athletics. You'll be leading a few teams, it's okay to be overwhelmed, focus on the task at hand.

Entering the teenage years:

Take care of your mind, body and spirit. Make health a priority as soon as you enter your teenage years. We only have one life and if you want to live a long time, you'll need to pay attention to what's happening on the inside and the outside.

Always do good. You want to be the bad boy. You want to break the rules. You want to be recognised. This is your ego looking for external approval. Always do good. It will make you feel good internally.

Listen to everyone. Listen to everyone, don't pretend to be the smartest man in the room, focus on making connections and relate to everyone. You will always have one thing in common with someone next to you. Listen to their story.

Learn to fail. The best lesson you can learn, keep on failing, the reason why I choose the quote from Michael Jordan is because I could relate to it; remember to stay in the middle continuum. If you fail don't be down, if you do well, don't be too high in emotions. Stay in the middle.

Education. I know you're not a fan of school and learning certain subjects, but learn why you're not good at them, practice, put in the hours needed, don't get lazy, education is free, make the most of it.

18 years old:

Fear no experience. You'll be entering a new chapter in your life, you'll be meeting new people from all walks of life, experiences new things, don't shy away from this.

Make self-development a priority. Start reading more and understand the keys to success, everything you do will be constant learning, never stop learning from books, others, family, friends and strangers.

Pick your passion. Through self-development you'll learn there are no shortcuts in life, despite what friends are doing right now. Find your passion even if that means you'll be going against the norm, go all in and don't look back. Be bold in your decision and stand by it, you'll have doubts, but trust yourself. You know best.

Physical is the vehicle. You'll find your passion through sport. Sport will always be the answer. Around this age you'll find what you truly want to do here, put in the work, start putting in your 10,000 hours.

Go against the norm. Don't worry if others are doing something else and you're not sure of what you want, it's okay to not go out drinking and partying every day. Do what you like to do.

20s and 30s:

Pursue your dream. Start creating a plan of action; you'll be graduating pretty soon. Start gathering information on what you'd like to do and nail it down.

Work hard, play harder. It's in the name, enjoy life, don't get consumed by one thing, relax and enjoy.

Team first. Ego is the enemy, the goal and mission is bigger than you. Serve anyone without expecting anything in return. Amazing things will happen once you shift your mindset and start enjoying helping others.

Respect Everyone. Respect – earned not given; respect each and every person you meet, you don't know who you'll meet, you may need them one day, so be kind and pay attention.

Travel. Travel broadens the horizon, this is pretty cliché, but remember there'll be a point in your life where you'll be able to travel anywhere in the world whenever you want, take advantage of this, you're in a pretty lucky place.

Change lives. You're in a unique position, your job will allow you to change lives forever, make sure you don't take this for granted, and be grateful.

Lastly, I'd like to thank Mark and Sharon Stokes for allowing me to write part of this book; we hope to inspire many of you reading this in the future!

LUKE MANN

Advice to your younger self

There is nothing so useless as doing efficiently that which should not be done at all"

Peter Drucker

ABOUT THE CHAPTER AUTHOR

Luke has enjoyed a long and diverse career to date. He has a mechanical and electrical background and originally qualified as a technical engineer for BT back in 1983. His time at BT represented a chance to combine his engineering bias with that of the commercial world and enabled him to become successful at product development and customer engagement. In 2000 he made the decision to end his 18 years of corporate life for the chance to be part of a management team of a start-up company focused on the construction of data centre facilities across Europe. This was a great opportunity to hone his skills, as part of a small team, and to become directly responsible for key decision making and to be accountable for the results of those decisions, both good and bad, on a new business.

He has subsequently worked for multiple organisations and has developed a specialism for the Energy Services sector. For the past 15 years he has run his own consultancy company, helping organisations to achieve more with their energy resources, and introducing alternative technologies and ways of operating to reduce their carbon footprint. This is a hugely active sector and one that keeps him very busy.

Luke lives with his family in Hampshire and is a keen field sports enthusiast and boater.

MY CHAPTER

Something that I find puzzling is that, as I get older, whenever I stop and imagine myself, from a God's eye perspective and looking down on 'Situation – Luke Mann', I still see myself as starting out. The image in my mind shows nothing that is behind me in terms of legacy, whether achievements or disasters, just what lies ahead and the options available for the route forward. At the age of 52 years, based on an average distribution of life expectancy, means that I am well and truly over the halfway mark, yet in my observational eye I still only see the things that lie ahead.

I find this a little disconcerting as it could perhaps indicate that I see little value in the past, with all the life experiences that anyone would have gained by this stage of their life. On the other hand, maybe, I should consider this a positive so as not to be influenced, one way or another, by what has happened previously. Perhaps there is an assumption that all previous life-learning, and advice received on the way, is accepted as a given and is automatically used to make decisions and steer the path through what might be the next four decades, if I'm lucky. One thing is absolutely nailed on, that path would have been considerably different, and probably negatively so, if it wasn't for the guiding hands and words from family, friends, colleagues and acquaintances who have provided valued and timely advice along the way.

With this backdrop in mind, I have set out to think about what advice, based on my now actual experience, has been the most useful to me and why I would like to impart that to my younger self. And in considering this, I believe there are two components to this offering, both equally as important as the other. The first being the message, the actual words and what they mean, and the other one, timing. In terms of timing, it's an important factor to think about when the words of wisdom may have the greatest benefit. Not perhaps from the very beginning, infancy/childhood, because there does need to be a general level of maturity to recognise good advice and an even greater sense of resolve to act on it. To me, good advice also needs to have some level of reference, so the recipient will have had some of their own life experiences to be able to register how perhaps a different approach may deliver a different outcome. So, I suppose my target age (for me as the recipient) would have been when I was about 25. By this time, I would have been out in the big bad world of employment for a few years, buying a house, possibly thinking of a family, building for the future. I would have hoped that I might have been just about ready for some words of encouragement and direction from the touchline. The second key factor is the message and how this might be considered and then acted on. With all things in life it is usually the subtle adjustments that we make, being easier to maintain, compared to mammoth changes that have real longevity. Just think back to all those New Year's resolutions – made and failed. The content needs to reflect this and perhaps only suggest a change or approach that is realistic and achievable, a bit like the 'Couch to 5K' initiative. I doubt very much this would have got far if it had been named the 'Couch to 25K' – certainly not for me.

So now I've considered the type and timing of my advice, now to my offering to my younger self. And in doing this I think back to a Wall Street Journal article written by a fella called Peter Drucker and was titled 'The Five Deadly Business Sins'. Now please don't think that my regular reading digest normally extended to the WSJ, nothing so highbrow. It just so happened, that at the time when I was about 25, I was spending some time working on a project in the States and one of my contacts there, who continues to remain a good friend, gave me this article and urged me to think about its content – and I did. Whilst, according to Drucker there were five sins, there are probably many hundreds from what I have seen. The one that stood out for me, and still does to this day, goes like this, 'Never slaughter tomorrow's opportunity on the altar of yesterday'. What he's saying here is don't miss out on what lies ahead just because it's not what you are used to or have today. I think those are probably the most valuable things one could ever impart to one's younger self, assuming that traits like being respectful and thoughtful towards others are a given. Now, Drucker's target audience would have been the business executives of the world, the industry captains, and his words were aimed at providing coaching on how to better run and manage enterprises of all sizes. But for me, those words of advice can be applied and benefit everyday life and the decisions we make along the way. I still have a copy of the photocopied article and whilst there were indeed five sins, I only really think about my favourite and the circumstances where it has benefited me – and there have been numerous times when I haven't heeded the words. Morose in my younger years.

I can remember one example vividly. It was back in 1998 and within the large corporate organisation where I worked, there were many development and training programmes available to the promotion-hungry pole climbers, such as myself. One particular initiative from HR was the Potential Senior Executives Programme (PSEP very corporate). A key component of this was to place potential candidates of stardom as Executive Assistants to some of the senior management heads across the business. This was supposed to be for a limited period, 12 months perhaps, and was aimed at exposing the person to the trappings of senior management and all that went on whilst operating in all that rarefied air. It was a very prestigious gig and looking back, quite an insightful programme. Many of the individuals that were selected went on to run big organisations, both within and outside of the business. It was with huge surprise that I, one day, had the tap on the shoulder by my manager to confirm that I had been put forward for one of these assignments. The role was to be working for one of the heads of our international division and would be based in Virginia, USA. This was a real big deal and for the first day or two after hearing about it, I was very excited and flattered. I happened to know the incumbent and made quick time to link with him to find out about what life might look like for me. At this time my wife and I had recently got married. We had also moved into our dream home, one that we thought we could never afford and had gone all out to buy. We had also just had a significant renovation project completed and to top it off, had lovely new carpets fitted throughout; it was truly beautiful – and ours. It was against this backdrop that I started to think again about the EA position, and as the days went on the excitement and attractiveness started to fade. This was now a compare and contrast – the chance to have 12 months gaining some of the most important business experiences that I was ever likely to have and a promotion path carved out for my future, against the lure of a new shag pile carpet – and I chose the carpet. Clearly this was not the explanation that I offered on declining the position and whilst I do think hard about why I really sacrificed that opportunity on my yesterday's altar, there were probably some deeper factors at play too. I now regret it. I couldn't perhaps see past the home comforts which was indeed a shame.

I didn't progress any further with the PSEP. In fact, during one follow-up session, when psychometric testing had recently been introduced, it was determined that my profile was a little too 'maverick' for the large corporate world and in the year 2000, after 18 years with the company, man and boy, I left to go to be part of a start-up technology business. Looking back, I was probably always that round pin in the square hole in the corporate machine which had taken some significant number of years to discover. This discovery allows me to indulge in my closely followed second piece of advice: if you don't fit the hole you are in, then move on – don't waste any more time because it's much better for all where you fit just right.

IAN MCBAIN JNR

Investing in YOU and focusing on YOUR happiness

"Winners are simply willing to do what losers won't"

Anon

ABOUT THE CHAPTER AUTHOR

Over the past 30 years I have experienced many exciting and daunting challenges. My working life started as an apprentice motor mechanic, which led to a period as a car salesman before I upped sticks and moved from Scotland to England to fulfil my boyhood ambition to become a Firefighter. Fast forward fifteen years and I have literally just sold my first business – a Removals and Storage company – that I started from scratch after catching the entrepreneurial bug, so that I could focus my attention on my new passion which is property investment and training. I am a Director of our family property business in Southend-On-Sea, Essex investing in Buy-To-Let, HMOs, and Serviced Accommodation and enjoy a fulfilling career mentoring others as they develop their own property portfolio.

I'm currently writing my own first book entitled "Firefighter to Financial Freedom" and am always happy to chat via Facebook.

www.ianmcbain.co.uk

MY CHAPTER

They say youth is wasted on the young, and whilst I don't believe that to be true, there is an element of reality to that statement. Imagine what you could achieve aged 20 given the wisdom you gain by the time you are 40. I've learnt much through my different careers, my travels, my friendships and my mistakes. The major lesson I wished I'd learnt earlier is to focus on your own happiness, not your wealth or status. I would advise my younger self to invest in my health and education, and I'd recommend working with a mentor or coach to help enhance those areas.

Investing in yourself may sound selfish at first, but ultimately, when you are happy, healthy and informed, you are able to perform at your best and give value to all that is important in your world, including relationships with friends, family and your occupation.

Some people are born with a sunny disposition, others are always serious and never seem to enjoy the lighter moments of life. It's impossible to be happy all the time; life throws everyone some curveballs, but it is only now that I truly appreciate how important it is to look for joy in the everyday, to celebrate the small successes, and to focus on what makes you happy.

I would tell my younger self to cut out the negative, make your environment a happy place. Eight years ago it was suggested to me by a friend that I stop reading the newspapers, watching the news on television or listening to it on the radio. At first I was seriously skeptical. He recommended I undertook a news detox for 21 days and report back on my findings. Well guess what? I felt happier than I'd felt in ages!

We are all effectively in charge of what information we feed into our minds. Keeping your own world calm and positive, without drama or sensationalism, is an absolute must. I wished I had understood the value of selecting what material I absorbed; the mind is a powerful tool and it is important to harness it with positive intelligence.

Under almost every circumstance your happiness is dictated by your health, which most people take for granted. If you lose your health, then you cannot function at anything else.

Although I have always enjoyed exercise in many guises, I wish I had sought a health and fitness coach years earlier. It has been one of my best decisions ever.

I've changed my entire lifestyle following the advice of my coach. He recommended the best foods for me to eat, and when and how to exercise based solely on the needs of my body. As I approach my 47th birthday, I am now fitter and stronger than ever, not just in body but in mind too.

I doubt my 17 year old self would ever have listened if I suggested cutting out the junk food and beer, but I now recognise that by keeping my blood sugars at the same level throughout the day, I lose all cravings for sugar and caffeine and I am less likely to eat food which can make one sick or weak. I also find I am considerably more positive, clear minded and productive.

Focusing on your happiness, interests and passions also holds the key to building a successful career.

My most fulfilling occupations have been achieved whilst working within areas that interested me; engaging in projects that genuinely inspired and motivated me. I wonder what I could have achieved if young Ian had actively pursued his passions at 17 as opposed to falling into a job that appeared to offer longevity and security.

I have learnt the essential lesson that it is never too late to chase those dreams and that in today's world it is considerably easier than in previous decades to refocus. Over the past ten years the idea of a job for life has become redundant. Slaving away for a company no longer offers any real security, nor is it valued in the same way it used to be.

With the advancement of technology and social media which allows you to discover and connect with the world at click of a button, it has never been easier to create a job or business based on your passions.

When your heart is invested in something, committing to it seems effortless; your enthusiasm will drive you further and longer than a financial incentive ever could, and yet paradoxically, this passion and dedication to your own cause is just as likely, if not more, to bring financial rewards. This is not to mention a huge sense of satisfaction and emotional well-being gained from pursuing something you are passionate about.

Working on something that lights you up enhances your life and that of those close to you. Feeling productive and happy is a priceless combination.

I now know I under-achieved at school, possibly because I was young and keen to get out into the world, and possibly because the subjects and way in which we were taught seemed old fashioned and irrelevant. I'm not promoting everyone should go to university when I say I wished I'd invested more in my education, I simply mean that learning and developing your mind is key to your success. Gaining and increasing knowledge in an area that you are passionate about will inevitably lead to success in that field.

I love educational and self-development books, it's phenomenal how much knowledge you can cram into your head in a short space of time. After reading 'Rich Dad Poor Dad' by Robert Kiyosaki ten years ago, I was hooked immediately and have since re-read it several times. I now regularly read a self-development or educational book each week and listen to podcasts on business, entrepreneurship, life hacks, travel and fitness most days. I have attended many personal development seminars and events, learning from the greats such as Tony Robbins and Dr. John Demartini. Having always been an avid (and fast!) reader, I so wish I had started consuming educational books sooner.

My career has spanned many years and many fields; each role seemingly disjointed from the previous one but each, in its own way, has taught me so much both in terms of business and how I work best, but also about myself and my values. Perhaps I never would have had the confidence to start a business with no prior training or experience if I hadn't spent eight years in the fire service, both witnessing the fragility of life and understanding my determination and mental strength.

I am so glad I appointed a business coach early on in setting up my businesses; I'd highly recommend learning from those who have the knowledge and experience you have yet to gain. A business coach will often help harness your visions and focus your efforts, quickly saving you time, money and helping you avoid expensive mistakes.

Starting a business can be daunting and scary but equally very rewarding, not just financially, but also by way of the job opportunities you create for others. Setting up a company and growing it to a profitable enterprise is something less than 5% of the population will do in their lifetime, but with technology as it is now, it is possible to start a business with the minimum of risks and a relatively low start-up capital.

Without doubt the best thing I ever did was start my own company. I discovered I had a natural flair for business. There is something very liberating about working for yourself and trying to live life on your terms.

I often wonder what my life would look like now if I had taken the leap years earlier and set up on my own. What else could I have experienced if I had understood the power of investing in yourself, in developing your mind and following your passions rather than simply joining the rat race because that was the norm. What if I had focused my energies on exercises that promoted emotional and physical wellbeing as opposed to just building muscles – and what if I had been as brave at 25 as I was at 35?

I know these will be lessons I will teach to my young daughter as she grows, but also ones I am determined to follow and embrace myself over the next 20 years, for I know now that quite simply we all deserve to be the best possible version of ourselves.

I have realised firsthand that when you feel happy, healthy and enriched you are able to accomplish so much more in all the areas of life that you hold dear. I have experienced how a positive and empowered attitude allows you to give more to those around you, to do the utmost for those that are important to you, and that for me is the secret to an enjoyable, fulfilling and ultimately happy life.

RAY MCLENNAN

Things I covered up and why I advise you not to...

"You will never reach your destination if you stop and throw stones at every dog that barks"

Winston Churchill

ABOUT THE CHAPTER AUTHOR

Ray has owned and operated 12 restaurants and at one time employed over 150 people. In addition, he has owned and sold three hairdressing salons, a Glasgow nightclub and a wine importing business. He co-formed the Copyright Protection Agency in Dublin in 1996 to advise SME's on intellectual property issues, blogs and tweets on legal, business systems and property investment matters.

He is currently trying to finish writing three topical business books.

Ray was the Regional Manager for Scotland & Ireland for Angels Den, which has over 18,500 registered, FCA Screened, High Net Worth Angel Investors on its database and finds funding for SME businesses up to £5m.

After raising over £1m in Angel investment for one of his own property projects in June 2014, Raymond was instrumental in September 2014 in helping create Property Angels Den (PAD), which matches High Net Worth Investors with property proposals of all sizes.

Ray joined the Progressive Property (PP) VIP Group in April 2015 and has attended various PP training courses such as 'Property Masterclass', 'Finding JV Partners' and 'Expert Speaker Revolution' in July 2015 as well as attending Elite Speaker Bootcamp in February 2017 and 2018.

Ray is also a Guinness World Record Holder and keynote public speaker.

Recent speaking engagements include: Progressive Property Glasgow, Multiple Streams of Property, New Start Scotland Exhibition, Napier School of Entrepreneurship, Entrepreneurial Spark, The Recovery Club, various Chambers of Commerce and speaking at a multitude of business clubs and law firms on topics such as:

- Creating a Remarkable Business
- Four Ways to Grow Any Business
- Survive and Thrive in a Recession
- How to Turn Your Law Firm into a Thriving Business in six months or Less
- The Power of Small
- Don't Let a Slow Start Hold You Back
- How to Raise Investment for Your Business in 20 Slides or Less
- Raising Angel Finance
- Skill Stacking for Success

and many more.

Ray is a shareholder in a number of private companies.

http://www.raymclennan.com/

MY CHAPTER

I know you're only 10 years old, the youngest of four by nine years and a little bit shy, but you're about to do something that I know you will regret, and I know this will not help you – and it certainly won't help others.

I am you, only older, and I've been given a fantastic opportunity to influence the past. I'm here, from the future, to give you some advice that will make a massive, positive difference in your life to come.

I know that you get the bus to school each day, crossing the city of Edinburgh in your regulation school uniform and that you cover it up under a very non-school regulation coat; your regulation school cap is hidden in your regulation school bag and the school bag is hidden inside a bigger sports bag. So, you see I know that you like to cover things up. Especially things that you think might get you into trouble, or worse still, might bring in the unfriendly verbal fire from the other undisciplined school kids who go to the bad, state school next to yours and who also get the same bus.

You keep out of their way on the bottom deck of the bus, even though I know you desperately want to sit on the top deck. But you know that sitting up there will exponentially increase your chances of some very unfriendly fire, both verbal and physical. Staying on the bottom deck provides sanctuary. Safety in numbers and numbers of older people who will defend you, just by their presence.

It's one of those older people that I want to tell you about, but, more importantly, I want you to listen to him and take his advice when he strikes up a conversation with you.

This is a time before we were told not to speak to strangers. Before children were so wrapped up in cotton wool that they had no opportunities to grow and develop by learning to navigate their way across the city at 10 years old. In fact, strange as it seems now, we were encouraged to ask for help if we got lost or were frightened.

So, when you were frightened and you sat down beside the old man on the bus and he struck up a conversation with you, you did the right thing by replying and asking him questions.

Yes, I know he's old – very old in fact. He's even older than your Grandad who died four years ago, before he ever had a chance to really influence you. But this man shared a common experience with your Grandad and to be fair, he has racked up a lot of life experience as well, so when I suggest you listen to him I'm suggesting you not only listen to him, his stories and anecdotes, but that you take his advice and put it into practise.

He advised you to read a book. He called it the greatest book ever written, full of the best advice, and, (in his opinion) the only book that any person should ever need to be successful in life.

This book suggests 13 Principles to live by and all have stood the test of time.

I know that you bought the book and that you started to read it. I also know that you covered it up with wallpaper as if it were a school book – why did all your school books have to be covered in wallpaper?

I know that you covered it up to avoid the unfriendly verbal fire that you thought would come your way from reading it, but fire, this time, from friends and family who you thought would ridicule you for reading it.

My advice to you is to read the book openly. Don't cover it up and don't be ashamed for reading it – you have nothing to be ashamed about. In fact you have everything to be proud of because one day, many years later, when you do openly read it and talk about it and encourage other people to read it, your life will change for the better in ways you can't imagine now.

There are two principles in particular that will make a massive difference to you, to your family and to people that you work with. I know now that you will be kicking yourself for not doing this sooner in life but I want to go back to the bus again, for just a moment, to suggest that you not only read the book openly, but that you use that valuable time to ask the man and the older people around you for their advice on each of the 13 Principles, because everyone has a story to tell and older people give the best advice.

You see, like your Grandad and the man who told you about the book, many of these older people had suffered greatly in their youth. Suffering can bring out the best and the worst in people, but that older generation had a collective set of skills, knowledge and experience that is unlikely to be repeated in our lifetime – they were true survivors. They not only survived a horrible war, they survived true hardship and real austerity as well as borderline starvation – they witnessed death and destruction on a scale we cannot imagine.

So, when they offer advice, it would be advice worth taking. It's advice gained by experience, which is the best kind. It's also advice that's timeless. Older people have the unique position where they can measure the results of their actions. They know what works and what doesn't. Most of our life consists of human interactions and since the beginning of time, that's something that hasn't changed. Fads and fashions can come and go but most human reactions fit into a narrow band; but it can take a lifetime to learn what they are.

Or:

By listening to advice;
Reading the right book;
Acting on the advice;

We can speed up the process and start to make a difference.

The book he told me about was "Think and Grow Rich" by Napoleon Hill. I hid it from view because I thought people would laugh at me for reading it.

My father, mother, brothers and sister all ended up self-employed. They all worked towards being different, being free, being responsible for their own future. They all did it in their own way. They would all have benefited from reading the book. We would all have benefited from discussing the book. By hiding the book from view, I denied us all the opportunity to grow.

How do I know this?

Because 30 years later when I eventually followed the two most important principles in the book:

1. The MasterMind principle
2. Know very clearly where you want to go

I embarked on a process that led me to my purpose and an exponential rise in satisfaction and income.

When I was younger I didn't know where to find a Mastermind Group or who to talk to about finding one. I also didn't know where I wanted to go in life.

So, my younger self, my advice to you is don't cover up your book. Don't cover up your feelings. Don't cover up your dreams and ambitions.

When you're open about these things, you will attract and encourage other people who feel the same and you will be stronger for it. So strong that the unfriendly fire that will still come your way will be deflected. It will bounce off you and you will be better prepared to deal with any that does get through.

So – don't cover up.

NELLIE MCQUINN

Live your best life

"Success is a journey not a destination. The doing is usually more important than the outcome"

Arthur Ashe

ABOUT THE CHAPTER AUTHOR

Nellie started performing for Australian television when aged seven. Since then she has had a successful career both in front and behind the camera, creating her production company Grass Roots Media, aged 19. In 2018, the company had grown to be one of the UK's most successful children's digital media service providers, with over seven billion views. It was subsequently acquired by UK start up, Moonbug, a global entertainment company that develops and distributes safe and fun content for children. As Head of Production, Nellie is now responsible for managing the production of the company's kids' entertainment brands, which are some of the largest in the world and have garnered over 20 billion views. Nellie is extremely proud to be at the forefront of shaping future generations, creating free and accessible entertainment and educational content for children of all shapes, colours, sizes and abilities.

Because Nellie doesn't like to sit idle, in 2016 she formed Property 165, a boutique property company specialising in residential flips and investments. It started as a hobby inspired by her Gran's love of property – however, it quickly turned into something more. Nellie was awarded 'New Property Investor of the Year' in the 2017's Property Investors Awards and she continues to build the Property 165 business alongside her work in children's entertainment.

www.nelliemcquinn.com

MY CHAPTER

When I was asked to write this chapter I was extremely humbled. However, as I spent the next few weeks contemplating the pearls of wisdom I should impart upon my metaphorical younger self (and by proxy all the future generations that would read these pages), I started to panic. I realised that I am not qualified to do this. I am barely holding it together. As I progress through adulthood, I am constantly faced with the reality that actually, I know less today than I did yesterday. Who am I to advise my younger self? Yesterday I was blissfully ignorant on what a deferred income annuity is. Today, I'm thinking I should consider annuities as part of a long-term pension plan and I'm cursing the fact that I haven't been planning for retirement sooner. I've only got another 30 years to go! The day before yesterday I had no idea that Chicago is home to the world's first skyscraper. A pleasant airhostess announced this as I landed in the windy city. How did I not know this architectural history? It feels like the sort of information my father, a consummate adult, would know. If I too want to be a proper adult, surely I should know this fact. As I pondered on what advice I should lovingly craft for these next few pages, I have become increasingly aware that actually, I don't know much at all.

The world is moving so fast. I think about the things I wish my younger self had known and from this is born an understanding that the world has moved on. I remember a particularly forward-thinking substitute teacher advising a class of thirty eleven-year-olds how to read the price of shares at the back of the newspaper. We plotted their changes for a week. Now I can track instant changes in the market in the palm of my hand. A maths teacher from the mid-1990s yelled at one of my peers that unless he intended carrying around a calculator in his pocket for the rest of his life, he didn't have a chance of holding down a proper job. I believe he's currently head of the finance division at an investment firm in Hong Kong.

How could I possibly advise that young girl growing up in the 1990s? Her world is not the one we're in now. Likewise, how can I possibly advise the children of today on what to do tomorrow? They will have access to a faster, smarter, more connected world than we have ever seen before. I am already a relic and my advice is already moot.

I am constantly filled with frustration that I don't know more. I am only now, in my 30s, starting to appreciate politics. Brexit spurned a desire in me to understand how modern policy shapes my life. I am only now, in my 30s, starting to appreciate the economy. Newly married, with a family on the horizon, my desire to consolidate finances, establish a portfolio of assets and plan for the future is coupled with a burning desire to understand how money actually works. Why didn't I care about this before?

I believe the school systems could do more to prepare us for life. When I graduated high school (in the top 1 % of the state, so I wasn't slacking!), I had no idea what the difference between a fixed rate and a tracker mortgage was. I don't think I even knew the nuances of how a credit card worked. Debt, credit, mortgages, pensions, inflation, managing household bills – probably more useful than the clothing females wore in the Ramesside period of Ancient Egypt (and even that information I promptly forgot after my last exam was completed). I constantly wish I knew more about these important day-to-day necessities, however, as with everything else, each day I learn more. Each day the landscape changes, and tomorrow I will learn again. I'm not sure that I was ready to learn about pensions when I was a teenager anyway.

When I'm not punishing myself for coming up woefully short next to Wikipedia, I settle with an appreciation that it is not about the destination, but the journey. I wasn't studying the stock market when I was in my teens (apart from the brief aforementioned foray into the dailies) but instead I was learning to dance and perform in the school musical. I learnt about musicality, performance and stage craft – skills which put me on a path to creating children's YouTube content and has led to my current position as Head of Production at one of the world's most exciting children's digital start-ups. Performing was my passion, and whilst currently I struggle to get my head around compound interest and curse that I wasn't paying attention earlier, I realise that drama led me to my husband. My journey was mine and mine alone. Wishing I were doing something else in the past means I wouldn't have my present.

So, here is my advice: appreciate the journey. It is not a race and there is no one else to compete against. It's OK to learn as you go. I am humbled by the fact that there is so much I don't know, and I am privileged to learn every day. You don't need to be the best. You need to be YOUR best and your best will take you on a journey that only you can experience. Never stop learning. Academia is only one small part of knowledge. Learn how to cook, how to travel and how to be a good friend. Learn to treasure moments with your parents and grandparents – you will regret all the time spent resenting them the moment they are gone. Say yes to things you wouldn't normally do. Read. Read. Read. Read fiction, non-fiction, the newspaper and blogs. Listen to podcasts. Go to the movies, appreciate theatre. Write. Write down the things in your head. You don't have to write a book, write about how you're feeling. ASK QUESTIONS. You have the world at your fingertips. If you don't understand something, look it up – there is a YouTube video explaining how to do almost anything. Don't stop your young inquisitive mind simply because you have responsibility and bills to pay. Live your best life.

In hindsight, my life journey has taught me skills that are all transferable. Drama lessons taught me how to perform to a room. I have used those skills in every job interview, for every pitch, presentation, meeting I have ever been in throughout my 'business' life. Having a childhood packed with extra-curricular activities has taught me how to juggle my hectic lifestyle – business, property and running a household. Studying for my HSC (A Level equivalent in Australia), has taught me a work ethic that far surpasses what I learnt in trigonometry. I spent a lot of this time, however, focusing on where I was going. I wish I'd enjoyed the ride a little more. This is the advice that I wish to impart upon my younger self, you the reader, and in fact, my current self. Far too often we are focused on the end, when the journey is what matters most.

HALSTEAD OTTLEY

If it's to be, it's up to me

"If it's to be, it's up to me"
William Johnsen

ABOUT THE CHAPTER AUTHOR

My name is Halstead Ottley and I live in Ipswich, the place in which I grew up and went to school. I am a Fitness Instructor and Property Investor. I started my entrepreneurial life at an early age by doing odd jobs for neighbours. I also generated a small income by singing in the church choir and assisting the local fruit and vegetable vender on his van at weekends.

I took up fitness due to my desire to be slightly taller. At the age of eight I was inspired by a film about a small boy who developed an exercise program that saw him grow to over 6ft tall – he ended up throwing the Hammer for Scotland. I in turn developed my own exercise program and although I did not grow to be over 6ft, I was much fitter and stronger as a result.

I am a qualified Fitness Instructor teaching Karate, Pilates, Aerobics and Chair-based exercise classes.

I buy properties to rent out to families and single working professionals.

Through my classes I help people, young and old, to fulfil their fitness goals. The Karate focuses on children and helping them to build self-confidence, be more active, increase flexibility and work on their social skills. The Pilates and Aerobics classes help adults to get into a sustainable exercise routine which works on both cardio and muscular resistance. The chair-based class is my work with a local charity for the older population in the community who have health challenges, due to conditions such as Parkinson's, Dementia and Strokes. I find offering help in my community to be the most rewarding part of my profession.

www.halsteadottley.com

MY CHAPTER

Exceeding Expectations

While I was in the sixth form, I took a part time job working for a Co-op branch within Ipswich; I worked every Friday after school and all day on Saturdays. My job was to tidy the warehouse after a whole week of deliveries and I'm sure you can imagine the terrible mess that awaited me every Friday. I remember my first day vividly: upon arrival my instructions were simply to just 'tidy the warehouse'. I was given no training or guidance, just left to get on with the task at hand. My shift was three hours long and, in that time, no one came to check on me to assess my progress or offer any help on my first day. The store was limited for staff and it was a Friday, which was late night shopping, making this their busiest day next to Saturday. Despite my lack of experience or training, I carried out the work to the best of my ability using logic and initiative.

The store closed at 7.30pm and with 10 minutes before closing, the manager came to tell me it was time to go home. I will never forget the look on his face – he had tears of joy in his eyes because the tidying of the warehouse was supposed to take me the entirety of Friday and Saturday and I had practically done it in 3 hours. As a result of my hard-working attitude, I was offered a Trainee Management position when I left school.

This taught me, very early on in life, that it's not about how much you get paid to do a job, it's about ensuring that you try your very best in every task you undertake. I didn't let my limited experience or lack of guidance stop me from acquiring this job and completing the task. Instead of creating excuses as to why I couldn't complete the task, I used sense and determination to make my first day of the job as effective as possible.

The advice to my younger self would be to always do the best you can and be the best you can because that's how you will get noticed. Although I lacked experience, I used pragmatic thinking to tackle the problem I was faced with. I carry this mindset with me in any task I do and this saw me go from strength to strength at the store as I quickly climbed the ranks to become the store manager.

Say Yes!

As a boy I belonged to a couple of groups among our community. I took pride in singing as part of a choir and the role I took up in the scouts. My mum was unable to drive, but when I was asked to sing at various Cathedrals around the country, or to do various activities with other scout groups, I always said 'yes' – and then figured out how I was going to get there and also pay for the trip. The fact that I might not know anyone attending never stopped me from taking on new challenges and experiences. I never let those things stop me from doing anything – I am a strong believer in following your own path and not letting others discourage you from pursuing the things you love.

The friends that I spent the most time with were not in either of these groups, and as a result it forced me to make more friends. They couldn't understand why I was doing any of these activities as these were not normal for most boys to do. That never bothered me because I enjoyed the experiences the different groups offered me and the life skills that I was able to develop from the range of activities I participated in.

As a result of this, I always face whatever challenges and problems that are presented to me with a 'there must be a solution' attitude.

This taught me to say 'yes' to any new and positive experiences that came my way. Sometimes you have to learn new skills, and this can be daunting, but if you know the outcome you are trying to achieve, then the uncomfortable feeling that you get at the start does not last for long. The people you surround yourself with teach you these new skills and support you in your journey for success.

By doing this you will create a broad and diverse circle of friends and connections which is something that I have found to be invaluable. Our closest friends have a colossal impact on our lives, whether it's the choices we make or the experiences we open ourselves up to. Always try to sustain a positive viewpoint on new adventures and most importantly, surround yourself with people that will expose you to new paths and help you say "yes!".

Never Giving Up

Things don't always work out the way we plan them, but that doesn't mean it was a bad idea or that we are not good enough.

When I was younger, I was crazy about football and would go almost anywhere for a game. I played for the scout team, but that was only twice a year, and us boys wished we could play on a regular basis. As I did not have the opportunity to play regular organised football, I decided to start a boys' football team for under-12s. It was tough. No one would help me. I ran and organised training sessions every week and I had the task of driving the boys to and from the games – and I even had to wash the team's kit.

In our first season we lost every game with dramatic score lines such as 16 – 1 and 12 – 0. The following season my boys were committed and trained hard every week. We didn't win any games, but we were scoring more goals. At under-14s we won 4 games that season as we began to turn our form around – you would have thought we had won the league as the boys were so happy. At under-15s the following year, our combination of persistence and hard work paid off. A few more players joined our team and I focused on the boys individually and created a culture of togetherness. We won the league that year and I was so proud of the journey our team had endured to be the league winners. At under-16s we were runners-up with another excellent finish in successive seasons. I took the team into a local Sunday league, as they couldn't drive yet, and we went on an amazing run of league and cup wins by persevering and training hard.

We can apply the lesson that I learnt from this journey to our daily lives when we don't get the outcome we want – it's easy to beat yourself up and quit. The lesson we can take from this is that once you know what you want to achieve and why, the results will come with determination. Don't be in a hurry when measuring your success. You might set a deadline to achieve your goals but if you miss the deadline, just try to review how to get back on track and carry on with pursuing them.

Keep working hard to improve yourself and you can't help but achieve success.

DIKSESH PATEL

Putting in the hard miles

"If the path before you is clear, you're probably on someone else's"

Joseph Campbell

ABOUT THE CHAPTER AUTHOR

Amassing a small Buy-to-Let portfolio alongside his career in Investment Banking, Diksesh has long held an interest in property. He went on to pursue various strategies such as Buy-Flip, offering turnkey solutions and HMOs.

In 2016 he left his career behind to pursue his passion and has not looked back; as he puts it, "if you want to build a serious business at some point, you've got to get serious".

Now a sought-after speaker on the property circuit encouraging the importance of building long-term relationships based on trust and adopting a risk-averse approach to business.

His business continues to go from strength to strength, based on strongly held shared core values with his JV partners and his Values Stack System of assessing opportunities. Diksesh also mentors a handful of people in their property business each year.

Diksesh is a firm believer in giving first and paying it forward, and now wishes to pay it back to the community that has helped him learn and grow over the years.

www.LighthouseCapitalGroup.co.uk

MY CHAPTER

As I write this, I have been reflecting back over my life, and asking myself what one piece of wisdom I wish I had not only been given but also taken on board. I hope you draw strength and courage from this to make the necessary changes in your life, whatever they may be – because it is never too late until it's too late.

Recently I have turned fifty, a milestone that many thought I would not make given how I had abused my body – at just 5ft 10in I was nearly 120kg (18 stone). I would get out of breath walking for more than a few hundred yards, suffering bouts of gout and verging on diabetes.

I had put all my time and energy into my property business and trying to be a good father to my two teenage boys, but I sacrificed my health. Often this would mean countless late nights networking, lots of unhealthy food and of course the glass or two of beer or wine to wash it all down with.

My dad died from a massive heart attack in his early fifties and at this rate I was heading the same way. From time to time I would go for a 'jog' which left me a sweaty mess and allowed me to fool myself into thinking I was actually doing something about it before stuffing more pastries down my gob. It had got so bad I often joked with my friend and mentor "Can't I just get liposuction?".

In business however I was doing well. I had learnt from past failures that despite the zero to hero stories that people love to share, except for a lucky few, there are no short cuts to success. Indeed, every time I sought out easy street, the quick way to turn a profit, I ended up losing a ton of money. Be it the 'high yield' property investments in the US that yielded nothing but losses, or the parcel delivery franchise that only delivered stress and heartache.

The turning point in my business was when I recognised that there were things more important than money – doing right by others and building relationships. By consistently going in with the mindset to help and connect other people, rather than what I could get out of things for me, I became a much-loved and well-respected member of the property development community.

These things don't happen overnight – they take lots of commitment and as I call it 'putting in the hard miles'. Building a strong network that stands the test of time cannot, in my opinion, be done from behind a laptop. Often I was out for three or four nights a week, added to which the numerous follow up coffee and lunch meetings. This was my life for several years.

I lost count of the number of people I saw at those events who would go once a month and wonder why their business had not grown – "all I need is someone to invest in my project, its got great returns" I would hear. Then there were those who were hawking their business services, such as the accountant who was on a mission to hand out his entire pack of cheaply printed business cards.

You see most people are not prepared to consistently put the effort in to make things happen, almost as if they are entitled to all the trappings of success without laying down the groundwork. Those that set themselves aside from the pack are those that adopt a mindset of commitment and consistency. See someone with a six-pack, they didn't get it by going to the gym once, and I can tell you that from personal experience – but more on that later.

After nearly a year of regularly going to an event, talking to the host and the guest speakers, I was asked to speak at a future event. I took that opportunity and in front of a packed audience, I shared my property journey. That talk kick-started things – I was asked to speak at other events and more and more people wanted to work with me because somehow my message resonated with them.

Now please don't think that all I did was networking and talking. I also spent much of my time trying to dig deep into all facets of the business and learn it inside out. This is stuff you simply won't find by using your favourite search engine. By being insanely curious about other people and what they were doing, not only did I expand my network, but I also found out a lot of knowledge which I now apply to my business, which is now highly sought after.

What the Proclaimers never said is that if you walk 500 miles and 500 more in the wrong direction, then you'll be 1,000 miles away from where you want to be. Blindly working hard and making sacrifices will not bring you success if you're going the wrong way.

Not only must you learn from others who have genuinely been

there and done it, take their wisdom and morph it into something that will work for you. Take the lessons from my fellow contributors in this book to guide your efforts and your journey will likely be much quicker – but please don't confuse this with a shortcut.

So business was moving in the right direction, but I can truly say my health had never been worse. I decided that something had to change. I no longer wanted to be embarrassed of how I looked in holiday photos and more importantly I wanted to be around for my kids.

I had tried and failed to do this under my own steam, trying one diet for a few weeks then giving up or even taking up cycling with my cousins (which was probably not a pretty sight for others). So, I did my research and found a personal trainer and nutrition coach.

At first progress was slow, and I was questioning the wisdom being shared with me despite the fact that he was buff as a Greek God and I was, well, a beached whale. The thing is that when you're in a rut your brain will do anything to protect the narrative you've been telling yourself for so long that holds you back – it's way more comfortable to do that.

Over time, by following his advice and putting in the hard miles (literally he had me doing lots of walking as well as going to the gym) I began to see and feel a change. Don't get me wrong, my body was rebelling at the food I was eating and the exercise I was pounding it with. But I had taken my first few steps on my journey back to health and it felt good.

It wasn't much longer afterwards that others began to see a change in me too, and yet whilst some people gave me compliments, not everyone was so supportive. I can honestly say that I have lost count of the number of times people tried to make me drink beers or eat deep fried food that my body had started to reject.

At first, I buckled on the odd occasion, bowing down to peer pressure but that left me feeling so awful that I knew that if I were to win back my health, I had to stick to my path.

When others see you putting in the hard miles do not be surprised if some, if not all, question your sanity, or worse still, try to disrupt your efforts. The sad fact is that people say they want to change but rarely are they prepared to make the changes necessary, and by seeing you they feel uncomfortable with themselves. It's easier to see you fail and conclude that it wasn't worth the effort of trying.

As I mentioned at the start of this chapter, I recently turned fifty, and despite the many doubters, I am in better health than I have ever been. I dropped 50 kilos, just under half of my body weight, and have had a photoshoot that would not have looked out of place on the cover of a Men's Health magazine.

My journey has inspired many others I know that it can be done, who have now started their own journey to turn around their health and fitness.

You can do this too if you're prepared to put in those hard miles. Whilst there are no short cuts, there are detours if you're not prepared to learn from others. This is true in pretty much anything you want to achieve in life.

My wish for you is that you go out there and make the most of this one life you have – for you and others around you.

Namaste.
Diksesh

CHRIS PATON

Advice at 34 to 20

"Every intention, every achievement has come from dissatisfaction, not serenity. No one ever said "Things are perfect, let's invent fire"

Fran Lebowitz

ABOUT THE CHAPTER AUTHOR

I'm Chris Paton, 34, from Newcastle upon Tyne. I'm a full-time Property Investor and newly-married husband.

I was born 'on the banks of the Tyne' in 1984 which apparently makes me a true Geordie and my roots are very much something I am proud of. I was brought up in the country in a small village called Longhorsley by my inspirational and hard-working parents, Lilian & Malcolm.

Admittedly never the most motivated of students! After school I opted to complete A-Levels, then I spent a year working in the construction industry before going on to College to study Design before going on to Northumbria University to study Three-Dimensional Design, graduating in 2008 – with a first-class honours degree.

My father, who started out as an apprentice joiner in the sixties, rose up the career ladder to become Operations Director of a regional construction company. Suited by day, he was forever building extensions on our home by night and I was his would-be apprentice from the age of two, which fuelled a deep and growing interest in construction.

Whilst at University I bought my first house to live in, converting it into a 5-bedroom HMO, carrying out all the work myself before finally renting it out to five students and moving back home. Little did I know this was the start of things to come.

Once I graduated, I gravitated into property development and focussed on the developing, high yielding, high specification, HMO properties in the North East of England. Today our still growing portfolio is managed by my growing and talented team.

Primary to what I do is to continuously strive to improve on everything. Small marginal gains have cumulative powerful outcomes, creating a superior product alongside a superior service with people who have shared values. This was recognised when we won the 'Best Small Student Landlord' for the North East of England two years running for our student portfolio.

One of the greatest rewards in this industry is the positive feedback you receive from tenants and witnessing the friendships that flourish in the spaces created. I think we have even had a marriage now.

www.chris-paton.co.uk

MY CHAPTER

Being asked to contribute towards a book on advice I would give to my younger self was, to be honest, a surprise. At 34 years old, in my eyes, I'm still young in the journey of life – my career is very much in its ascendancy and I rarely allow myself time to reflect on what we have achieved. I initially felt I have not yet earned my right to offer guidance, so to spark a process of deep reflection about advice I would give and at what age I see myself in need of this advice, has been both an interesting and humbling process.

I couldn't pin down a specific event which may have had a different outcome had I known what I know now – personally I found that too narrow and only applicable in one particular scenario. Instead I want this to be advice which hopefully will be relevant to people of different ages and from different walks of life. It had to be advice I could continually remind myself of so it affected my everyday actions, improving the outcome of various decisions.

When I started to peel back the layers of advice I could give, I was looking for that one golden nugget which may have improved a time or outcome. I asked myself each instance: is this the absolute best advice I could give, or could there be better yet to think of?

The result – I came up with two pieces of advice as I couldn't choose one over the other. Interestingly, whilst reflecting on these, I realised the reasoning for both centred around my core values. Values based on family, caring and giving, and of commitment.

Advice – To wind the clock back. When I look back on my time at school, my over-riding feeling is one of enjoyment. I liked learning, but liked socialising more and quickly developed a reputation. I count myself as lucky in reality as I just sort of drifted through school without ever really working hard and without ever having much drive or ambition. My parents never pushed me and I am unsure where they thought life would lead me.

Fast forward 20 years and I feel I am unrecognisable from that carefree and unconcerned 14-year-old boy. Driven, motivated, ambitious and determined are all things I recognise in myself today, yet I feel blessed for spending my teenage years in a slower gear. I enjoyed the journey and this is my first piece of advice: *'Enjoy the journey'*.

The time in my life which I would offer this advice was an easy decision for me. When I started to study at college, when I was 20, I had matured a great deal and developed a real work ethic following a year in the construction industry. It was at this time I started to develop ambition, drive and a determined and industrious side which had not been prevalent before.

I found during these years and beyond, I would often develop tunnel vision. I would be so absorbed in what I was doing that little else would matter. This was born from a desire to be unashamedly the best.

Whilst my friends were off travelling the world or going to festivals, I would at times be so immersed in what I was doing, I rarely took time to breathe – I would work continuously, striving to achieve the best outcome possible. This was a trait which I had developed and then took with me into working life. Even to this day, I find I become too absorbed in what I am doing and need to remind myself to take a step back. We can easily forget the reasons behind 'why I'm doing what I'm doing'.

Enjoy the journey – In the end, doing what we love can become unpleasurable and we can become resentful of it when we become so absorbed in achieving a certain outcome. We are only on this planet for a short amount of time, so it is paramount that we enjoy as much of it as possible. Doing what you love and enjoying it is one of life's great pleasures. Look after yourself and life will reward you in so many more ways.

My second bit of advice that I would give to my younger self is: 'Walk before you can run'. It seems generic but for my younger self, this would have great resonance.

Walk before you can run – One time stands out to me as being the first instance where this advice would have benefited me immeasurably. At the time I started my third year in university, my lecturers had praised me for my second year achievements and said they expected me to have a very positive third and final year. At this point it was logical that I would set the bar incredibly high, producing not just quality products but also in quantity.

This, given the hindsight of what is now 11 years, I know was a real mistake. What I ended up with was neither the quantity of work nor the quality that I expected of myself. Granted, my bar was very high, but it was an extremely disappointing time and I felt that I had let myself down and also my lecturers whose expectations had been set by my intentions. The latter I found very hard to accept.

What made this an especially challenging time was the unquantifiable amount of hard work which went into this outcome, meant I really struggled to enjoy my third and final year at university and at times I started to resent the subject which I loved very much.

Had these words of wisdom been shared with me by my 11-year-older self, I would have done things differently. I would have slowed things down, enjoyed the process alongside enjoying the final few months with the friends I had made. Such was the strength of disillusionment with design that, after I graduated, I moved into property development and the rest, as they say, is history.

I don't profess to be any form of expert in offering advice. I have made many mistakes in my career to date and will surely make countless more in the future but having pondered this subject, these are the two pieces of advice I would love to have shared with my younger self – but I would also add, making these mistakes, learning about yourself, your limits, your values and your goals is all part of life's wonderful journey.

Enjoy the ride.

TATIANA PREOBRAZHENSKAYA

There is no time like THE PRESENT and no present like THE TIME...

"There is no time like the present and no present like the time..."

Anon

ABOUT THE CHAPTER AUTHOR

I am a 35-year-old investment actuary, working in the consulting and insurance industry for the past 12 years. I am a mother of two children and a passionate property developer and investor. There are many things I like about my life – my family, my friends and an interesting and well-paid job. I have a supportive boss and a motivated team!

MY CHAPTER

Mark intrigued me with this question when he asked me to contribute to his new book and I must admit I did not know the answer until I started writing. So, I took a step back to reflect about my present and the journey I've made so far. Who am I and who could I have become if I'd done things *DIFFERENTLY* or *SOONER?*

WHAT AM I MISSING?

TIME. Time to be with my family and friends, to look after my health, to do what I ENJOY. All my thoughts and efforts are directed towards creating more time, whether it is through efficiency or leverage. I do not wish to reach the FORBES pages; for me the financial freedom is defined by my ability to control my time and not to sell my hours for financial compensation. I am still working hard to put the infrastructure in place to let me and my children LIVE our lives whilst supporting our lifestyles.

Looking back, here is **MY ADVICE TO MY YOUNGER SELF:**

1. VALUE YOUR TIME – It is so obvious, but it took me 10 years to realise this truth. It is our time (and not the money) which is the scarcest resource. By trading our time, we are selling away our lives (at least the best younger years) often without the realisation of how precious it will become to us later in life.

2. LEVERAGE YOUR RESOURCES – The key to wealth and financial freedom is leverage. Only by leveraging other people's time (and money) can we continuously grow our return on time. Mastering that leveraging of skills and recognising the power of the compounding effect will inevitably lead you to financial independence.

3. FOCUS ON YOUR STRENGTHS – We all have our strengths and weaknesses. In early life we are programmed to focus on our weaknesses to reach a particular standard/school grade and many people (including myself) make the mistake

of continuing this pattern in our adult life. In my case I was always 'good with numbers' so in my early career I spent a good part of my day (and my evenings!) 'networking' with clients and team members as this was my widely recognised 'area for development'. Thinking back, I regret this wasted time when I was trying to become something I am not, rather than focussing on my biggest strengths which will ultimately distinguish me from my peers.

4. DO WHAT YOU ENJOY – When we force ourselves to work just for money, it becomes unnecessarily hard simply because we do not enjoy it. We quickly become tired and exhausted and it impacts our performance and people around us see it.

    I can still remember my first internship in a marketing department in Frankfurt, where my first boss – a lovely lady called Ute – could not believe how useless I was in coming up with a poster advertising VARTA batteries! At the same time, when it came to planning logistics and budgeting, I could do a better job than my senior colleagues. This is because I always loved optimisation, analysis and numbers and no matter how hard I tried, I could not distinguish between the two posters with different colour schemes as long as they both said the same thing.

5. KNOW YOUR SELF-WORTH – If you want to make it to the top management in a corporate world, you need to get others to value you. This is only possible when you value yourself. I coached a number of junior team members and always found it fascinating how some people's view of self-worth differs from the perception of others. How often did I come across very talented and bright individuals who did not

have the courage to speak up in meetings? I came across a few opposite examples as well, but the truth remains – if you do not value yourself, others won't!

6. CHOOSE THE RIGHT TEAM – Knowing your self-worth on its own is not sufficient. It is as important to choose the right team. The people we work with (especially our direct manager) often dictates how we feel about our job, our contribution and potential which ultimately influences our level of confidence. Work with the people who value you and create a team where the members complete each other rather than compete with each other. I would highly recommend 'Roger Hamilton's Wealth Dynamics' framework which I apply when building my team. However, a number of behavioural tools exist to help create a positive and productive environment in our workplace.

7. CONTROL YOUR OWN ECOMONY – I cannot stress how important this is. Your personal economy comes first. It does not matter how hard you work and how high a compensation you receive, if you do not have the right structure to manage your personal wealth, you are passively giving away your savings and your financial freedom. I have worked in an investment management department for a good number of years and I could see investment savvy and talented individuals making double digit returns for their employers whilst keeping their own funds in a 0% yielding current account because they had no time to sort out their own finances. As a result, personal wealth gets eroded due to low returns, lost compounding effect, inefficient tax structures etc – the list does not stop. Putting this right could

save years of your LIFE and preserve what you have earned for your children.

8. MASTER TIME EFFICIENCY AND FIND YOUR BALANCE – Each of us has our own balance formula depending on our internal goals. Reaching this balance is an ongoing effort as we try and prioritise our competing priorities. In my view, the key to finding this balance is building the right team and delegating. I wasted a number of years by trying to get everything done myself – it does not work, we ultimately run out of time, become stressed, emotional and we start making mistakes. Our time spent on various activities has different return rates (whether it is financial or emotional return). Identify key 'high performing' activities, where your return on time is maximised, and delegate as much as you can from the list of 'low performing' tasks. Try to optimise and streamline your processes as much as you can and you will start to see the light at the end of a tunnel.

9. DO NOT BE AFRAID OF CHANGE – I realised only recently that 'security' and 'stability' are not only very hard to achieve (if not impossible), but the desire to achieve them actually constrains our progress and development. My internal objective has shifted from 'stability' to 'flexibility' – I believe my ability to adapt and navigate through changes to be my greatest strength.

I feel particularly strongly about the last one at the moment. I have put a lot of effort into 'securing' stability, both in the workplace and in my personal life, only to realise this is a myth. Change is a part of life and is a catalyst of progress. Rather than avoiding it, we need to learn how to influence change to steer our ship in the right direction. In the meantime, enjoy our PRESENT rather than wasting time trying to control the future.

JUSWANT RAI

What other people think of me Is none of my business

"If your actions inspire others to dream more, learn more, do more and become more, you are a leader"

John Quincy Adams

ABOUT THE CHAPTER AUTHOR

My background was just a traditional one. Education, working my way up the career ladder and working until retirement – that was my plan. That was my programming, that was what I believed was the right thing to do. My dad came over from India in 1955. He had one job the whole of his working life while mum had two part time jobs for most of her working life. So I came from a background where it was 'work hard for your money'.

It was around 2004/5, after about a 20-year career in IT, that I was given a book called *'Rich Dad Poor Dad'* by Robert Kiyosaki, by Sylvia. This was a huge game changer for me. Everything I knew leading up to that point got flipped on its head. It was all about multiple assets and income streams.

In 2005 I started my new journey, initially in property. From there Sylvia and I were inspired to launch a property networking event which became the biggest in the UK for nine and a half years. I joined a network marketing business which I am doing well in, and it all came about by creating multiple income streams.

It came about by creating something that would give us a lifestyle that we would enjoy. We wanted flexibility and security – we found that through our businesses.

It's an ongoing journey because one thing is for certain: things will change whether you like them or not. It's one hell of a ride and well worth it. You get to become the person you were always meant to be – not the person others want you to be.

www.thefutureispurple.com

MY CHAPTER

One of the most important phrases I have ever heard is **"what other people think of you isn't really your business"** – as long as what you're doing is legal, moral and ethical. IGNORE what other people think unless they are already hugely successful in what it is you want to do and you are willing to learn from them.

I spent way too much time worrying about the opinion of others and seeking advice from people who had no clue what they were talking about.

Pre-2004/5 – I got my advice from people like me who worked 9-5, safe and secure in their career. Working hard until they got to the point where they'd built up enough of a pension pot to retire.

Of course, having read 'Rich Dad, Poor Dad' blew all that to pieces.

I went on a journey of learning – not academically, but personally – expanding my beliefs, knowledge and mindset.

I just want to share with you some things to think about:

Fixed vs Growth Mindset

Who you are is not set in stone. Whatever it is you are doing right, is not the sum total of your ability. Your friends, family and colleagues will want to pigeonhole you and label you. That makes them feel safe and secure. The moment you break that mould and step out, they will not understand why and they'll try to bring you back.

Remember Mr IT, Mr 9-5, Mr safe and secure gave all that up to learn how to invest in property, run the biggest property networking event in the UK for 9+ years and build a successful network marketing business.

If you are always willing to learn and say to yourself "I don't know how to do that YET but I can learn how to", things will always work out.

Books, Books and Books (plus audio)

Always be either reading something that is going to improve your thinking, mindset, belief or knowledge. If you don't think you have time to read, then listen to audios whilst commuting in the train or car.

The mind is like a garden – if you leave it alone, weeds will creep in. So be constantly aware of what you are watching or hearing.

Ask successful people for book recommendations.

Learn from Success

When we first wanted to get into property we wanted to get into HMOs and a lot of people told us to stay away as it was too much effort.

Before I asked someone for their opinion on HMOs I would ask:

"Are you doing HMOs?" and "How's it going?" If they said "Yes" and "It's going really well" then I would want to sit down and have a coffee with them, make friends and pick their brains.

That became my way of finding out about how to do things well – Are you doing X and how's it going?

Only go to those who are truly successful in what you want to do next and take advice or guidance from them.

Step into the Unknown

I have learnt far more from not playing it safe and not sticking to what I know. Going out there and trying new things and falling flat on my face a few times has taught me to be resilient, persistent and consistent.

There is always another chance, another opportunity and another go. Take the leap – it will always be alright.

Have Belief and Decide

Having massive belief in what you are doing will make a huge difference to your results. At the start it may be just blind faith, but the results will come from the activity you do. If you are on the right path and taking the right steps, have the belief it will work.

Decide what it is you are going to do and stick with it. I don't mean for 90 days or a year. I mean for three, seven, nine plus years. True success takes time to really appear. The compound effect of everything you are doing isn't going to kick in for months, if not years down the line. Decide, act and be patient.

Beware the Dream Stealers

There are two types of dream stealers out there and they can both play a huge part in your future if you let them.

First are people you know well – family, friends and acquaintances. They will know you for who you are and what you do. When you embark on something new, they may be a little bit confused, scared and not supportive. Most of them will be doing that because they want to keep you safe. Some will do it because they want to keep on a par with you and not see you excel.

That's fine, just let them know you appreciate their concerns and you keep doing what it is you want to do.

The second is an interesting and fascinating group of people. They will generally be people you have never met, or they have no clue who you are. They will attack you, try to undermine you and just be idiots.

They will want to share their opinions with you about what you are doing and why it won't work, having never tried it themselves.

Only take advice from those who have succeeded in what you want to do. Everything else is just an opinion based on little or no actual facts or data.

You will become a different person as a result of the journey you are on and some of the people you know will not like it or agree with it. That's fine. You keep doing what you must do. You can help far more people with your success than you could by playing it safe.

DO NOT try to keep everyone happy. YOU will fail and make yourself miserable!

Begin with the end in mind

One thing you need to do is sit down and work out what it is you really want from life. If money was no object, what would you be doing, living and enjoying the most?

Write down a simple list – bullet points of 50 to 100 things you want to do. They can be small, medium or big and what could seem like outrageous goals. Daydream and let your imagination go wild.

Once you open up the doors of possibilities, your mind will start to see and find opportunities to make it real. You will start taking steps consciously and sometimes subconsciously. That will take you closer to your goals.

If the pace is slow and you don't feel fully committed, maybe the end goal isn't right. You will know when you have hit the mark. Your energy, your thinking and actions will all align to take you to the end goal effortlessly – or so it seems.

Finally, I would just say have faith in your own limitless potential and go for it.

ANGELOS SANDERS

What is your destiny

"Someone once told me that time was a predator that stalked us all our lives, but I rather believe that time is a companion who goes with us on the journey and reminds us to cherish every moment, because they'll never come again. What we leave behind is not as important as how we lived"

Capt. Jean-Luc Picard

ABOUT YOUR CHAPTER AUTHOR

My name is Angelos Sanders and I am an entrepreneur, Number One bestselling author, property investor, mentor, property network meeting founder and host, podcast host and huge Star Trek fan (no one is perfect) ☺.

I started my entrepreneurial journey aged 23 and life hasn't been the same since. I started by building a significant property portfolio that has allowed me to buy back my time and to become the master of my own destiny. This was achieved with lots of hard work and sacrifice, alongside working with joint venture partners who would earn a great rate of return on funds invested. If you want to go fast, go alone. If you want to go far, then go together.

Not one to sit still for too long, I started a property and personal development network group that has grown exponentially. Together with our members we provide a great and supportive community of fellow property investors in the South West of England. The group has benefited from local, national and international guest speakers, who give their time freely to come and inspire our audiences. Six years on and the group continues to grow, support and inspire new people.

Working with my co-host, we co-created a podcast called 'Your Success' that focuses on what success is all about. That too has inspired many people around the world helping them to become the best version of themselves. The success of the podcasts spurred us on to co-author a bestselling book about how to become successful. Now I am writing two more solo books which I am looking forward to publishing soon.

In my spare time I enjoy learning about Ancient Greek and Roman history and have embarked on archaeological expeditions to Greece. Scuba diving is where I truly relax as it is the closest experience of being in another world.

MY CHAPTER

Who is in charge of your life?

Are you a passenger or a driver of your destiny? Can you take control of your life's course and plot your journey as the Captain of your life's ship, or are you happy to simply drift from shore to shore hoping that something comes up? This is a choice we all make and it is usually determined when we are quite young. Whilst neither is right nor wrong, the real decision is do we wish to feel powerless or powerful? I imagine you, dear reader, are more attracted to a journey where you are the Captain.

These are the questions that I ask, and often challenge myself with, on a daily basis: Am I doing the things that truly make me happy and are they aligned to the goals I have set myself, in both the short and long term?

In life there are few certainties and many people hop from career to career, never truly working out what it is they truly want from life and what really fulfils them. Whilst we cannot control everything that is around us, we can control how we respond and how we take the lessons that life's challenges throw at us. If you can find, or even create a meaningful career and life for yourself, then you are already many steps ahead of the rest of society.

Plotting your journey

Life isn't easy. No-one owes us anything and we must carve out our own path to success. The sooner we accept this, the happier we will be. It also means that we take back control and responsibility for our lives.

It is difficult to know where we are all headed on our individual journeys through life but that is also one of the joys of life, the unpredictably of it all. We are fortunate enough to live in a world where we are only limited by our own beliefs and imagination.

Try and realise that a lot of what happens to you is down to chance or luck and that is exactly the same for everyone else on this planet.

All of us are trying to make a decent life for ourselves but if you have something burning within you, perhaps a passion to do something or create or improve lives for others, then you have a responsibility to society to unleash your talent. It is the person who adds value to society who is the best rewarded.

Discover what really drives you

What is it that makes you jump out of bed with enthusiasm for the day? Can you make this into a living? Can you monetise it? Does money even drive you? I am not advocating going on a hippy retreat on a remote mountaintop, it is important to really discover what your values and drivers are.

Remember, you are either serving your own purpose or someone else's so always bear this in mind whenever you are dealing with people or situations. Who is helping you to achieve your goals in life and who is distracting you from accomplishing your goals? It is sometimes great to be altruistic but remember to value you and your time and not give it away too freely. After all, money can be replaced, time cannot. Our time is one of our most valuable assets.

Which way to go?

Think of life as a snooker table with yourself holding the cue. You aim one ball at the hole and you encounter other balls in the game. These 'balls' should be considered as either opportunities or obstacles that can either help or hinder you. Remember when dealing with obstacles and setbacks you are either earning or learning. Ensure that lessons from setbacks are fully utilised as, firstly, you do not want to repeat the same mistake and secondly, you will now be armed with an experience that your peers might not have within their arsenal. Take negative experiences and turn them into useful positive experiences. This way, no matter what life throws at you, you will always feel ready to take on anything!

I am 35 years old at the time of writing this and although I am still relatively young in the grand scheme of things, I would like to quote Indiana Jones, "It's not the age, it's the mileage!".

Sometimes the sheer volume of challenges can make you feel older than your years and at other times, really young and invigorated. If you are on a path of entrepreneurship or business or something other than the normal 9-5 job routine, then the sheer amount of passion, perseverance and persistence will determine your success.

Heads-up

You will need bucket loads of perseverance as it most certainly won't be easy on your journey. No journey is – whichever path you chose. I can guarantee that there will be periods when you are up against the wall and you will be hit (metaphorically, I hope) with setbacks. It is the mark of a strong and determined person to choose to take those hits and get back up swinging.

When we are younger, we often believe that we know a lot more than we actually do and have the (sometimes misplaced) confidence, or even arrogance, to ignore the advice of more experienced people. We do not know everything – seeking help from people ahead of us on the journey is a wise course to take. It can provide some amazing shortcuts on our journey and helps us avoid wasting time making painful and costly mistakes.

Be fearless in life

If anyone ever tells you that life will be easy, they have either had success handed to them or they have won the lottery (but even then, people can end up worse off than before). Achieving success is about focus, hard work and perseverance and ensuring that you enjoy the journey as well as the end results.

I never want to look back at my life and say the two saddest words in the English language, "if only".

Embrace new opportunities (provided they are aligned with your values and goals in life).

There have been many milestones that have changed my life but I would like to share a couple of them with you.

I have always enjoyed acting and when I was younger, I was offered the role of an Emperor. My character had to make a grand entrance at the Theatre Royal Plymouth main stage where 200 people were sat in the audience. My entrance involved me walking out in uniform singing. I remember the first time I had to make my entrance – I was backstage and I did not anticipate any nerves. Suddenly there was a twang of apprehension, but then the logical part of my brain kicked in and offered me a choice – either get out there and sing or walk away. Needless to say I got out there and loved every minute of it.

After that play and another production concluded, I decided to stop acting. This is perhaps one of the few regrets that I have in my life – I wish I had continued acting. But that wasn't the end of my acting 'career'. I did not realise it at the time but I managed to fulfil that side of me by creating a networking group. The focus of the group is to learn and inspire others with their property journeys, but along the way we have had great role plays where I have portrayed a dodgy Mexican property bandit, along with other amusing characters. The confidence from acting on stage has helped me in many situations throughout life.

Second, was buying my first investment property. I had finished university thinking that working 9-5 for others, and then being promoted, was the way forward in life. Luckily, I was encouraged to buy my first investment property and my eyes were opened to another way of making a living. Fast forward many years and having built a significant portfolio, property has allowed me to free up my time to achieve many other amazing things such as becoming an author, mentor, host a popular podcast about success and spend time with my family.

Quick tips to help you lead a happier life

1. Learn how money really works and the value of money. Mastery of money is not really taught at school in any great level of detail and most people leave school uneducated when it comes to generating wealth and dealing with debt. Arm yourself with knowledge that will serve you and your family well.

2. Keep fit all the way through your life – little and often beats an unused yearly gym membership. Our health is the most important thing in life, but we can take it for granted and neglect it when other matters take priority.

3. Enjoy the journey otherwise what is the point? Take regular breaks to recharge and reassess how things are going. The downtime will help you move forward with a renewed vigour. If you are consistently unhappy with what you are doing, then you need to look within and change it. You are

a free person to do whatever you wish.

4. Surround yourself with great people who are more experienced, wiser and wealthier than you. This will help push you forward as their ambitions and characteristics will eventually inspire and rub off on you. Appreciate the people who have helped you along the way.

5. Make time for your family and friends as they are usually the first ones who are relegated to second place when working on our mission.

Thank you for reading, feel free to connect, and I wish you the best of fortune ☺.

AVNIE SHAH

The art of being present – stop, breathe and listen

"Don't wait for the perfect moment.
Take the moment and make it perfect"

Anon

ABOUT THE CHAPTER AUTHOR

From a young age I enjoyed drawing, painting and experimenting with different materials. I recall a time when I told my mum that I'd won a competition at school and she was so proud of me. She told me I was a 'born artist with a creative flair' – so I guess, this became my destiny!

Although art was an integral part of my life, in my teenage years, deep down I felt my talent was not good enough to sustain a successful career so at university I followed the path of a Graphic Designer, thinking it would be more prestigious and rewarding.

Post-graduation: I helped set up a business in Dubai. My primary role involved managing properties as well as Branding, Graphic

Design and Advertising. During this time, I began painting for multiple exhibitions and sold my artwork to both corporate and residential clients – 'a dream I once had as a child'. I then moved to England and put my art on hold again to focus on motherhood.

My life now, decades later, is a different picture as I have moved back into painting. I am currently an Abstract Artist and a Graphic Designer, both of which have reached new heights. I am also a proud mother of three beautiful children, who are with me on this roller coaster journey and teach me something new every day.

One thing I have learnt is living for the moment is the most precious gift one can give to themselves and others around them. This lesson came at a crucial point when my life was chaotic. I found peace in art, which is why I now host art events for adults and children to give them an opportunity to unleash their creativity.

I share my experience with many valuable creative exercises in my upcoming book **'The Art of Being Present'**, due to be launched by the end of the year.

www.artbyavnie.com

MY CHAPTER

To my beautiful younger self

You look so strong and happy with a hopeful light glistening in your big brown eyes, more beautiful than you will ever know. You have a loving personality that will convince friends and family you are OK, and on the outside you show this, but I know behind that façade is a different story. You often feel lonely and vulnerable, struggling to express your emotions. You are so unique, yet trying to be the same as others due to the fear of rejection, which takes over your very being and hides who you really are. Well, I am here to tell you that you have a choice, your life is like a blank canvas and YOU are the artist.

You are young, the canvas is raw, and your masterpiece is in constant progress, so take control and make it your own. This has been the most important transformational learning from the 43 years of my life.

Unable to say no to anything and feeling like you are on a constant treadmill is exhausting. The pressure to do more, be more, and trying hard to maximise every moment is unhealthy. It eventually shows up through your tone of voice, skin and body. I know you've heard the phrase 'quality over quantity'. You, being young, think you must work hard to be successful but the more work you do, the less quality is produced, and your overall effectiveness is therefore compromised. Paint your canvas smart! It's all about escaping from being who you really are. I am here to hold your hand and to keep you away from the treadmill. Stop, breathe and listen – follow these words and the chaos will be gone. Being busy doesn't always mean greater progress, so stop pushing and fighting with yourself. All your actions are screaming for help, telling me you think you are not good enough, striving for more, when actually you already have everything you need. YOU ARE ENOUGH!

Being a 'doer' can have its advantages, but not when you are a people pleaser. It sucks up all your energy and leaves you dry and empty. You always 'do' without thinking, with no goal or destination – where you are going? I see you climbing the ladder as fast as you can, do you even know where that ladder leads? Its only when you stop, you can see where you are and can make a conscious decision on which way to go. Remember: stop, breathe and listen.

How innocent you are, taking on the load to make life easier for those around you with no expectations, doing the very best you can at playing the role of a perfect daughter, sister, student, wife and then a mother. What are you trying to prove? You are too hard on yourself, living your life behind a wall, so high that no one can climb it.

This wall became even higher after mum suddenly passed away at the young age of 52. Your world was shattered yet you continued with life as if nothing had happened. I wish I could have told you to cry and keep crying till you could not have cried anymore. You did not even shed a single tear at her funeral; instead you were the one hiding behind the camera lens taking photographs and not confronting your true feelings. Even now it's not too late to grieve and deal with it, as it doesn't go away, so share with your close family and friends – let them in and feel your pain. It's natural to feel the way you do; there is so much love for mum, now at a standstill with nowhere to go. Channel it towards your loved ones and have faith in God – she is gone and there is nothing you can do to bring her back. It's time to let go of what has happened and leave the past behind you, where it belongs. You can prepare and be hopeful for the future, but the only place you can make a difference is in the present.

I wish I could put my wings around you, hold you tight and tell you that it's going to be OK. In fact, it's going to be more than OK as you are going to get through this, lighten the weight and the heavy heart. This is YOUR time and YOUR moment, which will never come again.

You have so much ahead of you, so much to learn and so much to give, with a capacity to make a big impact – but first it must start with YOU. Look inwards and feel your heart beating. That alone is enough to know your true worth and just how special you truly are.

Believe in yourself. You know you are not alone – your family love you and they will always be there for you. There is a bigger force guiding you so trust it and flow. Don't try to question or fight it, just flow and enjoy the warmth of the sun, the fresh scent of the flowers and the dancing in the rain. It is these little things that are taken for granted, things that you will remember in your later life.

Focus on the blessings hiding in our daily life; acknowledge the way things are rather than how they should be. Accept complexity, its highs and lows and appreciate this is the beauty of life. By accepting and allowing yourself to live in the now, you will slowly start simplifying; feeling lighter, happier and able to make choices with a clear mind.

Now you are wiser, you know you are at your best when you are relaxed, so give yourself the gift of time. Time to stop everything – just stop, breathe and listen. Let your thoughts come and go and allow yourself to awaken and see things as they really are – not better and not worse. Accept imperfections and understand 'nothing is impossible'.

Your art has now become a form of meditation, where often you are alone, the world is sleeping and you paint away. The music becomes a background noise, time stands still and your journey of creating art becomes a prayer, where you feel free and your authentic self shines through. It truly is a great feeling! The art of creating is like a dance where you mix colours, apply strokes, re-apply the strokes, flowing with your emotions and feelings. A safe place to allow your heart to lead, as nothing can go wrong and there is no such thing as a mistake.

This is not a dream; it is reality. Life sometimes will often feel surreal to you, due to the wonderful phenomena of the universe. Just think about the chance that all this exists, you will then feel ultimate gratitude understanding how precious you are.

I am so proud of where you are today and excited about your future. Every day is different – it may not always be a good one but there is always a lesson to be learned which you can continue to document and share with the world through your paintings and writing. I hope my words on this paper will help you fulfil your dreams and remember – it is your canvas, so make your painting as beautiful as YOU!

Thank you for all the experiences you have given, for making ME be ME.

ROBERT SPENCER

A letter to my younger self

"Wherever you go, go with all your heart!"
Confucius

ABOUT THE CHAPTER AUTHOR

Rob Spencer is an independent marketing consultant who has previously held senior leadership positions within a wide range of consumer-led organisations ranging from start-ups to small enterprise to large corporates. He is a serial entrepreneur with a track record of innovation which includes, amongst other firsts, the UK's first Fairtrade juice. He believes passionately in ethical marketing, sustainable development and the value of purpose-led brands and has long been an advocate of corporate social responsibility. During his career he has developed a wide range of health and wellness initiatives across the food, drink and nutrition sectors. More recently he has applied his experience to the non-profit sector where he is a firm believer in providing the tools, training, education and skills to allow people to develop sustainable futures for themselves, their families and the communities around them. In his spare time Rob is a keen musician and an avid independent traveller.

MY CHAPTER

Dear Younger Self

"Long-time no speak! How the devil are you?"

"Actually, don't tell me because I already know."

Your parents give you all the love in the world. You're a bright, inquisitive kid, full of energy, keen to explore the world and all it has to offer. It seems like you're cruising through school, popular in class and in the playground and largely unruffled by the trials and tribulations bubbling around you.

All good then. What could possibly go wrong?

Well, young man, the answer is ANYTHING and *at some point it will!* Go wrong that is.

The good news? *It doesn't really matter!*

Here's why:

1. Nothing in this world is certain – It may surprise you to learn you are going to fail your eleven-plus exam, but your success, your happiness, will not be dependent on what happens to you in this exam, or indeed on just about anything that happens to you in the coming years. What matters is not what happens but how you react to it. Your success will be decided first and foremost in your mind because that's the only thing you really control. Here's the truth: you're going to face highs and lows. My best advice is to embrace them equally. Each peak and trough will play itself out. Success and failure are ultimately both illusory and transitory.

2. It's good to dream – Some people have a big dream, a lifelong ambition. They are wonderfully blessed, but don't feel any less of a person if you don't feel that absolute clarity. That's not to say it's not important to have goals, far from it – you need goals in order to make objective decisions. It's also important to leave yourself open to influences and to be alert to opportunities, being ready to seize them when they arise. You have a varied and fulfilling career ahead of you by doing your best and being happy in what you achieve. That doesn't mean the absence of ambition or settling for second best. It means recognising what matters. In time you'll look back on things that seem critical to you right now and wonder what all the fuss was about.

3. Your life is not a destination, but a journey – I know it's a cliché, but to enjoy the ride you must live in the present. There will be times when that's easier said than done. You might find yourself dwelling on the past or obsessing about the future. It's natural to have doubts and to turn things over in your mind. There will be times when you feel low. That's OK too. Acknowledge those thoughts and then put them to one side. What's gone is gone. Learn from it. Move on. What's yet to come cannot be guaranteed, no matter how much you wish it so. The present is the only moment we have, the only experience we can touch, feel and know for certain that it is real. So, don't waste it. Right now, you don't know what irony is but I'll give you a clue: it's ironic that we can only live in the present and yet in our search for success and happiness we often get hung up on re-living the past or attempt to tie down the future. In doing so we risk missing out on the pleasure of today. Here's a little secret from your future self: when you acknowledge the past, embrace the present and remain open to the future – it's amazing how often the future sorts itself out in your favour.

4. Perspective is critical – There will come a day when a company restructure gives you the opportunity to take voluntary redundancy. Your boss will question your decision to take a year out and travel. "You're very well thought of here," she'll tell you. "If you stay on, you're in line for a big promotion." Your response will be that this opportunity might never arise again and that you believe the experience will make you a more capable, rounded person. Just as importantly you know you're at a suitable crossroads. You've established a strong network of people in whom you trust and who trust you and, while nothing is certain, you're confident they will be open to discussion when you return. So off you go. And guess what? Your next role leads to bigger and better things. So, don't be afraid to take a breather now and then, mentally and physically. Travel makes you realise just how fortunate you are, but it doesn't have to be travel and it doesn't need to involve a career break. Anything that broadens the mind and gives you perspective is beneficial.

5. It's not all about taking risks – In your early career you'll have a charismatic boss who persuades you to join him when he sets up his own company, but he's short of cash so, with promises of great adventure and reward lighting up your eyes, you lend him your hard-earned savings. The company fails and he walks away without a backwards glance in your direction. Some people will tell you life is all about taking risks, but that's not strictly true. It's more about knowing WHEN to take risks. There are going to be times when you're torn between playing it safe and embracing new experiences. The important thing is to do your homework and take advice from others before making a firm decision. Of course, you're going to make bad decisions – that's life. If you are tempted to play it safe, ask yourself why? It may be absolutely the right decision. At other times you'll know deep down it's time to take a risk. Learn to recognise the truth of what your gut is telling you. Whatever decision you make, embrace it, own it, take responsibility for it and remain positive, because whatever direction you choose, it's only a step on your journey and the experiences you gain along the way are a vital part of your growth.

6. Get to know yourself – This might sound a bit daft to you right now. But you'd be surprised at how tough getting to know yourself can be. It's easy to motor along without asking yourself hard questions: "What is my real motivation for doing this?" or "Why am I not doing this?" Find out what really makes you tick and embrace it. Only by getting to know yourself can you truly believe in what you are doing, and only by believing in what you are doing, will you feel truly fulfilled.

7. Everything doesn't have to be perfect – If you insist everything must be perfect nothing will ever get done. Aim high but know when to say, "it's good enough". Don't be too hard on yourself, you won't always reach your goal but don't let that put you off. Every experience, positive and negative, is a building block and can be used constructively in creating a more fulfilling future.

8. Share your vision – There will come a day when you interview for a role with a blue chip multi-national corporation. All will be going swimmingly well. You are told that your responses to the tests have been outstanding. Then you meet the big boss and he casually asks, "So, Rob, where do you see yourself in five years' time?". You swallow the temptation to say, "Doing your job" and instead you go with, "I'm sure I'll do a great job and make progress here. If I'm happy and fulfilled, I'll judge that a success". You won't get that job because it's not good enough simply to do a great job. You must explain how and why, give people confidence that they can trust in you to make a positive difference in their lives. Which brings me nicely to my next point.

9. Your good intentions matter – You're good at speaking up, right? What's more important is knowing when to do so. Think about the impact you have on others and how best to put your message across constructively. Make time for people, especially your friends and family – your good intentions are key to your journey. Resolve to be a positive force, have a purpose in what you do. You don't need some world-shattering altruistic ambition, simply do the little things that matter, the day-to-day incremental acts that add up – you'll find the ripples will spread. The reward? Not only will others benefit but you'll feel a whole lot better than if you remain focused merely on yourself.

10. Maintain your faith in human nature – You are going to encounter some situations which will test your faith. Don't be put off from trusting people, rather learn to ask the right questions. Cynicism and anger are simply destructive. For every bad person in the world, there are hundreds with good hearts. Be smart at judging people. Find good people and hold on to them – your life will be far richer as a result. Of course, you'll make mistakes. Don't let that deter you – life is short. Don't look back and say: "What if?".

MARK STOKES

The power of anticipation

"Does it make your car go faster"

Frank Williams

ABOUT THE CHAPTER AUTHOR

Mark has been married for over 20 years to wife Sharon and they have 4 amazing children: Ben, Jack, Katy and Emily.

Mark had a successful executive career of 25 years operating companies and deploying complex infrastructure globally, spanning four continents and dozens of countries. As well as operating multiple organisations, Mark had additional responsibilities which entailed extensive corporate 'trouble shooting' and business restructuring which added a further dimension to his vast experience. He retired from corporate life in his mid-forties to concentrate on creating multiple businesses that create shared value in society, as well as enabling him to focus on creating a powerful multi-generational legacy.

Mark is a multiple number one best-selling author with *'SSAS Pensions: creating extraordinary levels of compounding wealth'* and

'Commercial to Residential Conversions: the essential manual for property developers'.

As a seasoned developer and businessman, Mark is also a specialist in raising private capital and is in high demand by those wishing to efficiently and effectively structure debt and equity fund raises in the market.

Mark enjoys networking and his vast connections over three decades in business has made him a sought-after public speaker and a prolific introducer and business facilitator. His tenacity and foresight led to the founding of SSAS Alliance in 2017 which continues its exponential growth as a leading independent organisation supporting business owners seeking to further control their personal economy, including their pensions.

He is a Trustee of a Small Self-Administered Pension Scheme (SSAS) and enjoys creating and growing diverse business interests including property development, a portfolio of mixed asset classes and a training organisation where he teaches and mentors many people in business, wealth creation and commercial property.

Being highly driven and focused has extended to his social pursuits where he has competed in ultra-endurance sports, including Ironman and has over 30 ultra-trail running races from 50 miles – 150 miles to his name including the iconic Marathon Des Sables.

www.markstokesuk.com

MY CHAPTER

A letter to my 4 children: Ben, Jack, Katy and Emily and young people of the world.

- If only I had known that.
- I really wish I had done that.
- I never even knew that was possible.
- How on earth did they do that?

Do you recognise some of these thoughts? Well, let's be honest, every one of us has from time to time in our lives. Well the good news for you reading this now is that many of these fears will disappear and be replaced with the incredible power of anticipation that is open to you NOW.

Why make the mistakes and stumble aimlessly in the dark when you can have a powerful torch with everlasting batteries that will serve you well, as you navigate the roadmap of life with conviction and confidence.

All you have to do is to start, to reach out and the Power of Anticipation will become available to you with the benefits beginning almost immediately – sometimes slowly, sometimes unnoticed initially, but the awesome power of the wheels of compounding will start to turn from day one.

Don't delay making today your day one!!

To help you create and navigate your roadmap in life, here are 49 lessons that you can start on immediately that have proven themselves time and time again over the years:

1. **Imagine your future:** Decide earlier to plan for the future. Not starting earlier is one of the most frequent regrets of many. Don't make that mistake and believe me – it is NOT

BORING at all!! It is some of the best fun you can have – so start now with a life plan and goals you want to achieve and make a start by planning for your future.

2. **No-one is coming to save you:** Control your destiny or someone else will! Many of us are fortunate enough to be surrounded by ones that we love – many are not. We get in life what we seek. Some choose to live a life of subservience and adopt an 'entitlement' culture. You are entitled to nothing in life. You work hard for every breath you take, every success you make, every step you take forward. YOU must be in control of your life – it is YOUR destiny to achieve – no-one will get you there for you. As Bill Gates said, "it is not your fault if you are born poor, but it is your fault if you die poor". Take responsibility for you. The things you give your maximum effort to seldom give you cause for concern – it is those things that you don't give that focus and effort to that often come back to haunt you! Don't ignore the things you know must get done. There is a great saying, "Everyone wants to go to heaven, but nobody wants to die". Think about it – what are you prepared to do to make your dreams come to reality, even if that means short term sacrifices for long term gains.

3. **Full immersion:** Become great at something by fully committing to your passion and define it as part of your life plan. Do everything with a sense of urgency and commitment – great results and learning will follow.

4. **Attitude is everything:** Be consistent and positive in everything you do. Your ATTITUDE will directly enable your ALTITUDE!

5. **The amazing power of YET:** This amazing three letter word transforms any thoughts you might have, eradicates any self-doubt, promotes self-belief and maintains your focus in any circumstance in achieving anything you aspire to – with the right mindset. Yes, 'YET' is that powerful!

   1. I haven't got that skill – yet
   2. I don't know how to – yet
   3. I haven't achieved that goal – yet
   4. I haven't found the money – yet
   5. I haven't got that new car – yet

   This simple word changes a very negative statement into a declaration of intent. It becomes a clear message that you will get there and are fully committed.

6. **The greatest resource is resourcefulness:** If you have an abundance mindset combined with one of action, you can find any resource you need. With the resources of skill, creativity, business acumen, anticipation and uncommon sense, you will have the resourcefulness to travel any path and attain almost any goal in your life.

7. **Be contrarian:** You do not have to be constrained by tradition. Challenge it constantly, establish an uncommon sense – you CAN be boundaryless!

8. **Don't sweat the small stuff:** NEVER get wrapped up in the minutia of the world. Leave that to others – they will be far better at it than you!! Your time is incredibly valuable, with massive opportunity and much to achieve. Do not allow other people to drag you through mediocrity and averageness. You set the angle of your trajectory!

9. **Take action:** In order to become successful, you must do something: Take action – NOW! Action feeds desire which feeds your faith to continue to act and evolve. The successful people in life are the ones who take action, repeatedly.

10. **The language of success:** Be the change you want to be in the world. Start now and create your personal brand on everything you do – it will be your hallmark of quality. This should be in the things you say, post, message and blog – your standards will define you.

11. **Business is fun:** It is also where real wealth is created in a highly tax efficient manner and where you can protect, scale and leverage to great success.

12. **The legendary power of compounding:** Do more than is expected, earlier than expected – go the extra mile and the compounding of results will astound you. Work hard when no one is watching – that is the acid test of commitment. Compounding is rightly referred to as the eighth wonder of the world and effects habits, money, assets – in fact, everything in life – and the longer you work at it, the faster the results grow.

13. **Be a leader and not a follower:** Question what others appear to do and challenge the norm. Plot and navigate your own roadmap in life but have the great sense to reach out for the wisdom of others you respect, to enable you to get there in the most efficient way possible.

14. **Thrive on creativity:** Become a dynamic idea generator and have a system that records, researches and plans ideas to either come to fruition or to discount and leave for another time and place possibly.

15. Someone else's opinion is none of your business: If you listen to everyone's opinion you will be a busy fool and it will get you down – and waste your time. The actor Will Smith said, "Other people's opinions are a really sh*t way of determining how we feel about ourselves". Only seek the advice of those that are qualified in that particular area of life to provide a valuable insight.

16. Courageous work ethic: If you want something badly enough you will have to make sacrifices and it may hurt along the way. There will be ways to ease the pain by working hard AND working smart, but it will take hard work and determination – there are no free meal tickets in life. Be brave and courageous and see beyond the inconvenience of today – set your focus on the long term that you have committed to. Your strength of resolve will be your omni-present companion in your constant pursuit of your desires.

17. Never settle for average, ordinary or mediocre: Being extraordinary is not a lottery – it is your duty to honour yourself. You only have one life – live it to the max!

18. Establish great habits: The quality of your habits will be your backbone of a life fulfilled. Great habits will provide you the framework, consistency and productivity that enables you to focus, evolve and improve over time, taking advantage of the awesome power of compounding. Do not expect these to happen immediately BUT make a start TODAY and fine tune frequently, trying to improve 0.1% every week of your life. Be a constant student of your own self development through evolution and not revolution!

19. Live your own life: Avoid watching how others live – it will seldom bring anything other than distraction, envy, frustration and dilution to your life. Here is an exercise for you:

1. Write down the hours you have spent in the last week watching other people's lives (Instagram, Snap Chat, Facebook, YouTube, global news channels, newspapers and Reality TV).
2. Now add those hours up and times that by 52 weeks of the year – it's a big number right!!!
3. Decide what you could achieve using those hours instead?
4. Make a change now and GO AND DO IT!!

20. Aim for version 10 but start with version 1: Ever wondered how all great things come about? Well they usually start with someone having the courage and passion to make a start. As the Chinese proverb states: 'A journey of a thousand miles begins with a single step'. Whether it is opening a notebook or iPad and starting a plan, sketching out the initial steps or reaching out to someone for advice – make that first step, knowing that it is the start, a cascade to further steps, each one of which will take you one more small step closer to achieving your goal.

21. Avoid the disease of procrastination: Nothing can ever be gained or learned from procrastinating or being indecisive. It is only from starting, trying, figuring it out, finding a better way along the way and learning from the lessons of experience, that true progress and achievement can be attained.

22. Don't expect perfection:

1. It is unachievable
2. It will take too much time anyway
3. By the time you have fine-tuned to the nth degree of detail, life will have passed you by and someone else will have swept past you with the next new idea!
4. Never in the history of mankind has someone waited to launch a product only once it is perfect. Things improve over time and in small, yet increasingly rapid, evolutionary steps

23. Do what you love: Do not spend the next 30 – 40 years of your life doing something you detest. However, understand that you will have to do things you don't enjoy, to attain your desires. 'Do what others won't, to achieve what others can't'. Find out what it will take to get you that next step closer to your target and what is more – be prepared to do it.

24. Be self-disciplined: It takes courage and guile to navigate the challenges of life. Being true to yourself and well-disciplined will serve you well in staying on track and not getting distracted or diverted.

25. Self-Belief: Believe in you. Self-confidence is a rare, valuable quality and is infectious for all around you. You are your best asset – equip yourself with the very best skills and lessons possible. Self-belief precedes all action.

26. Desire: One of the most powerful principles you can have is to have desire to achieve something. When I mean desire, I mean something so compelling and overwhelming that, coupled with self-belief, you just know what it is you will achieve. In his iconic book 'Think and Grow Rich', Napoleon Hill refers to it as a 'white hot' desire – it is that intense!

27. Stay humble: You will never know everything, so avoid arrogance and you will have a thirst for self-improvement and have the ability to learn something from every experience and every situation. Learn this most valuable life skill: 'Walk a mile in another person's shoes' – they may have valuable experience, input or connections to aide your life's journey. Be sure to have your filters engaged though, to ensure you do not get distracted along the way with trivia!

28. Solve problems for people: If you can continuously identify solutions to the problems of others, they will appreciate and value your service and pay you well, and often, for the privilege!

29. Don't wish it were easier, wish you were better: Focus on the things that matter and have the courage to discard the distractions. There will be things in life you can control and those that you can't. Be aware, but don't worry about the things you can't control and focus your time and energy on those that you can control. You are responsible for you!

30. Take control of your personal economy: Master the skill of managing your personal wealth and create habits and systems to:

1. Make money – Earn
2. Manage money – Save
3. Multiply money – Invest

4. Protect money – Secure

31. Keep your costs under control: Always live within your means – never spend more than you earn. Combined with the 4-step system above, always make sure you spend as little as possible. Every penny you spend you will never get back so make your choices wisely. This is a life skill you MUST master.

32. Value your time – it is all you have: Don't settle for make a living – make a life. Several decades ago, many people had the same job for life. In the increasingly fast-moving world we live in, that is no longer going to be the case in the future. You can either:

1. Work for someone else and accept there may be uncertainty and job changes ahead
2. Have a life plan and work for a reason that fulfils your higher life plan
3. Create a business and you employ others

33. Create Shared Value: In everything you do, recognise that you are achieving value for others AS WELL as yourself, rather than value at the expense of others. The chances are you will lead a much more enjoyable, enriched and amazing life if you can serve the needs of others, whilst fulfilling your plan too.

34. True Grit: Possess grit, courage, determination and rigor – it will serve you well in everything you set out to achieve.

35. The Power of anticipation: This is one of life's great skills and something that overlays everything you do in life.

Whatever area of passion you pursue, make it all-consuming in finding your pathway to success. Anticipate the challenges and opportunity you will have along the journey and do not be afraid to correct your course or change direction.

36. **Remove regret, remorse, anxiety and envy:** In today's world of social media, have you ever thought that the grass is greener on the other side of the fence, how everyone else's life seems great? Well, I have some news for you – mostly it is NOT! Those pictures of people showing yachts, super cars and expensive watches is often to lure you in – it is called marketing and quite frankly has ZERO bearing on your life. Pave the way for YOUR life – don't waste it as a spectator watching the lives of others.

37. **You will not remain at your current age:** Avoid just living in the moment. The world is your oyster – you can decide what you want to achieve in your life. Make the decision that YOU are in control of YOU. Build the life you want, one part at a time, step by step and expect it to take a while. Make a record of what goals and vision you are committing to achieve and find out what great looks like to you in 5, 10, 20, 30 years' time – that time will soon be upon you.

38. **You get what you tolerate:** In life you will get what you accept and expect as well as tolerate. You will be bombarded with challenges – the news and media, lateness, low income, disrespect, poor nutrition, 'essential impulse purchases' and the list goes on. Set your benchmark standards that you must abide by and expect, to maintain your personal performance:

    1. If you tolerate poor standards you will migrate towards

poor standards

2. If you tolerate negative people you will migrate towards their habits
3. If you tolerate distractions, you will gravitate to their thoughts
4. If you tolerate poor nutrition, you will become unhealthy
5. If you tolerate 'news' you will have less time

39. Surround yourself with amazing people: A consistent factor in ALL the successful people I have known is that they keep the company of interesting, driven and great people. Surround yourself with inspirational people who will help you move forward positively in life – avoid negative people who will pull you down and suck the energy out of you.

40. Mindset of success: Have the confidence to understand that you are on an amazing journey of life and you can achieve whatever you set out to achieve. The way you approach success, before and during, will be YOUR hallmark of success that you lead your life by, and may include:

1. How you hold yourself in front of others
2. How you treat others
3. Respect
4. Levels of performance that you tolerate and expect from yourself and others
5. How you dress and act
6. Being humble
7. Being in control
8. Knowing when to listen and when not to

9. How you do things when no-one else is watching

10. Are you the inspirational positive achiever that people want to be around?

41. Failing is how we grow: You will fail – expect it and get used to it. Failure is healthy, it is how we grow and mature. It isn't always easy though, so grow a thick skin and don't listen to the judgement of unqualified spectators! Be confident enough to take risks, but wise enough to minimise failure by taking great advice. Here are 10 reflections on failure:

1. Fail small and often – it is called evolution

2. Don't fear failure or let it slow you down

3. Failure is a product of making a start which is great!

4. Fail early and quickly

5. Learn from failure

6. Fail forward and build momentum

7. Learn from the mistakes of others – it is cheaper!

8. Anticipate risks and minimise them if you can

9. Grow a tough skin!

10. The mindset of failure is one of making progress, learning and absorbing incrementally valuable, compounding lessons towards achieving your major goals in life

42. Delayed gratification: It can feel good to choose to have something now but making the effort to have the discipline and resist impulses can enable you to have bigger and better rewards in the future. If you can improve your self-control and delay gratification, then you will allow the benefits of compounding to take hold in everything you do and enable you to achieve larger targets quicker.

43. **Leverage:** Every successful venture has had to come to terms with how to increase in scale. That could be through more time, money or other resources. Have an abundance mindset – you can secure as much resource as you like if you have the skills. You should NOT be short of money or resources to achieve the right thing. Become a master of bringing the power of leverage into your personal and business life. You MUST use leverage to create anything of scale and to grow. It will also help you gain your time back to do the things you really want to do in life.

44. **The power to say "No":** I am going to give you one very important possession that no-one can ever take away from you. It is the power to say 'No'. We are bombarded with everyone else's opinions, products, services, worries and issues. YOU have the power to set up boundaries in your life and to decline involvement. Preserve your time wisely, otherwise you will dispense it freely and liberally to everyone and become a passenger in your own life. There will be many times in life you will say "Yes" but saying "No" should happen much more often!! Be confident, yet diplomatic. Not many possess this powerful discipline – make sure you master when and how to say "No".

45. **Give freely:** It is a wonderful feeling to assist others without expecting anything in return. It is called the 'Law of Reciprocity'. Allocate a proportion of your time and resources to support others. Everybody wins when help is given unexpectedly and, over the long term, surprising and pleasurable things can materialise in very unexpected ways.

46. **Remain Curious:** Never lose the joy of being curious; find out how things operate, why systems work and how you can

improve that extra 0.1% every week. Curiosity and open-mindedness can uncover a wealth of exciting opportunities to improve and evolve – embrace it!

47. Have intensity of purpose: Life is too short for dilly-dallying or meandering. If you are going to do it, make a start and get on with it. As Yoda said, "Do or do not, there is no try" – coupled with self-confidence, this is a game changer. This urgency is crucial in creating momentum and starting to move the great wheel of compounding forward.

48. Don't be afraid of being different: Constructively challenge the status quo that society traditionally dictates. There is no future mapped out for you – it is yours to create and define. You shine bright with your self-confidence – a contrasting blend of humility and self-belief is a rare and wonderful gift in life possessed by all the great leaders in their area.

49. Be calm under pressure: Life will throw many obstacles in your way. Remain composed, calm and collected even when emotions are rising all around you. It is the person and team with clarity of vision, purpose and thought that will be able to absorb and process all that is happening around them and make the well-informed decisions necessary to capitalise on opportunity and head off any risks confidently and effectively.

Anticipate where your life is going. Desire and be in control of your destiny. Your self-confidence and uncompromising will to achieve, through self-belief and action, will direct you to achieve the most amazing things in life.

"Whatever the mind can conceive and believe, the mind can achieve"
Napoleon Hill

Love. Dad xx

KIM STONES

Thoughts from a life of experiences:

"When you are looking, luck happens"

Anon

ABOUT THE CHAPTER AUTHOR

I was born in Denmark in 1961. My mother decided it would be a great idea to name me Kim – a common Danish name. However, not such a great idea considering we lived on a council estate which was a bit rough at the time. I was bullied and so I started learning the martial arts. I started Taekwondo at age 14 and received my blackbelt at 16, become an international at 17 and went on to win six British, three European and three World championship titles, at both team and individual level.

At 22 I started teaching Taekwondo full-time all over the Yorkshire area in sports centres until a friend told me about a better way. At age 36 I connected with an American company and got on a plane to New York to 'steal' all their ideas on how to professionally run full-time martial arts centres.

Upon returning, I turned my Doncaster school from a 70 member, £3 per person per night class into the UK's largest single-centre school with 540 students grossing £25K per month and netting over £10K per month, which was unknown at the time in the UK.

Identifying the demand, we formed a consulting company that ended up consulting over 250 client schools of which many went on to become hugely successful centres in their own right.

I was late to property investing, buying my first buy-to-let in 1999 aged 38. However, I got the property investing bug quickly and bought over 70 in the following nine years including some commercial properties. In the past several years I've invested in the HMO market. Four years ago, with my daughter Chelsea, wife Coral and half the family, we formed Kimcoh Properties Management and Lettings which has grown into Doncaster's largest HMO management company.

I get bored easily so I'm always looking for the next thing, always open to investment ideas, joint ventures and any opportunity to 'make a few quid'.

In 2006 I sold my two full-time martial arts schools, plus the consulting company, to go full-time into property although really, I'd been full-time since 2003.

During the busiest year I bought 31 single lets; man, those were the days – no money down etc! I've never had much money so when I do get hold of it, I want to buy property!

kimcoh@hotmail.co.uk

MY CHAPTER

What would I say to my younger self – where do I start? Well here are some random thoughts from a life of experiences.

1. In the beginning be patient, talk to anyone you know who has property investment experience (long-term not the Facebook term!) and ask investors for a coffee – you will find they are up for a chat as many can be a bit lonely!!

2. Buy a single-let property: There's no training in this world that teaches you about pulling the trigger and having financial responsibilities so make sure you know all about what you are buying.

3. Don't spend £25K on a course! If you learn where to look you can find out what you need more efficiently and gain valuable experience on the way.

4. PASSIVE income is a load of bollocks the way it is often taught! Yes, passive income through rents can come in whilst you are out with the family and can make a living, but it's not the usual reality. I am not sat on a beach whilst I get richer, even if that is possible. Often, it is not passive whilst you have responsibilities. Having a great team around you makes it more passive, but not fully.

5. Staff: Some days you will love 'em, some days not so much, but boy try and live without them!!! Always try to understand them and get inside their brains, systemise and create KPIs as much as you can. Your staff won't like it at first, but they will eventually, and the more you take the thinking out of your business, the better.

6. YIELD: Ignore it at your peril. Yield pays the bills and capital growth is the cream. I've been lucky in that the yields in Doncaster have always been good actually – as rents rise, the yields are getting better but this will last only a couple more years as the capital growth comes a knocking again (it's been a while in Doncaster!). Gross yield is a fag packet quick exercise, net yield pays your bills, be mindful of costs etc.

7. Other People's Money (OPM): That's the way you create more, but my advice would be crystal clear at the start. Understand where you are now and who is responsible for what. A shareholder agreement is essential – it has legal costs but a great investment to avoid trouble later. Make sure you have a clear plan of how you will make the money – does it stack?

8. Boring usually means it's making money; be patient! Property investing is a long-term approach, not a get-rich-quick scheme – that is a lottery ticket – and yes, I still buy one every Saturday!

9. Critical naysayers: They are all around, sometimes the closest people to you are the most negative. Drown out that noise, it's not their fault, they are usually just concerned about you BUT listen to them – they may be correct in some ways. Mitigate this 'white noise' by doing due diligence but ultimately you will need to pull the trigger.

10. Less is often more: Ego can make you but it can also destroy you. In investing (20 years plus) you will face many challenges; try to see those challenges ahead of time.

11. Pay yourself first: Yes, but pay your bills also. I've seen many

pay themselves first, they buy the Porsche, then realise the bills need paying.

12. Slice and dice: Buy properties that can be split into two or three units or develop say a 2-bedroom property into a 3-bedroom property. Always add value.

13. Below market-value deals: Yes, they are out there and always go for a large discount on the actual price. Always give a reason to a seller to justify your offers BUT try to find the ones that you can add value to also.

14. Pay good tradespeople on time: That way you will find and build relationships with the best one's as many aren't used to that – so benefit from the goodwill.

15. The best and most productive deals I've done have been direct to the vendor although you will need a good relationship with the agents.

16. BE PATIENT

17. EXIT: What is your end game and also, what is your exit if things don't go to plan? What is your plan B? Don't go into a deal without a plan B – if you don't have one, don't buy it; cover your arse!

18. RISK can be where the reward is: That is calculated risk and not risk for ego's sake.

19. If I had my time again, what would I do? BUY 3, SELL 2, KEEP 1 – then repeat. I would trade much, much more – cash in your bank will give you choices, the choice of acquiring that

fabulous net deal! I've been buying and selling for a while now, as a combination with investing – it's the best thing I've done and I should have started earlier, like 20 years ago when I started investing.

20. Having a business that creates a steady drip-feed of cash flow, whilst investing in property, will lead to great wealth over time.

21. People sell to people they like – become likeable and focus on the sellers' needs.

22. Have some fun along the way: Enjoy the ride. Reward yourself, and the people around you, and when times get hard you will be in a very supportive community.

Good Luck.

AKASH VAGHELA

Don't be afraid to take the road less travelled

"You will get all you want in life, if you help enough
other people get what they want"

Zig Ziglar

ABOUT THE CHAPTER AUTHOR

I'm Akash Vaghela and I'm the founder of an online body transformation company called RNT Fitness, where we specialise in helping regular, busy people get into the shape of their lives. The difference we make extends beyond the physical change we elicit, as we aim to use the physical as a vehicle to create change in all areas of life.

I was born and raised in London, and when I'm not helping transform lives, I love bodybuilding, exploring new countries and trying out the best rib eye steaks in town!

www.rntfitness.co.uk

MY CHAPTER

As far back as I can remember I always wanted to be a lawyer. My father was a lawyer and after witnessing his work ethic, the respect he'd earned in our community, and his ability to look after our family, I wanted to follow in his footsteps.

For me, being a lawyer was the dream and so I'd steered my entire early education to head in that direction. I picked the subjects at GCSEs and A-Levels that would favour a law degree, and I travelled the world for work experience, spending two weeks at a law firm in Aachen (Germany) and close to a month mixing between the courts and a highly established practice in Mumbai (India). It was all fun and games.

This all happened between the ages of fourteen and seventeen, which can form a critical part of your formative years, and how the next chapters of your life unravel.

At just shy of seventeen, I had what now stands out as a life defining moment. During a school lunch break, one of my best friends said to me, "Akash, why don't you come along to the gym with me? You'll like it". Despite regularly playing tennis and dabbling in some boxing, I'd yet to step into a gym.

I trained with him, and I was hooked. I was no stranger to exercise, but this was different – it felt euphoric. As I continued to train, I started to see and feel my whole body transform. My confidence sky-rocketed, and this only pushed me to keep digging deeper and learning more about my body.

Fast forward 6 months and heading into my final year of school, I asked my father if I could do a few weeks work experience at the firm he practiced at before school started again.

What happened shocked me.

I hated every minute of it. Law just didn't truly interest me. What sounded exciting at the university open days felt far-fetched in the real world. What felt like a dream when completing work experience in Aachen and Mumbai was merely an extension of the feeling of being on holiday.

At the end of my time at his firm, I realised I'd been so single-minded in following dad's footsteps (which he never pushed onto me either) that I'd blocked out all other options. I'd never exposed myself to anything new, or even the idea of anything different beyond this pre-set path I'd given to myself as a young teenager.

As I returned back to school, it was time to submit university applications. Still not knowing any different, I prepared mine geared to Law, and had them all ready for submission.

A few days after completing the preparation, the second life defining moment happened. I was with the same best friend who took me to the gym, and we were in the computer room together during a class. I was paying no attention to the teacher (I know, probably not the best place to admit this!) and instead, I was planning my next workout while thinking about how I could optimise a particular nutrition variable in my day.

My friend caught me and said to me, "Why don't you scrap Law and do something in Health and Fitness? It's clearly what you're passionate about. I don't think I've ever heard you once speak or read about Law".

Until this computer class, there'd always been one singular road for me. All of a sudden I was at a crossroads with two options: the trampled, beaten down road, or the road less travelled.

The next week involved some of the most difficult conversations with myself and others I've ever had.

I first had to discover what I truly wanted. Not easy at the age of seventeen, but after much thought, there was only one clear winner – It had to be health and fitness.

What helped the decision?

Well, a day before my sixteenth birthday, I was taught in the harshest way that life is too short. My first cousin was taken from us with a brain tumour at the age of nineteen, and it rewired my thinking in a manner that only showed itself during this decision-making process.

After scouring the Internet for potential university degrees, careers and opportunities thereafter, I realised this was a seriously up and coming field with great potential. Step one complete.

The second challenge was to break it to my parents. While law was never pushed upon me, there were (and still are) significant social norms that needed to be challenged with regards to career choices in my community. As a South Asian, if you aren't pursuing finance, law or medicine, you aren't doing anything worth pursuing. Crazy, I know, and while these stigmas are reducing, there's still work to be done.

As expected, my choice went down like a lead balloon, and the immediate response I received was, "How do you expect to pay the bills?".

Understandable, and quite frankly, I had no idea. I just knew I'd make it work because I'd spent the last two years engrossed in the field, using my body as an experimental model, and was only now waiting to test my theories on others!

After much discussion and showing them the potential of what I could do, I won them over. Writing this, a decade after the event, is serendipitous as my parents have been my biggest supporters since, and the effect the decision has had on our community has been truly transformative. Parents have become more open minded to their children's choices, teenagers are thinking outside of the box of what they could do, and people of all ages are now inspired to followed their passion, which brings me great joy and reinforces the fact that I made the right decision.

The last piece of the puzzle was to change my application to Sport and Exercise Science and tell my Head of Year, who gave me a slight look of disappointment and concern when I did. At this stage however, my choice was made and I'd taken one step on the road less travelled.

The journey doesn't end there, but for the purpose of this chapter, I really wanted to hone in on these few years as it's rare that a week goes by where I don't say to myself, "what would have happened if I hadn't changed my path?". Perhaps it would've happened later, or perhaps it may never have, you never know. What I do know is that ten years later, it's still the best decision I've made.

And so now when I speak to teenagers, which is either before or during the time they need to decide what to do after school, I urge them to experience and explore as much as possible.

Think outside of the box, pursue as many hobbies as possible, and never be boxed into the singular thinking that schooling can often cause. My biggest mistake early on was believing a fantasy of a career I truly knew nothing about, while simultaneously blocking out any potential opportunities that may arise in other fields. It took a push from my best friend, inspiration from my late cousin, and difficult conversations with myself and my family to steer me onto the correct road for me.

As parting words, I'd encourage every one of you reading this to try as much as possible. Especially the activities that scare you, challenge you, and cause you to think and be different. You never know, they may end up being the making of you, and allow you to grow and develop in ways you wouldn't have done otherwise. And when it comes to deciding on the road you want to travel on, take your time to understand in yourself what you want to do. It's not worth following something for the money, or if it is what society is pressuring you to do, or if it's all you've ever known. Success is worth a lot more and it's often found on the road less travelled. Don't be afraid of it. Have courage, stay resilient, and be relentless in your pursuit of what you want in this life – It's short and you only get one chance at it!

BRONWEN VEARNCOMBE

Banker turned property professional shares her life lessons

"I've learned that people will forget what you said, people will forget what you did, but people will never forget how you made them feel"

Dr. Maya Angelou

ABOUT THE CHAPTER AUTHOR

Property Investor and coach, Bronwen Vearncombe, has built a successful business over the last few years and been able to give up her full-time corporate job and find freedom.

Having been told she'd not be able to retire until aged 67, she knew there must be a way to escape and to spend more time with her husband and two children – and maybe even be her own boss!

Learning from the best, she and her husband worked hard to get a great education and to understand the risks and opportunities that property can provide. This led to a portfolio of single lets, multi-lets and commercial guest houses in Hampshire, often purchased with private investor funds, and most importantly created to provide a passive income. As an ex-banker, she certainly isn't afraid of borrowing and lending and is particularly skilled at finding investment and working collaboratively with others. Bronwen has her own SSAS pension realising that her own final salary pension could be better deployed by becoming the trustee!

Featured in national property media, leading a monthly property networking group for two years and a property Mastermind programme in Winchester, Bronwen loves to share her knowledge and to help others get onto the investor ladder of success. Her programme of pre-recorded webinars and coaching enables easy, but supported, learning of the very foundation steps and uses examples from her own portfolio too.

Whilst starting to follow her dreams, she travelled the world as her husband did the Clipper Round the World Yacht Race 2017-18. She was able to use technology to combine her adventures with the business and coaching too – she is proving that a passive property income can really work.

https://propertyinvestingfoundation.com

MY CHAPTER

1. Understand what interests you in life, the subjects, the activities – try things out and expand on them

What do I believe I would have liked to have understood at an earlier age? If I'd known some things, or come across certain gurus, might I have made different decisions in my life, or might I have made the right ones sooner?

My childhood was pretty amazing. Not only did my parents choose me – I was adopted as a baby – but they gave me so much love and support, encouraging me to try new things and pursue things I enjoyed. I had a brother (also adopted) who had the same up-bringing of course – but chose a very different path to me. I often wonder what made the difference. I believe we had similar values to life though, but maybe some more genetically different elements. What I believe is that my values were definitely shaped by expectations and the role model from my parents and my father in particular. A very humble, quietly confident man, he would often shape my interests by finding ways for me to learn more or take part in practical experiences. For example, wildlife and nature fascinated me. I joined the World Wildlife Fund at an early age, avidly reading their monthly magazines. My father encouraged and paid for me to go on their kids' residential holidays, which not only overcame my shyness at the time, but encouraged me to make new friends too. I realised that to enjoy something, sometimes you have to go beyond your comfort zone, or overcome your fear to find the good things. That built my self-confidence from an early age.

In my early teens I dreamt of becoming a doctor, but the early work experiences the school/college provided, helped me realise that perhaps it wasn't the right path for me, but my values were probably unchanged. So, this real-life experience was essential in helping me understand if it suited me or not.

As a businessman, my father understood the elements of the financial world. When I found I couldn't pursue my passion of medicine, he quietly suggested and researched some broad business degrees that were modular based. He realised that whilst accounting and law were not necessarily a passion, the other subjects around this like marketing, business, economics etc could stand me in great stead in understanding the world. I also continued my interest in wildlife too through my hobbies.

My lesson for my younger self is: Try different things, understand different roles and jobs, get some experience if you can – even volunteer for free. Never think 'I can't do that' but 'how can I do that?'. Go to university only if you have an interest and passion that you would like to learn more about, but above all be inspired by something.

2. Personal values/drivers

Are your values shaped and influenced by the paths in life or are they inherited – and we don't have a huge amount of choice in these! What determines what drives you?

These can be really hard questions to answer but what I've learnt is that to understand them can make a huge difference. A book by Jo Simpson called 'The Restless Executive' is a great read to help understand this topic better.

Creativity, belonging, exploring, making a difference, honesty, discovery, adventure, freedom, energy, commitment, clarity, excellence, authenticity, love, fun, security, courage, etc are all examples of values. They are what you stand for and would not compromise on. To find out what they might be, ask yourself the following questions:

- What's important to you and why? What does it give you?
- What do you enjoy doing?
- What frustrates you and therefore what's the flip to this?

Write them down and put them into priority order for you

If you are in tune with your values, you can feel so much more fulfilled and in tune with life.

My priority values include honesty, adventure, helping others, energy and commitment. When these have been to the fore, I've been much happier in life; when jobs I've done clearly didn't resonate then I've been very unhappy. It's easy to look back and understand why. It also helps when you understand other people's values and how they differ to yours.

I use values when I'm looking for teachers, coaches, advisors etc. It's important to me that the person or company aligns to my values. An example for me was when I was looking to learn about property investing – one organisation told me that I could buy a house with a credit card! That went against my core value of honesty and alongside their hard-sell approach, I knew I wouldn't be choosing them to work with.

3. Know and build on your strengths

Well, my big lessons came from a career in Banking. I was lucky enough to be chosen for the fast track graduate scheme where I would be trained up and supported over a couple of years and into my first managerial position. Many lessons taught were on leadership, people management, customer service and understanding my own strengths and weaknesses. We were put through many different models to test our leadership skills from Myers Briggs to Belbin which helped me understand how people were so very different in their approach and thinking. But the key issue I have now is that much of the focus was on improving the weaknesses, not driving the strengths. Through my property education I used the Wealth Dynamics model which, as an entrepreneur, really helped me see the variety of strengths needed across a team.

My advice now to a younger self is to really understand your strengths, build on improving them, not worrying too much about your weaknesses but being aware of them. Find a role in life that really focuses on these core strengths and the values, then you'll be good at what you do, and you'll enjoy your job too.

4. Assets and Liabilities

As a banker I thought I knew everything about finance! Well that wasn't true when I embarked on my property training. A revelation moment came in a book on our reading list called 'Rich Dad Poor Dad' by Robert Kiyosaki. This helped me realise that what I had thought were assets – a house, a well-paid job, even a pension – are not really assets at all.

I realise now that the advice of getting a good job, getting promoted, working your way up the ladder, and retiring at 65 (or older these day) is not necessarily the best way to build wealth and freedom in your life. Trading your time for money in a job isn't security, because if that job were to disappear, there is no more money. Also, you are working hard to achieve someone else's strategy, not your own. If you have a house you live in, you need to maintain it and pay the mortgage to keep it – it earns you no income. A pension may be a pot of gold in the future – but how can you influence how much that might be worth in the future?

Property investing education taught me that the second property you own, that you can rent out, is a true asset. It puts money into your bank account every month, even if you're asleep or in another country. Building any business can be the same, as long as you can delegate the work at some point to create a more passive income. The great thing about property is that it's a scarce resource in the UK. It's hard to get on the ladder because of the costs – we are not building enough houses for the demand and many people have to rent. So, with the economics you not only have the opportunity for rental income, but also the capital growth in the longer term too.

To really progress with property as a business I had to make sure that I worked with others who were successful in the same field. If I'd listened to many risk averse friends, or believed what I'd read in the papers, I would never have continued. So, here's another lesson to my younger self: surround yourself with positive people and experts in the field you want to be excellent in. Don't believe anything you read on the media or newspapers!

In summary, my advice to my younger self is to really think carefully about whether what you do in your work is fulfilling, enjoyable and giving you skills to grow. Does it meet your core values? Get the best financial education you can get through understanding how to create assets in your life. Work with experts who can help you learn. You are never too old to learn! Ultimately, this will create the freedom to follow your dreams.

My dream of volunteering in a wildlife sanctuary in Namibia came true last year and I'm back there again this year – thanks to my property investing business. Oh, and I'm still a member of the World Wildlife Fund too!

SHAZ WATKINS

Know yourself and have the courage to do the things you'll be proud of

"I know the plans I have for you" declares the Lord, "Plans to prosper you, not to harm you; plans to give you a hope and a future"

Jeremiah 29:11, The Bible

ABOUT THE CHAPTER AUTHOR

Shaz Watkins is a professional violinist turned property investor and coach, who also loves travelling and scuba diving.

Although she and her husband Chas (yes, Shaz & Chas!) live in SW London, they mostly invest in properties up in Macclesfield.

Shaz works almost full-time as Director of their property business Maison d'Etre Property Solutions Ltd (www.maisondetreproperty. com) sourcing, project managing, working with investors on their "flips" (Buy, Refurbish, Sell business model) and building their portfolio of rental properties.

Shaz is also YOUR Property Coach – offering mentorship and

coaching to clients who are looking to begin their property journey or take it to the next level, specifically through refurbishment, HMO or rent-to-rent routes.

Shaz plays in a number of chamber ensembles including her string quartet and ceilidh band and works with several folk musicians including Emma Tricca.

www.maisondetreproperty.com

MY CHAPTER

What does it mean to be 'Proud of yourself?'. The dictionary definition is:

'feeling self-respect or pleasure in something by which you measure your self-worth'.

I would like to encourage readers of this book, whatever your age, to take the risks you've always dreamt of. I promise you, it will make you proud of yourself.

You won't regret taking that leap of faith.

Once you find your raison d'etre (your purpose) you will feel 'in flow' and you will experience the rush of fulfilment and pride at having achieved your dream.

It may take a first leap of faith for you to grow enough to discover what it is to be authentically you.

Believe in yourself and put those beliefs into action.

Take that calculated risk, have the courage to step out into the unknown.

There will always be nay-sayers; those who try to warn you off taking that step, but their cautionary tales speak more of their inner story than the reality that awaits you. Live up to your own expectations – even when it feels as though you're leaving others behind. If they are meant to be part of your life, you will reconnect with them later.

One single, enormous step taken in January 1999, contrary to many friends' 'better judgement' is responsible for me blossoming and growing into the person I am today, and I am very grateful for the experience.

Born into a Scottish family, the stereotypical, frugal nature of things held true.

My Father, William Forbes had a successful career in finance. He taught me the fundamentals of money management, borrowing, investment and debt that have stood me in good stead.

Many who knew him would say that he was 'Risk Averse' but I believe he would have described his risk profile as 'Cautious' (a measured approach to research and risk taking).

My mother, on the other hand, is terrified of risk (especially financial) and would rather not consider any of the outcomes but predict the worst in most situations!

This combination meant that I grew up in a solid, but slightly fearful environment.

My father was transferred to London when I was only four, so I had an enviable combination of frugal heritage mixed with all the ideas and opportunities of the London scene.

Education and hard work were very highly regarded in our home while I was growing up, but I always had the sense that I was more prepared to take a risk than our family tradition extolled.

I am SO proud of myself for 'biting the bullet' in January 1999. Almost out of the blue, packing up my life in London and heading out to Azerbaijan to have violin lessons with a professor I'd never met, live with a couple I'd only ever spoken to by phone and to immerse myself in a culture I knew almost nothing about!

That year in Baku changed my life forever. I began to become the person I am today. I learnt so much about myself and others, and life in general, which I would never have done had I stayed in the safety of the UK.

I had always been fascinated by Russia; its history, unusualness, unconventionalism and sense of danger, but holidays there were not an option.

During the previous year I completed my music college degree, and, thanks to the encouragement of my teacher Oliver Butterworth, I embarked on a summer of travel and music. I took a train (well, actually, about nine trains and a ferry!) from London to Brno in the Czech Republic.

It was the biggest step outside my comfort zone I had ever taken.

Travelling alone, I visited several cities on the way, took my first overnight train, stopped off in places where I could not speak the language and I loved (almost) every minute of it.

I subsequently learnt that I was not the first person in my family tree to have been so brave, so reckless, so inspired. My father's sister Maud had, at the age of 19, trained to be a nurse in order to leave the tiny fishing village in Scotland that she had grown up in ('where everyone knew as soon as you sneezed') to travel to America on a two-year Visa. It turned out she loved it so much that she never came back to live in the UK! She was the first person to tell me they were 'proud of' me and I am forever grateful.

How to take a calculated risk.

Very little in life works out exactly as you hope for and therefore it's impossible to plan with 100% certainty. Trying to do so will lead to confusion and inertia. You can and must however, mitigate the risks as you see them.

It is important to know your own risk profile.

Whatever it is, don't lie to yourself. Trying to make decisions which do not match up with your profile will give you sleepless nights and diminish the joy of the enterprise undertaken, even if it's successful.

Whatever your risk profile, you must research as much as possible using the internet, books, social media, networking and learn directly from people who have already done what you are driven to do. Be careful not to create evidence to back up what you want to do though!

If it's a property venture:

Learn asking and sold prices, rental market value, how to add value, local refurbishment costs and the demand for your end product. Speak to agents and other investors in that area and have them look over your numbers and ideas.

If it's travelling to another country to study:

Research the country, city and educational establishment. Speak to your proposed teacher and other students. Take a language course or buy a dictionary!

Once you have identified the potential risks, you can mitigate against them.

For instance, when I went to Azerbaijan I had a return ticket so that if it didn't live up to my expectations, I could come home again immediately.

Getting to know yourself.

This is a lifelong quest.

The journey through life, with all its twists and turns will inform the person that you are, build your character and mould you into the human being that best reflects your values.

It was not until I had lived in Baku that I learnt to ask better questions of myself.

It turns out for instance, that I work best to a deadline. I wish I had known this as a student. Perhaps my parents or teachers knew this. Sadly, none of them spoke to me about it so it has been something I learnt later in life.

I also know that I am not a morning person and that my most productive time of day is the evening. I use this information to serve me.

Now I know most of my best work is created under pressure I can ensure that I set myself up for success. I make sure my diary is populated accordingly; I create sufficient space to do the work just before any deadline.

A revelation I gained in my 40's came after reading 'Quiet' by Susan Cain in which I discovered the difference between being shy and being an introvert. Although they often look the same, they are different:

- Introverts enjoy and need time alone to recharge. They get emotionally drained, spending a lot of time with others so their preference is for environments that are not over stimulating.

- A shy person doesn't necessarily want to be alone but is afraid to interact with others. Shyness is the fear of social disapproval or humiliation.

Once you know yourself better, your dormant, innate confidence will rise.

Having grown into myself a little whilst at music college, I discovered that it's okay to say that you do not know or understand something, and I developed the courage to say so as my shyness abated.

Not knowing or understanding is not a sign of weakness. Asking for help and guidance is a show of strength.

Being shy I felt compelled to pretend I knew what someone was talking about, even when I didn't. Now I know why.

In our formative years we're always asking 'Why?' – yet it's a shame that being inquisitive is somehow 'grown out' of.

Peer pressure is not a thing.

It is merely an excuse.

Your peer *group* however does have a huge effect on your output and outcomes.

It's said that 'you become the average of the five people you spend the most time with'. Therefore, always try to be the least experienced, wealthy or successful person in your group. Find people who are doing what you want to do and emulate them. We always have things to learn from each other, but if you put yourself in an environment where you constantly need to 'step up', you will develop more quickly.

Ultimately, life is tough. It will throw you many curveballs.

How you deal with them is what you can be most proud of.

ROB WILKINSON

The people who think they are crazy enough to change the world are the ones who do

"The people who think they are crazy enough to change the world are the ones who do"

Steve Jobs

ABOUT THE CHAPTER AUTHOR

Rob Wilkinson is an award-winning co-founder of FCA approved property crowdfunding platform 'Crowd with Us'. He heads a specialist team that provides investors with a variety of debt and equity-based property development investments. Rob is also an experienced Master Mariner. After leaving school Rob spent the next 18 years traveling the world by sea, in both the commercial and private sectors, working his way up to Master Mariner on some of the world's largest and most prestigious privately owned yachts. In this role, he was responsible for managing assets and relationships for Global Leaders and Captains of Industry, including a senior member of the Saudi Royal Family and former world's richest man with a net worth of over $60bn USD. In this role, he met and dealt with well-known world leaders such as Donald Trump, Tony Blair, Barack Obama, and many others. Before his career as an entrepreneur in proptech and fintech, at the age of 20 Rob bought his first property in London and continued to grow his property portfolio in his spare time. He built his own house and eventually moved into property development and fundraising for property development. This eventually culminated in the founding of Crowd with Us. Alongside his family, Rob's other passions are sports and helping others through his various charity commitments.

http://www.crowdwithus.london/

MY CHAPTER

I'm a Master Mariner (Ships Captain) by trade, having been awarded a scholarship to study as a Navigational Officer Cadet at the age of 16. Prior to my first trip to sea at this young age, knowing that I'd be surrounded by and leading men much older and experienced than myself, my father gave me two pieces of advice that I've never forgotten. "Don't ask others to do what you wouldn't be willing to do yourself" and "Speak to others how you'd wish to be spoken to".

These two principles came to serve me well as I progressed through the ranks of life at sea. Up until around my 25th birthday I'd always been the youngest person on any ship I sailed on and had been leading teams on a daily basis for most of my career, up to that point. I've always asked myself the question, "would I do this?" before asking something of someone else. In many cases, especially in new environments where it's important to gain the trust and respect of those you're working with, or where the personal safety of others comes into play, I'll often carry out the task alongside my team to demonstrate my ability and the fact that I'll happily do anything I ask of others. The above said, you can't expect to know everything, so it's also incredibly important to always show humility. There may be instances where you have no choice but to ask someone to do something you wouldn't do yourself, for the simple reason that you don't know how to do it. In these situations, I'm always honest with those I work with, explaining that they are the experts, that I don't know how it should be done and that I need to learn from them. This is a much better position to take as opposed to claiming to know something you don't, as those that do know will easily identify you as a fraud and any respect or trust you've built up will quickly erode.

My father's second piece of advice goes without saying really, but is easy to forget, especially when we find ourselves in positions of power. This could be anything from being promoted to the Captain of a sports team to running a deck full of grown men. By speaking to people how you'd want to be spoken to yourself, rather than at them, you'll get a much better reaction. This is where effective communication comes into play. Mastering the skill of interpersonal engagement is fundamental to our personal and social development. It sets rules, boundaries and steps to attain desirable results and success. The ability to communicate accurately with others is a vital life skill that should never be overlooked and is, in my opinion, the number one tool for a successful life, whether that be in personal relationships or business. Think of the most successful people you know, and I guarantee they'll all be amazing communicators.

Whatever it is, the answer is YES!

We grow as people through experiences, however we're not

always ready for what life throws at us and there's nothing more uncomfortable than being out of your comfort zone. As such, the natural reaction is for us to wait until it feels right! This is often a long way off in the future. The strange thing is, the best place to grow and flourish as humans is when we're in this place of discomfort and unease. As the saying goes: 'pressure turns coal into diamonds!'. I've always made it my goal to jump at every opportunity that presents itself to me. However, there have been times where I was so uncomfortable that I've made excuses or procrastinated so much, I've lost the chance. Whilst I may have experienced immediate relief, once this subsided it became replaced with regret. As such I'd suggest you say **"YES"** to any opportunity for growth and run with it! If you don't know how to do something, or even how you'd find out how to do something, say yes anyway and figure it out as you go along! The mind is amazing at solving problems and I guarantee you'll figure it out! That said, don't take shortcuts, as they rarely pay off. One of my mantras is, 'don't do something because it's easy, do it because it's right'. Whilst I'm all for carrying out tasks in the most efficient manner, shortcuts are rarely shortcuts and inevitably result in you having to do something twice, so I'd always suggest doing it right the first time around.

Failure = Feedback

What's the worst that can happen? We're often so concerned with failure that it clouds the bigger picture – So what if we fail? 'What will our friends or family think?'. Who cares! I believe the only failure is in giving up. If you don't succeed the first-time round, take a step back and analyse what you did, what went wrong and why? What could you have improved upon? Work on getting better then try again! If you've failed an exam for example, re-book it the same day you find out you didn't pass. Whilst it's OK to be disappointed, don't dwell on the result, focus on doing it better the next time around and I guarantee you, your friends and family will be just as excited when you do get the result, whether it's your first try or your third! Approach failure with excitement and positivity. How thrilling, inspiring and stimulating it is to get a chance to do something again. The more you fail, the better success feels after all.

The importance of Mentors

Always seek out mentors. Try to spend as much time with people who have achieved what you aspire to and less time with those who pull you back. You're the average of the five people you spend the most time with. Just think about it. If you want to learn to drive, do you try to teach yourself, have someone else who can't drive teach you, or do you employ the services of a qualified driving instructor? I'd probably go one step further and interview several driving instructors to find out from each how many of their students passed the first-time round in the last six-months and go with the one who had the highest success rate! Whether you want to learn a new sport or want to rise to the top in your career, spend some time identifying the best person in that field/industry and become their friend. In many instances, those people haven't made it there alone, they'll also have had mentors and will be very open to helping you. That said there are two important rules that follow this. Number one – listen more than you talk; and Number two – if they set you a task, make sure you follow it through and report back.

In the same way that mentors are important, if you notice anyone in your life pulling you back and taking more from you than they give, start spending less time with them. Whilst if you're lucky you'll be surrounded by fans, those family and friends that support every success with you, you'll find there's another subset of family and friends that struggle with your progress and try to pull you back. The more successful you get, the more they'll talk to you about the 'unnecessary risks' you're taking and that 'it's all going to end in tears' and how they'd do it much differently. Whilst this is never easy to hear, it's very common that your success pushes them way out of their comfort zone and results in them projecting their fears onto you. Don't pay attention to what they're saying. I find it best to limit time with these people and generally over time they'll adjust to your new level of being and will come back into your life.

Don't work to live, live to work – The importance of goals!

It's so easy these days to get bogged down by work, to get caught in the rat race with your only focus being on making money and living from one month to the next. Money is important, but don't lose sight of the bigger picture! We're only here once so let's ensure we have the best time possible! Set goals and work towards achieving them. Work out what you want out of life and ensure your life revolves around making them a reality. It doesn't matter how crazy or 'out there' your goals seem, write them down anyway. Bigger goals are much less daunting when chunked down into more manageable bitesize pieces. If you want to learn a new language or play a new musical instrument, you may ask yourself how on earth that could be possible. However, spend 20 mins a day for three months practicing, and you'll look at this once impossible task from an entirely different perspective.

Look at your goals every day and review them regularly. Are you progressing towards them or moving away from them? Accountability is a massive factor in ensuring success and can be achieved in a number of ways. A friend with similar values who can question you and help you stay on track, or announcing your goal on social media, are two strong accountability tools I use. Have short, medium and long term goals and most importantly, when you achieve one, ensure you celebrate it!

Have goals beyond your comfort zone, because in order to do something you've never done, you've got to become someone you've never been.

If you'd like more info on how I go about setting and reviewing my goals, feel free to contact me direct.

ZOE WILLIAMS

Being human – following your internal compass

'Whether you think you can, or you think you can't, you're right'

Henry Ford

ABOUT THE CHAPTER AUTHOR

Zoe Williams, originally from a small town in the North East of England called Alnwick, was brought up by a father who was a serial entrepreneur and risk taker and a mother who was a risk adverse, steady provider, as an accountant.

Alnwick is on the coast, so I love being by the sea, in the sea and on the sea. The energy of a wild coast really humbles me and helps me ground myself when all the craziness of modern-day life is being felt.

I have spent my life learning about what it means to be human, through observing myself and others, travelling the world and immersing myself in many cultures and environments. I always choose the path of most resistance to grow and develop myself, and others who care to join me.

I am now a transformational life coach, working with some of the largest corporate companies in the world to raise corporate consciousness. This will have a dramatic impact on the way the world does business, shifting from ego-centric leadership to a more united and conscious leadership style.

The difference I make is allowing the people I work with be seen for who they truly are and then creating the clearing for them to show up as their authentic self.

MY CHAPTER

It has taken me 40 years to discover the truth of being human and living a truly authentic and fulfilling life.

If I could tell my younger self one thing it would be this:

'The pain, the challenges, the loss, the sadness and joy, the heartbreak and exhilaration, the fear and anger that you will feel throughout your life is simply what it is, to be human. Try not to resist this, try to see it for what it is, being human. You have an internal compass to guide you through all of this – and we spend many years trying to silence our internal guidance system. Listen to it, don't let it be silenced'.

I realised when I was around 15 years old, I had a desire to really understand people and I wanted to help them. I didn't know what problem I wanted to help people with, but I just felt that humans were suffering unnecessarily, and I wanted to help people with that.

I bought a book, called 'The Basics of Psychology' – it spoke to me and that is my first memory of following my internal compass without a thought.

This felt good, as up until that moment as far as I can remember, my brain and thoughts and 'logic' made decisions for me. This was different, the book spoke to me, something stirred inside. I devoured it, page by page, absorbing every word and all of a sudden, the world around me seemed to make more sense.

The Hard Truth About Living a Fulfilling Life

After that moment I knew what I wanted from my life – I wanted to help people demystify what it means to be human and travel the world doing it.

The journey to achieving my dream has not been easy, and it is in this sentence I want to tell my younger self that 'life will not be easy if you follow a dream'.

Life can be easy, by staying safe and small in life. This means doing what others expect from you, not being fully self-expressed, only saying and doing what is acceptable to others. Living a life that others expect you to live is easy and it is not what I believe is being alive.

You eventually feel numb inside, from years of over-riding your inner desires and your internal compass with behaviour and actions that aren't your own. Many people in this world are living like this.

My Wake-Up Call

I was 29 years old, and I knew for certain by this time I was living a life that was not my own. I was married, living in a small town in the South of England, working in a 9-5 corporate job as an accountant.

So far removed from my dream! My dream to travel, see the world, help people and learn all there is to learn about being human was not being realised. And this was because I was making choices that others expected me to make and I was waiting for someone else to create the life for me that I truly wanted.

I was delivered the hardest of lessons. I became terminally ill and had to face the possibility of losing my life several times over. I cannot tell you the power of these moments in my life.

It sounds cliché and we hear it so often, but I cannot stress enough to you the realisation of your life almost certainly coming to an end before you've given yourself the opportunity to live it as you dreamt, is chilling.

The Smallest Decisions have the Biggest Impact

All the small daily decisions I made, taking me in the opposite direction of my internal compass came to the fore. I could see them all, the desire to feel safe inside the opinion of others, my parents, my friends, my husband – everyone who was not now looking at the prospect of having only weeks left to live and no second chance to fulfil on their dreams.

There are so many subconscious daily decisions we make that can either create a future we want or take us away from that future little by little – decision by decision we allow our dreams to drift.

We want to please those around us, and eventually when we realise how much time we've spent maintaining the status quo, time has passed us by and we've created a life around us that isn't for us, but for others.

It was through this experience that I realised two very important things I want to share with you:

1. Those people around us we are trying to please only want us to be happy. They don't really mind what kind of life we live, as long as we are doing what makes us happy. My family were shocked to hear that I had not been living my life for me, and they mostly supported my desire to address that.

2. The stories we tell ourselves about what is possible, are not true.

The second point I feel deserves some explanation! We only know what is possible based on what we know. We cannot know what's possible, if we don't know it – right?

I know this might be confusing, and it is supposed to be! It took me years to get this and I hope you can accelerate your path towards achieving the impossible before I did!

If we entertain the idea that after giving up living our lives for others and accepting that living a fulfilling life will, at times, be hard (because being human and fully alive means feeling the good with the bad), we can then explore the 'what's possible'.

Creating a Possibility for your Life

If we allow ourselves for just one minute to dream the biggest dream – what would you LOVE your life to be about? What would make you feel like your life had been worth living? What is your purpose?

When I asked myself this question I came up with the answer,

'I would like to have impacted positively on millions of people worldwide for me to feel that I had fulfilled my purpose'.

Just thinking it felt absurd.

Then the first time I said it out loud it felt even more ridiculous.

And, despite that it is what my inner compass was saying to me – the same feeling I had when I saw that book aged 15 – help people be free from whatever suffering they were experiencing.

I had no idea HOW I would achieve this, and I certainly had no idea if it was even possible for me to achieve such a possibility.

I worked with some amazing coaches and guides who helped me see that all I needed was belief in the possibility, and for that purpose to ignite me daily with a feeling of motivation and enthusiasm.

What I needed to let go of was the HOW. I needed to let go of certainty and control and things turning out the way I wanted them to. I had to let go of everything I knew about how to manage my life. Previously I had always had a plan, always knew what was going to happen next. This was stepping into the unknown and trusting myself to be able to make minute by minute decisions that would take me closer towards my goal.

Remember when I mentioned that when I was in hospital fighting for my life, I saw all the daily decisions that had taken me on a path away from my dream?

The process of finding your way towards your dream is to see it as possible, have belief in yourself. Allow yourself to get excited, inspired and motivated by the possibility. Don't allow the limiting beliefs to get between you and this elevated feeling of belief.

Then, every day take actions inside of this belief – they will be small actions, they will all add up.

Just as the actions I took daily, small and unnoticeable, moved me further and further away from my internal compass. The daily choices and actions we take in line with our life's possibility will eventually guide us there.

This is not easy, which is why I opened with the truth about living a full life – it is hard to get up again after setbacks. It is hard to keep the internal and external voices at bay telling you it's not possible. It requires belief and acceptance of all that it means to be human.

Feel the good, and the bad. Accept advice from everyone with grace and keep your internal compass as the loudest sound and brightest light guiding you daily towards your future.

NEVILLE WRIGHT

I should have. I would have. I could have

"Everybody is a genius, but if you judge a fish by its ability to climb a tree, it will live its whole life believing that it is stupid"

Albert Einstein

ABOUT THE CHAPTER AUTHOR

Hello and welcome to my world – a bit unpredictable, a bit fast, a bit different, a roller-coaster ride shared by two 15-year-old non-descript kids that have mainly gone up and up over the years with a couple of downers, when we just missed the bottom by the skin of our teeth; when I say 'our' I mean the girl and I.

Marilyn – we met on the 25th June 1966. In those days, boys around Peterborough, where we come from, called them 'birds'. Well my bird was free to fly whenever she liked and sometimes when the going got really tough, I don't know why she didn't. But she stayed, and I feel everyday so very lucky that she did.

We are both 68 and still on the ride of our lives with two married daughters and four grandchildren – plus one on the way. We do, and are many things, but mainly builders providing much needed homes. We also build industrial buildings of all sizes which, in our small way, helps businesses grow.

The following is about what advice I would give to my younger self. Given my circumstances at such a young age, I don't think I would have dared to have followed this through. Well, vulnerable children and adults need someone to look out for them at some time in their lives, but I never had that. All this started from when I had the unfortunate experience of being incarcerated in a place called a school that had a curriculum that was, and still is, alien to me and I believe the system has never done any good for the majority of people. Oh yes, nearly forgot the brief. The name – **Neville Wright**.

www.Nevillewright.com

MY CHAPTER

Looking back, from the very start, I was frightened of going to school. I would tell my mum that I didn't want to go, then I would say that I was ill.

I would like to say that it was because it took my freedom away, but I am sure it was just because I didn't understand what was going on as the other children seemed to have taken to this new way of life so easily, but I found it very strange.

I believe it was because I had a problem understanding how the letters made a word – everyone seemed to have no problem with this but for me! The letters just kept moving about – why, why, why me? Well, it was because I was dyslexic, and it was only years after leaving school that I discovered that I was.

Anyway, in the meantime, I was classed as stupid and disobedient. Until the age of 15, when I left school, and after that until I was 24, I had a conflict with myself of believing that I was thick but wondering why, or how, I managed to buy a house at the age of just 18, and by the age of 24 I'd had 17 jobs, bought four houses and sold three of them.

Before starting my own business, the house that I owned dramatically dropped in price and was now worth half of the value of the mortgage, which was half the price of the house. Then having got fired in the recessions of 1974, finding myself penniless and on welfare, it was time to change.

Advice to my younger self

So now I would tell my younger self, as the child just starting school, that everyone in the world has something special to give, and once you find out what it is that you can do, then you will be happy.

And I would say to my younger self that it's not always possible for teachers to see what you can see. So, tell them and tell mum and dad so they start to understand that you are not being naughty, like everyone says you are.

As I got older, nine onwards, I would tell my younger self not to be afraid to ask my parents if I could be taught at home as for the last two years, the teacher had made me stand in the corner of the class so I could only see the wall, while others learned.

By now I would say tell your parents that you are being beaten and called stupid at school, not only by the teacher but some of the other children too – and you didn't know why.

At 14 years old I would say to my younger self that you can carry on with your gardening work and odd jobs such as collecting scrap metal and old clothes etc – you don't have to work for another person, just like all the other children in your class are going to.

At 16 years old I would have told myself to not be afraid to ask Marilyn's Uncle John, who is a well-educated person after going to a private school, to teach me how to speak properly. I would tell me that he wouldn't ridicule me – he would be delighted to help me to become a better able person to give a speech when I marry his niece.

At 17 years old I would say, don't have good teeth pulled out when they only need filling, just because you have been hurt with the drill when you were a child.

I would explain just how teeth are connected to different parts of the body to keep it healthy and pulling them out would be detrimental for the rest of my life.

I would say look after your body – a 9-stone lad without training must refuse to lift 15-stone sacks of pig food every day resulting in 22 years of agony. I know you could have been sacked but you must not worry if that happens, as when one door closes, another and often a better one, will always open.

At the age of 20, having got married and expecting a child, I would say just because you are doing two jobs – one on shift work, and one every day around that job – keep calm and be glad that you have been given not only the day, but a lovely wife and child instead of always thinking, life's not fair.

By 23 and having virtually demolished our house with not a clue of how to put it back together, and besides not having any money to do so, finding ourselves living in a ten-foot caravan throughout that winter, thinking things just cannot get any worse – then I got fired.

I would have said do not get into a depression – do something, anything. Just tidy up the house and garden, clean the caravan and the car that is not taxed or insured, but don't stop in bed all day. This will pass, it's just a matter of time.

24 years old on welfare I would have told myself that I didn't have to think of myself as I did. I thought of myself as scum and a beggar, the lowest of the low, with no hope of getting a job with millions unemployed – what hope had I got? I couldn't even read or write and had a very bad attitude.

At this time, I wouldn't have told myself anything because I knew it all – if you had put me in a dark room then switched the light on, I would argue with my shadow.

Then I had to be left alone. I thought that I was dumb, stupid and worthless, but at the same time I knew I wasn't – nobody who was dumb and stupid could have done what I did in such a short time. The problem was I wasn't taking responsibility for my actions.

My brain kicked in after having an argument with the welfare and then I knew that I was the only one who was responsible for my family's life.

A kick up the arse – he got the kick up the arse that he needed when the welfare person said, "if you want more money, just have another child". He knew that if he did, that he would be on welfare for the rest of his life.

Now I would be able to talk to him. I would say you're doing the right thing by looking after yourself and working every hour that you can is the best thing for you.

Subliminal teachings from the age of four my father told me he should have gone into business with a person who owned a shop. If he told the full story once, he told it 10,000 times and I didn't take any notice of him – or did I?

I would be with my younger self all the way for a few years as he took every opportunity, every day, to grow the business which he had started with 37p for a window cleaning cloth. With Marilyn working with him there was no stopping them as, throughout his life, the thing that had kept him back was his mind. He told himself that he couldn't read or write and that he was stupid – but I wasn't stupid when I refused to have another baby. I was angry.

Anger – having anger can propel you in a positive or a negative way, but dad had said he should have taken the chance that he had been given, but didn't, and ended up reprimanding himself for not taking the opportunity to look after his family for himself throughout his life; now what was I going to do?

Education – I would say to my younger self, education is something everyone needs to survive and that education is different worldwide. I think if a person is educated to survive, they will seek further education as and when they are ready, so there is no need to stress or mentally beat a child that really can't grasp a subject.

This is what I mean – unbeknown to anyone, my dyslexia affected me playing ball games, but I wouldn't get punished when I couldn't learn the rules of cricket or football, so why did I get punished when I couldn't read?

Sprouts – you wouldn't say a child is bad and an underachiever if they didn't like brussel sprouts, or any other food for that matter, so why is the school curriculum designed to get them into boxes that they don't fit into? Then give them an unrelated score for what they are good at, which doesn't have a box, leaving the child thinking he's a failure for the rest of his life.

Mind – I would tell my younger self, if there is one thing that will really help you in life – do your best to learn the rules of chess, and one last thing – whatever you can conceive in your mind and believe, you can achieve.

I would say they may hit you and belittle you, steal from you and tell you that you won't amount to anything, they can exclude you and produce evidence that you are no good at any one of their subjects, but they can't stop your brain from believing in yourself – they may stop it for a while but that's temporary, just like pain is temporary, but just remember what Zig Ziglar said:

"You can get anything that you want in life if you will just help enough other people get what they want".

AARON YAHAYA

The intentional life – principles for a prosperous life of purpose

"We are all self-made, but only the successful will admit it"

Earl Nightingale

ABOUT THE CHAPTER AUTHOR

Aaron Yahaya is a Guinness world record holder, a keynote speaker and an award-winning entrepreneur whose business experience has spanned over two decades. His multi-industry experience covers hospitality, retail, publishing, learning and development and commercial property development.

Today Aaron works with individuals and institutional investors balancing their investment portfolio in property. As a director of EnSpirit Global, a tech platform for the development of entrepreneurial thinking, he uses his insight and expertise to provide a visionary and pragmatic approach to entrepreneurship.

With a background in Economics and broad leadership experience in strategic management cross-sectors, Aaron's passion is seeing businesses get created and grown. As part of this passion, he actively gives keynote speeches around the topic of accelerated business growth and resilience.

In his spare time Aaron is a keen runner, competing in half marathons and 10K races supporting UK and Nigeria-based Alpha thalassemia charity organisations, as well raising his son Joshua.

www.Aaronyahaya.com

MY CHAPTER

Hey Son,

We have opportunities like no generation before us; we live longer, live better, live more varied lives and get to make more of an impact. Never before in history have so many individuals had the ability to make a local, regional, national and international impact.

Never before in history have a few individuals had the ability to control billions of people.

Now is the time to strike out, wherever you are, with whatever you have – start with that right now.

Whilst I push on, here are a few things I think are important that you need to know for when you decide the time is right to break out on your own.

I have made a lot of mistakes and there is a lot I wish I had listened to, so I guess my first word of advice is to listen to your elders – you might hear them more than once, but listen.

For everything we do, there is a bedrock of personal things that we need to have, a foundation on which to build our lives, a bedrock from which things spring that we need.

So, here are my principles.

On Personal Guiding Principles

1. Do not take shortcuts, always look to finish your tasks and to work things out the way they are designed to. Earn the right to make modifications; if you do want to give out instructions one day, you have to learn to follow them. There is no wrong time to do the right thing.

2. Enjoy the process – do not keep wishing for tomorrow, you will only be living in today, so stay present. And if today doesn't turn out as you hoped, there will always be a tomorrow.

3. Accept your humanity and know yourself. You are not perfect, your significant other isn't either, neither are your parents so make peace with it. You are unique as an individual, a one-off in the history of mankind.

4. Have faith and trust your gut. Sometimes you are just going to have to act from a deep sense of conviction. You'll have to start moving to your destination before the direction is clear – in these moments, have faith and carry on.

5. Develop good habits, never underestimate the effect your habits will have on your life. Some studies speculate that over 90% of what we do on a daily basis is habit. Get your

habits right and create the life that you want on auto pilot. Exercise – never stop, because it will be much too hard to restart.

6. Watch your health and watch your diet. Watch them now because it will be much harder to break your habits the older you get.

7. Mastery and Focus – do not ever intend just to get by; do your best, test your limits and commit to mastery, one area at a time. Do not make becoming the best your aim, instead focus on continual progress, pushing your limit and building on the foundations you lay day by day. You might just find, when you look around, that you have set yourself apart from, and in front of, the rest.

8. You can do anything, and you can do everything, but you can't do everything at the same time. Some things are simultaneous, others sequential – lean on others to know the difference.

9. Getting things right is over-rated – get the feedback. Do not be obsessed with getting things right first time. Sometimes you'll win, other times you'll lose but you'll always get an outcome and will always learn if you stay open to it.

10. Time will pass. It is inescapable that the days progress without our intervention. Often, I have acted like I could suspend time – this is a fallacy. Learn from my mistakes and act with consistency, act with urgency, start it today, complete it today, do not worry about what people say – this too will pass anyway.

On People & Relationships

1. Smile at strangers. Everyone has a story and you never know what a stranger's story is. You can change the world one smile at a time; it never hurts to be of a cheerful disposition. Be a bright light in a world that has lost its sparkle.

2. Be polite, kind and generous. It is often said 'manners make a man'. Let it be said of you that you were a delight to be with, a breath of fresh air and good company. Be kind and of unshakable character. This means being sincere and principled, even in uncomfortable situations. Do not shy away from tough but necessary conversations; however, being sensitive, gracious and diplomatic is always appreciated. Compassion not condemnation.

3. You are in partnership with people. You need people to help you with your goals – remember to be the kind of person that people want to help and to partner with. Be the best partner you can be, be a friend whose friendship is worth cultivating.

4. Watch your tongue. The Bible talks about the power of life and death being in the tongue – this is food for thought. There are four things to consider before speaking, this framework will serve you well:

    1. *Does this need to be said? (Is this necessary, or can it go?)*
    2. *Does this need to be said right now? (Or can this wait till a better time?)*
    3. *Does this need to be said by me? (Or is there someone else better placed to have this conversation instead of me?)*

4. *Does it need to be said this way? (Paying attention to the 'tone' of your verbal and written communication)*

5. Keep your word. It is necessary to be dependable, to be reliable and to be able to be counted on – do whatever you must to keep it. However, you must be prepared to acknowledge when you are unable to and be prepared to accept the consequence of this.

6. Be punctual. Time is an irreplaceable resource, cultivate the punctuality habit early on whilst it might cost you very little. A failure to do so costs you so much more later on.

7. Treat all people equally. Every human being deserves respect, they should not have to earn the right to be treated decently. This should be your standard. Status is not relevant to your commitment to treat human beings with dignity.

8. Friendships – keep good company.

On Business

1. Watch your cash flow and know your numbers. Jealously guard your expenditure.

2. Excellence is a habit – cultivate a high-performance culture, lead from the front and make excellence the standard, not the exception. Be proud but not prideful, confident but not conceited, content yet still ambitious.

3. Wherever you are, that's where your morning starts; start wherever you are with whatever you have right now. There is a first time for everything.

4. Play the long game. Shortcuts can make your business and working life short lived. Play the long game – always.

5. Keep perspective, remain focused on your objectives.

6. Get mentorship. We climb higher when we stand on the shoulders of giants.

On Community

1. Be a contributor, support a charity, give to those less fortunate. Make a difference.

2. Be a good steward, leave things better than when you found them. Ensure they can be handed down to the next generation.

3. Create Value – leave things to be handed down to the next generation.

My advice to you Joshua is to ponder on these words, reflect on them and add to them for your children. I know that this advice will serve you well.

Here is to your success.

Your father
Aaron

FINAL THOUGHTS

Throughout the amazing collection of real-life business and life experiences, lessons and reflections freely shared in this collaborative book, there are many common recurring themes that emerge – rivers that run through it.

These could not have been predicted at the outset of the book nor were they manufactured.

They are the product and the findings of over 2,000 years of aggregate experience from the authors and certain factors have emerged consistently – did you spot any of them?

You have a choice in life.

You have the same amount of time each day, week, month or year, as the next person.

What you do with that time is priceless and precious.

You are in charge of your life and no-one is coming to save you; that is YOUR responsibility and not just to survive – but to THRIVE!

Each and every one of us has the ability to be a catalyst in 'Creating Shared Value' and 'Making a Difference' in the world.

We are all geniuses at something – do not allow society's inevitable judge to sway you. Forge your sustainable roadmap and enshrine it with continuous action and evolution – and you WILL achieve amazing things.

The knowledge contained in this book is extremely valuable – it can be a potent force in defining your life of success if understood, absorbed and implemented.

The compounding benefits of consistent implementation over future years will deliver exponential growth in wealth for you, in so many different forms, and not just economic wealth!

This compounding wealth can be used as a 'Force for Good', creating enormous value, changing lives and creating a momentum that can enable a multi-generational legacy for you, your friends and your family's future.

On behalf of all the chapter authors we wish you every success, happiness and a wealth of pleasure as you pursue your passion, achieve greatness and fulfil your massive potential.

We believe in YOU!

A SPECIAL SURPRISE FOR YOU!

Have you ever thought of being an author or maybe harbouring a long-held urge to put pen to paper?

Becoming an author was a 35-year itch I wanted to scratch and finally, at the age of 48, I self-published my first book. Within 12 months I had published two further books!

During that time, I have learnt the joy, the deliberation and the satisfaction of drawing together a wonderful collection and array of thoughts, experience and reflections to help others.

Becoming an author can be a daunting prospect for some, to say the least. However, I have a special opportunity for you.

If you are interested in becoming a chapter author in the next publication in this series, volume 2, then follow this link

www.markstokesuk.com/ATYYSapplicationform

for more details and your application.

And maybe we will have the privilege of working together in the near future.

With warmest regards.

Mark

OTHER BOOKS BY THE AUTHOR:

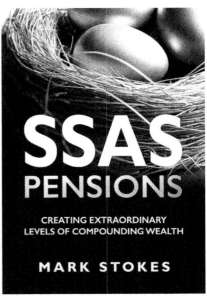

Available now on:

MY ACTIONS

MY ACTIONS

MY ACTIONS

MY ACTIONS

MY ACTIONS

MY ACTIONS

MY ACTIONS

Printed in Great
Britain
by Amazon

31355063R00214